Killing

the

Witches

Killing
~ the ~
Witches

THE HORROR *of*
SALEM, MASSACHUSETTS

BILL O'REILLY
& MARTIN DUGARD

ST. MARTIN'S PRESS
NEW YORK

First published in the United States by St. Martin's Press, an imprint of
St. Martin's Publishing Group

www.stmartins.com

Design by Meryl Sussman Levavi

Library of Congress Cataloging-in-Publication Data is available upon request.

ISBN 978-1-250-28332-0 (hardcover)
ISBN 978-1-250-28333-7 (ebook)

Our books may be purchased in bulk for promotional, educational, or business
use. Please contact your local bookseller or the Macmillan Corporate and
Premium Sales Department at 1-800-221-7945, extension 5442, or by email
at MacmillanSpecialMarkets@macmillan.com.

First Edition: 2023

1 3 5 7 9 10 8 6 4 2

This book is dedicated to Therese Janow

"Thou shalt not suffer a witch to live."

Exodus 22:18 (King James Bible)

Killing

—the—

Witches

Prologue

T he woman with less than an hour to live does not accept her fate.

Dame Euphame MacCalzean prays silently in her dirty prison cell. She is the mother of two boys who died in infancy and three grown daughters. Not yet forty, a Catholic and woman of means, she kneels in a thin dress, the fabric offering no padding against the cold rock floor. Her hands are soon to be bound in tight thick rope for her ride to the burning stake. Jailers will parade her up Castle Hill, there to be executed.

Effie's fervent prayers belie a simple truth: she is not guilty. She stands accused of possessing dark power and promoting the vilest evil—even casting a spell on twenty-five-year-old James VI himself, king of Scotland. The king will leave behind a great legacy, including the first royal postal service and commissioning a translation of the Bible that will be named in his honor. Yet he is terrified of witches, convinced they are trying to kill him and his young Danish bride. He has authorized the prosecution and torture of all such women.*

---

* James VI will also become king of England in 1603 after the death of Elizabeth I. His contempt for witches was so well known that William Shakespeare will write the play featuring witches, *Macbeth*, during his reign. The opening scene contains a reference to King James.

Justice plays no role.

Edinburgh is a center of manufacturing, known for its fine wool. The growing city is a filthy, hardscrabble town of twenty thousand. A great castle rises on a steep hill at the city center. Much of the Scottish capital is a chaotic mess, rife with typhus, cholera, and bubonic plague. Cattle walk the streets. Existence is hard. Death comes easily and too young. Streets are cobbles, cold mud, and trenches where residents dump chamber pots from high windows to the warning cry of "Gardyloo!"*

Entertainment is scant, though always a welcome diversion from the grind.

Such as today.

The Royal Mile is crowded with townspeople making their way up the southern slope of Castle Hill on foot and in carts. Most witch burnings are held on Wednesday, which is thought to fetch a larger crowd. But even on this Tuesday, there is no lack of spectators. Many want to be part of the show, clutching dry timbers to throw on the flames. It is a noisy, excited procession, forming a ring on the castle esplanade around the tall stake to which Effie will be tied, then set alight.

There are rumors His Majesty will be in attendance.

In fact, James is here in the Scottish capital on this bright summer morning. Wife, Anne, teenaged queen of Denmark, travels at his side. The paranoid ruler will not attend the execution and has the power to pardon his subject.

But James is determined to rid his kingdom of Satan's spell.

So Effie MacCalzean must burn.

---

* "Gardyloo" was a brisk warning to jump out of the way as waste was being dumped in the streets. The term comes from the French *prenez garde a l'eau*, meaning "beware of water." With buildings often as high as twelve stories, the splashback could reach the second floor. Edinburgh's 1749 "Nastiness Act" required that waste could be thrown out only between 10 p.m. and 7 a.m. Despite the presence of a modern sewage system in that city, the Nastiness Act is still in effect.

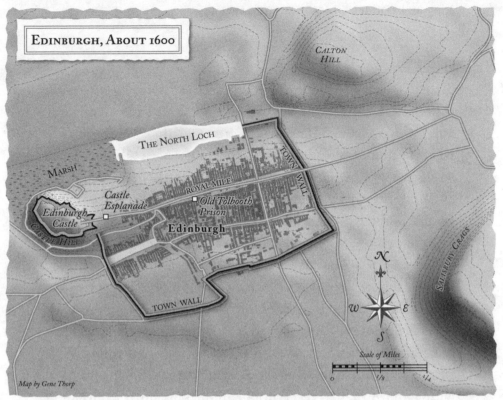

EDINBURGH, ABOUT 1600

CALTON HILL

THE NORTH LOCH

MARSH

Castle Esplanade

ROYAL MILE

Old Tolbooth Prison

Edinburgh Castle

CASTLE HILL

Edinburgh

TOWN WALL

TOWN WALL

SALISBURY CRAGS

N
W E
S

Scale of Miles

0   1/8   1/4

Map by Gene Thorp

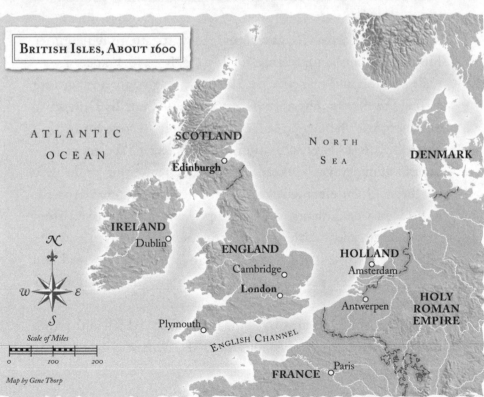

BRITISH ISLES, ABOUT 1600

ATLANTIC OCEAN

SCOTLAND

Edinburgh

NORTH SEA

DENMARK

IRELAND

Dublin

ENGLAND

Cambridge

London

HOLLAND

Amsterdam

HOLY ROMAN EMPIRE

Antwerpen

Plymouth

ENGLISH CHANNEL

N
W E
S

Scale of Miles

0   100   200

Map by Gene Thorp

FRANCE

Paris

✢ ✢ ✢

Sixteen days ago, Dame Effie was charged with twenty-eight counts of sorcery, including "bewitching two children to death, attempting to murder her husband, attending four conventions of witchcraft, and sitting next to the devil himself—while handling a wax image of King James."

Dame Effie's trial is the talk of the town. The prospect of a mother of three young women being tried for witchcraft is a salacious scenario—one that provides diversion and even amusement.

The man who has ruined Effie is David Seaton, a court magistrate living on the edge of financial catastrophe. He is also her brother-in-law. After Seaton's brother, Patrick Moscrop, marries Effie in 1579, things go bad in a hurry. Effie is known to be unfaithful and not in love with her new spouse. Within twelve months of their nuptials, she allegedly attempts to kill her husband with poison—though succeeds only in making his face break out in spots.

Effie MacCalzean is never charged with attempted murder. Her hapless husband, fearing for his life, flees to France. Eventually, Seaton takes revenge. In 1590, the magistrate arranges for a young twentysomething maidservant named Geillis Duncan to be arrested on the charge of "acting strangely"—code for being a witch. This is an easy accusation for an officer of the court. Under questioning, Ms. Duncan denies having anything to do with witchcraft. Then the interrogation becomes more intense. According to court documents, she is stripped naked and shaved from foot to head, and her thumbs are crushed with screws known as pilliwinks. A rope is then wrapped tightly around her head and twisted until her neck almost snaps, a slow torture known as "wrenching."

As this painful drama plays out, a birthmark, which authorities consider a "devil's mark," is found on Ms. Duncan's naked torso.

She finally confesses. Humiliated, hands mangled, her face a mask of rope burn, she capitulates and begins listing a variety of men and women she considers to be witches and warlocks conspiring against the king. At the top of the list is Effie MacCalzean. After her confession, Geillis is thrown into the dreaded Old Tolbooth Prison, where she will soon die of deprivation.

But Geillis Duncan will outlive Dame Euphame MacCalzean.

✤ ✤ ✤

Effie is imprisoned in May 1591. Her trial begins on June 9. Scottish law demands Dame Effie be provided a defense. Six legal advocates represent the wealthy woman, yet each knows her fate is preordained. No member of the fifteen-man jury is mad enough to defy the king—particularly when it is well known that James has taken a special interest in Effie's fate.

The accused is the illegitimate daughter of Thomas MacCalzean, an aristocrat possessing vast land holdings outside Edinburgh. He recognized her as his legal heir in 1558, when she was a young girl. Upon his death in 1581, Effie became owner of Thomas's estate. If she is executed, her substantial inherited lands will, by law, go directly to the Crown. Effie's own daughters have no legal standing. So, while King James VI is terrified of witches taking hold of his soul, he has no issue with gaining control of Effie's lands, haunted as they may be.

Effie MacCalzean's trial lasts four days.

The unanimous verdict is guilty.

James is delighted to hear it.

✤ ✤ ✤

The time has come. Her jailer approaches. Effie stands. She is barefoot. Her eyes blaze with fear. The condemned woman is led to the cart that will take her the short, steep distance up Castle Hill. Effie does not resist. Her executioner says nothing. If he is afraid the Devil will make him pay for ending Effie's life, he does not show it.

The journey to the stake begins.

The crowd is close, clamoring for the moment when smoke will rise, followed quickly by flames. Then the screaming. The audience can't wait. Many have never witnessed something like this. In most Scottish witch executions, the victim is tied to the stake, then strangled to death. *After* which the fire is lighted. It is believed a witch's dead body will continue to cast spells unless destroyed by flames.

But Effie MacCalzean will not receive that mercy. She will be burned alive.

So it is that Effie is now tied to the stake.

The executioner lights the pyre with a torch. The crowd is hushed, but not for long. They roar as one when Effie panics at the first puffs of flame and smoke. She is an agent of the Devil, after all, so the crowd has no problem cheering as she struggles against her binds. But then the sight of a human being burned alive becomes all too real. The smell of scorched flesh overwhelms the aroma of woodsmoke. Parents put protective hands on the shoulders of their children. Still, few turn away. Effie is an example: this is what happens when you associate with the Devil.

The flames rise.

Effie MacCalzean screams, a piercing shriek unlike any the spectators have ever heard. She begins suffocating from the smoke. Extreme pain sends her body into shock. Within five minutes, she will be dead.

Her tunic burns easily. So does her hair. Effie's screaming diminishes, then stops.

The spectators remain transfixed. What was once a woman is now charred flesh. Her eyes have melted. Her face is no more. The audience is disappointed that King James has not attended. But as the crowd walks down the hill, the people are satisfied. Smoke continues rising into the air. Conversations are hushed. Justice has triumphed over evil in Scotland. The witch is dead.*

But the Devil is not.

And soon, he will be on the move.

---

* Witch trials continued in Scotland until 1736. Four thousand individuals were accused of witchcraft during that time, of which an estimated 2,500 were executed.

Chapter One

The New World beckons.

It is a cool English day as John Alden, a twenty-one-year-old barrel maker and carpenter, stands at the rail of the merchant ship *Mayflower*, watching the chaos on the wharf just below. He is about to risk his life on an extremely dangerous voyage. What he sees terrifies him.

Today is Sunday, a day of rest, yet dozens of workers are loading provisions onto the ship. It looks unlikely there will be enough to last the 102 passengers as well as roughly thirty members of the crew and officers the entirety of the ten-week voyage. In addition to the lack of food, some of those who have booked passage are growing apprehensive about the journey because the Atlantic Ocean has been wracked by gale-force winds. In fact, many of them refuse to board.

Even though Alden is young and a relatively inexperienced member of the crew, he knows this is not an orderly departure.

And perhaps an omen of troubles to come.

The truth is that the *Mayflower* should have been long at sea by now. The planned three-thousand-mile voyage to the American coast is harsh even in the calm summer months. But the North Atlantic turns mean in autumn. Two previous attempts to depart in good weather ended when the *Mayflower*'s companion ship *Speedwell* began leaking. Repairs failed and the small vessel eventually had to be abandoned in port. As a result, the *Mayflower* will have to carry far more people and belongings than originally intended. One of the leaders of the venture, Robert Cushman, writes to a friend, "If we ever make a Plantation, God works a miracle."

John Alden, a husky blond adventurer, understands this risk. He knows that only one other English settlement has survived in America. That is Jamestown in Virginia, where as many as 3,000 of the 3,600 settlers have perished since the colony's founding in 1607. Those colonists are members of the Church of England, a faith swearing loyalty to the king. Many of the *Mayflower* voyagers are Protestants of the Puritan sect, often known as "dissenters" due to their strong disagreements with the king's religion. This is their reason for seeking a new life in America. But for some on board, such as Alden, faith has nothing to do with the journey. It's just a job. Furs and tobacco can be very profitable when shipped back to England. No matter the motivation, all are willing to sacrifice comfort—and perhaps their lives—for a better future.

This is not the first time the Puritans have fled England. Twelve years ago, they sailed to Holland because the Crown was persecuting them. However, the Puritans, mostly farmers, found it difficult to purchase land in Holland. They were relegated to working in the wool industry, where wages were low. In addition, Puritan leadership believed the Dutch were corrupt—the Devil was working among them in Holland. Thus, the group returned to England, knowing they would eventually have to find another place to settle.

Almost immediately, the Dissenters and King James clash. Puritans believe in religious law but reject the laws of the Crown. That is unacceptable to James. But rather than punish them, the king sees a chance for the Puritans to actually *help* him: the fundamentalists would be allowed to sail off once again, on the provision that they establish an English colony in the Americas.

At first, the Puritans consider going to South America but eventually decide that Virginia might be a better place. A British merchant company agrees to support their settlement in return for profitable exports from the New World. Thus, the *Mayflower* is chartered by the merchants. For this reason, the Puritans are also required to take on board many other paying passengers that do not share their extreme faith.*

✣ ✣ ✣

Finally, the *Mayflower* is ready to depart. John Alden notices that a number of Puritans have refused to board—their places taken by "Strangers," as the nonbelievers are called.

The voyage begins with a solemn prayer.

As the small ship floats away from the dock, "a prosperous wind" soon fills her sails. *Mayflower* is hardly a large vessel, just 25 feet wide and 106 feet long. She is "square-rigged" with four masts. As the ship sails out of the English harbor into the turbulent Atlantic, the passenger list is an odd mix of men, women—three of them pregnant—children, and two dogs. Among the group is Myles Standish, a mercenary. At age thirty-five, Standish is a tough, hardened taskmaster who will provide protection to the Puritans and Strangers.

But it is John Alden who is, perhaps, the most important man on the ship. As the barrel maker, he is in charge of maintaining the beer supply. *Mayflower* passengers have only two beverage options: water or beer. Water is easily polluted and can make people ill. However, the microorganisms that make people sick can't survive in alcoholic beverages. So beer will become the primary source of liquid nourishment. And just as important, Alden is the

---

* All passengers were required to pay the merchant company more than $3,000 in today's money in order to come to America. That payment and their commitment to build a settlement gave them each a share in the New World profits, which they used to pay down their substantial transportation debt.

beer keeper—ensuring that each passenger is allotted no more than one gallon a day.*

Mayflower is known as a "sweet ship," because the leakage from wine casks over a decade has left a pleasant aroma in the hold. But that will soon change. One hundred and two passengers living in tight confinement below the main deck quickly turns the space dark, damp, and malodorous. Living quarters are divided with curtains. Ceilings are just five feet high. Passengers live by lantern, rarely knowing if it is day or night. To make this fetid hold even more crowded, all materials needed to build a settlement—from seed to cannon, from Bibles to cauldrons—are also stored below. The Puritans believe themselves to be a peaceful people, but they are also realistic, and well armed to defend their new colony from pirates, the French, and local Indian tribes. They have dragged on board muskets, fowling pieces, swords, daggers, and several heavy guns, including two 1,800-pound sakers, three 1,200-pound minions, and four smaller cannon.

As the Puritans and Strangers soon learn, the *Mayflower* has not been built for this type of voyage. She is a sturdy merchant vessel, built to carry 180 tons of cargo in her hold. In more than a decade at sea, the *Mayflower* has carried a wide variety of goods, from wine to furs, to European ports—returning to England with brandy and silk. The ship has never attempted a voyage of this length with so many passengers.

Autumn storms soon turn the Atlantic treacherous. Winds blow so strong that, at times, the ship is forced to "lie ahull," lowering its sails and being carried on the waves. Puritan leader

---

* John Alden entered history in 1858 with the publication of Henry Wadsworth Longfellow's epic poem "The Courtship of Miles Standish." In this fiction, Alden supposedly spoke for mercenary Myles Standish in asking Priscilla Mullins for her hand. Her response, "Why don't you speak for yourself, John," became quoted throughout the English-speaking world.

William Bradford writes, "The ship would be badly shaken. Conditions aboard are dreadful."

This is true. Passengers are subjected to hardships they have never known. Meals are cold: hard biscuits, cheese, smoked and pickled meats, salted fish. It is always wet and filthy, with no relief from the incredible stench. They recline side-by-side with absolutely no privacy or hygiene. The air is barely breathable and the only activities are card playing for the Strangers and Bible reading for the Dissenters.

The ocean becomes the enemy. The ship is tossed like a cork in a hurricane. For their own safety, passengers stay in their own cramped space. Going on deck is dangerous and mostly forbidden.

Many become seasick. There are no sanitary facilities—slop buckets are used for relief and remain unemptied until they can be dumped overboard when the seas calm.

The first death comes on September 23, seventeen days into the voyage. A member of the crew, "sometime sick with a grievous disease," according to the ship's log, "died in a desperate manner." His body is "tossed overboard."

Another fierce storm buffets the ship. Most passengers remain calm, having long ago put their fate in the hands of the Lord. Suddenly, the *Mayflower* is hit hard by hammering waves. An ominous cracking sound rattles the vessel. Damage has been done. A number of leaks appear. The Atlantic is fighting to destroy them.

The crew makes a quick inspection. A main beam has cracked. The fate of the *Mayflower* is now in jeopardy. The crew knows it. They begin arguing about how to deal with this. Some of them want the ship's captain, Christopher Jones, to turn around and sail back to England. Others believe they have no choice but to press forward.

Belowdecks, this fear reaches the passengers. But there is no panic. William Bradford and the other Puritan leaders hastily climb up onto the deck to meet with Captain Jones. He is direct:

there is hope. The *Mayflower* is damaged but remains seaworthy. He explains that buried deep in the storage hold, among the furniture and cookware, is a large iron implement. It had been brought to help the passengers build cottages when they land. Captain Jones has an ingenious plan to put it to use.

As soon as the winds subside, the crew goes to work. Carpenter John Alden is in the middle of it. Using the great screw to reconnect the broken pieces, the cracked beam is successfully raised back into position. There is widespread relief among the passengers. Captain Jones maintains course for America.

The Puritans gather to say a prayer of thanks—and guidance. For their situation is still precarious. The harvest moon shone brightly in the early days of the voyage, but now the nights are black and visibility is limited to less than a half mile. There is no sign of land and no way of determining how long the voyage will last. Sails across the Atlantic in these stormy high latitudes have been known to take up to two months. At this slow rate of progress, the precious beer supply will soon run out.

However, life continues. In late September, a child is born to Elizabeth Hopkins. The boy is named Oceanus—Latin for "ocean"—because of his Atlantic birth.

But with life there also comes death. Shortly after Oceanus Hopkins is brought into the world, William Butten, an indentured servant to Dr. Samuel Fuller, dies of an unknown ailment.

At about that same time, a bizarre incident unfolds. Gale-force winds howl without ceasing, but the *Mayflower* is riding steady. Twenty-seven-year-old John Howland is weary of being kept belowdecks. It has been about a month since Howland breathed fresh air. So he climbs a ladder, pushes open a hatch, and lifts himself onto the main deck. He stands on the damp wooden planks, eyes closed, taking deep breaths. It is a glorious moment.

But this is a fool's peace. The ship bucks. Howland loses his balance and starts to slide overboard. In desperation he tries to grab hold of a rope, a cleat, a rail—*anything!*—but fails. Howland is swept into the raging sea.

Yet in that final moment before wind and waves pull him under, John Howland's fist somehow wraps around a rope. That halyard some sailor forgot to adequately secure is used to raise and lower *Mayflower*'s upper sail. Howland holds on to this lifeline with a death grip as he is dragged beneath the sea. To let go is to die.

Several crew members witness Howland's plight. They immediately search the ocean for him, knowing this is not an event men survive. Suddenly, the sailors are stunned to see the young man surface, still clinging desperately to the halyard. Sailors grab the rope and reel him in, finally pulling Howland back on board with a boathook.

Alive.

It is a miracle.*

✦ ✦ ✦

The forlorn passengers remain stoic. They endure hardships largely in silence. It is only at prayer time when voices are raised. Surely, God will save them, just as he did John Howland.

On November 9, 1620, crew and passengers exhausted, seagulls are sighted floating on the ocean. It is Wednesday, November 11, when the cry "Land ho!" is heard throughout the ship. One seaman has died, as well as a passenger. A baby has been born, the ship's officers, crew, and more than one hundred settlers have reached the shores of America. "They were not a little joyful," writes Puritan leader William Bradford.

✦ ✦ ✦

But where are they? After sixty-six days at sea, navigation is inexact. The *Mayflower* has crossed horizons few Europeans have ever

---

* John Howland would live another fifty-three years. He and his wife, Elizabeth, will have ten children and eighty-eight grandchildren. Among his many descendants are Presidents George H. W. Bush and George W. Bush.

seen. Captain Jones believes the ship is far north of what will become known as the Hudson River and knows that the merchant's charter does not apply in this region. So Jones decides not to make landfall. He orders the *Mayflower* to sail south to Virginia.

It is an unfortunate decision.

Within hours, the winds and tide turn against the ship. The *Mayflower* sails unexpectedly into the rocky shoals and hidden sandbars of what was later named Pollock Rip—a treacherous area just south of a place known as Cape Cod.*

Racing waters create white-capped breakers. The winds shift yet again, and there is a real fear the *Mayflower* will founder on the jagged bottom. Captain Jones tells his passengers that he is abandoning the effort to reach Virginia. Instead, he will sail north, back to the New England mainland.

This causes great turmoil among both Puritans and Strangers. The charter granted by King James does not apply to that region. This land is desolate. It is known Indian ground. They have no legal right to settle there. As passengers and crew watch the seemingly endless woodland flow by on their port side, they accept the reality that after months at sea their true journey has just begun.

The next morning, *Mayflower* drops anchor in a sheltered harbor, the northernmost hook of Cape Cod. They name it Provincetown. A group of elders meet in the main cabin to forge an agreement about a settlement. This will become known as the "Mayflower Compact." The youngest man to sign the document is John Alden, who has had his fill of life at sea. He will stay in America rather than make the perilous return to England.

Five weeks later, Captain Jones decides to make the short voyage to the mainland rather than stay in Provincetown, which is far

---

* British explorer Bartholomew Gosnold gave this stretch of coastline its name in 1602, due to the enormous schools of codfish in the region.

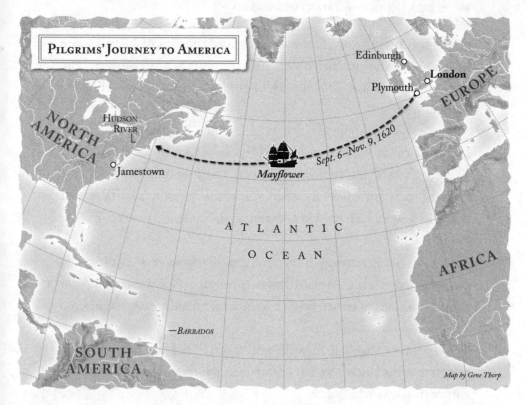

PILGRIMS' JOURNEY TO AMERICA

NORTH AMERICA

HUDSON RIVER

Jamestown

Mayflower

Sept. 6–Nov. 9, 1620

Edinburgh

Plymouth

London

EUROPE

ATLANTIC OCEAN

—BARBADOS

SOUTH AMERICA

AFRICA

Map by Gene Thorp

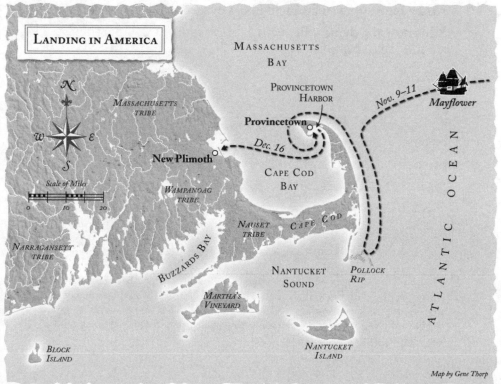

LANDING IN AMERICA

MASSACHUSETTS BAY

MASSACHUSETTS TRIBE

N
W E
S

Scale of Miles
0   10   20

PROVINCETOWN HARBOR

Provincetown

New Plimoth

Dec. 16

Nov. 9–11

Mayflower

CAPE COD BAY

WAMPANOAG TRIBE

NAUSET TRIBE

CAPE COD

NARRAGANSETT TRIBE

BUZZARDS BAY

MARTHA'S VINEYARD

NANTUCKET SOUND

POLLOCK RIP

ATLANTIC OCEAN

BLOCK ISLAND

NANTUCKET ISLAND

Map by Gene Thorp

out in the Atlantic. Winter is coming and the people need a more permanent location. There are already six inches of snow on the frozen grounds. The *Mayflower*'s log reports, "Snowed and blowed all day."

Myles Standish leads the first landing party. Some of the land is already cleared, and on December 11 the settlement is named "New Plimoth." The eighteen adult women on board are allowed to disembark—and then spend the day doing laundry. But there is danger. Indians are encountered. Some are peaceful, some are not.

A high point provides a sweeping view of the surrounding area for security. A clean stream flows through it. However, the passengers and crew return to the *Mayflower* at night as frigid cold sets in.

Poet James Russell Lowell will claim, "The little shipload of outcasts who landed at Plymouth are destined to influence the future of the world."

They have survived an incredible voyage.

But now the dying will begin.*

---

* In legend, the voyagers set foot on a large granite rock, which became known in history as Plymouth Rock. There is no evidence this is true. The first mention of the massive gray rock came during a celebration more than a century later. It is highly doubtful the passengers and crew would have risked their footing stepping onto a wet, slippery surface.

Chapter Two

MAY 1628

COASTAL NEW ENGLAND

MORNING

The verdict is guilty.

Captain Myles Standish and his well-armed men stand outside a modest dwelling. They have come to arrest Thomas Morton, the leader of a small settlement forty miles north up the coast from Plymouth. Morton arrived in America aboard the *Unity* in 1624. But he wanted no part of the Puritan settlement at Plymouth.

Instead, the forty-nine-year-old lawyer from Devonshire established a small settlement where settlers could do pretty much whatever they wanted to do.*

So now Standish has arrived to arrest Thomas Morton, who is himself armed and not pleased about the situation. Supposedly his crime is selling guns to Indians, but his real transgression is that his settlement, named Merry Mount, offers religious freedom—and is growing more rapidly than Plymouth.

There are two types of people in the New World, the flamboyant Morton has written: Christians and Infidels. It is the Infidels, the

---

*The libertine Morton is also a writer. His controversial three-volume work *The English Canon*, describing his adventures in America, was published in 1637 and is considered the first book ever to be banned in the New World because it was critical of Puritans. It was printed in London.

lawyer believes, who are "most full of humanity, and more friendly than the other."

Thus, Thomas Morton is rebuking Plymouth by allowing libertine exhibitions in Merry Mount, including male settlers "consorting" with Indian women. The raucous celebrations are held around a giant maypole, eighty feet high, with a pair of buck's horns nailed near the top.

The Puritans are horrified by this pagan symbol.

Governor Bradford, based in Plymouth, describes these festivities as "the beastly ye mad Bacchanalians." So Bradford, who ridicules Morton as "a Lord of Misrule," orders Standish to put an end to this "school of Atheism." The standoff doesn't last long. Morton and his men are too drunk to resist. Morton surrenders and is immediately put in chains. The maypole is pulled down. Eventually, Merry Mount is burned to the ground.*

The power of Governor William Bradford and his Puritan advisers is absolute. The *Mayflower* long ago sailed back to England. Settlers stood on the rocky shore, watching uneasily as ship and crew disappeared over the horizon. Seven years later, they are alone—and many fewer. The dying season has lived up to its name.

Upon landing at Plymouth in 1620, Puritans and Strangers forged a legal foundation for the settlement. The leaders began by agreeing on a loose form of government combining British law and harsh religious beliefs. The next step was to build a town. Plymouth is laid out in the shape of a cross. Two intersecting streets make defense easier. A two-story fort is built on the highest point overlooking the town and bay. The work to

---

* Thomas Morton is exiled to a deserted island where Indians help him survive until he is rescued by a passing ship and taken to England. By the time he returns to the New World, Merry Mount is deserted. Morton attempts to return to Plymouth in 1642 but is arrested and imprisoned. He dies in Maine in 1647 at the age of seventy-one.

build nineteen residences is underway when the "sickness" begins. Hunger. Scurvy. Winter fever. Frostbite. There is no safe place. There is no one to help.

The illness spreads as the English begin running out of food and beer. Myles Standish understands the colony can show no weakness to the native Indians who lurk in the forest. So the disease-ridden are used as ploys. "They set up their sick men with muskets upon their rests and their backs against the trees," writes William Bradford. "They did that to convince the Indians the colony is able to defend itself."

The ploy works, but there is no relief from struggle here in Plymouth. Frustration soon becomes anger. While the Puritans and Strangers mostly manage to get along for their mutual survival, it is never entirely harmonious. In January, a fire destroys the common house. By March 1621, forty-nine of the original *Mayflower* contingent are dead—almost half those who set sail from England. Only five women survive the winter. One of them, the teenaged Priscilla Mullins, has lost her parents and brother, leaving her completely alone in this strange place.

The fight for survival is communal. Supplies continue to dwindle. Settlers catch fish and seals. They also manage to shoot some fowl and deer, but it is not enough. Rations are cut by half. There is only one place to turn for deliverance.

That would be God.

Puritans pray, for they believe the Lord would not bring them this great way just to abandon them. They are looking for a sign that they have not been forsaken in this desolate place.

The sign arrives almost naked.

✤ ✤ ✤

Indians have been watching the English since the first landing party. The settlers find signs of them all around: smoke rising in the distance, a cache of corn found buried in the ground. "Indians came skulking about," Governor Bradford reports. "Once they stole [our] tools."

Early in December, a Puritan landing party is attacked. Furiously howling Indians materialize out of the woods, firing arrows. Captain Standish stands calmly directing the defense. Several arrows whiz close by, but no one is hurt. His men return gunfire. An Indian is heard shrieking.

The First Encounter, as it is labeled, does not last long. The Indians disappear into the thick woods. The settlers give chase, but the enemy is gone. The Puritans kneel and offer thanks for their safety.

Myles Standish knows the hostiles will return. This is their land. Native Americans have lived here for ten thousand years. Plymouth is the home of the Wampanoag Nation, a name meaning "people of the first light." There are almost seventy other nearby tribes. Many of them are peaceful. But not all.

The specter of Indian violence covers every decision. Standish well understands that. So his men drag a cannon to the top of Fort Hill, where they build a fortification around it. When the Indians attack, they will face that cannon.

And so the settlers are shocked in early spring when a tall Native American, his black hair short in front and long in back, walks confidently into Plymouth settlement. He is wearing "only a leather around his waist with a fringe." The settlers quickly grab their muskets. They look around for other intruders. Then this Indian says the one word they never expected to hear: "Welcome, Englishmen."

And he says it in English.

He also asks for a beer.

The visitor is named Samoset. The Puritans are astonished to find an Indian who speaks English. How is that possible? Samoset explains he comes from an island to the east, where he has been taught the language by English fishermen. Samoset also says that the Patuxet tribe, who cleared the land around Plymouth, are all dead. Four years earlier a plague spread through the area. The Great Dying, Samoset calls it. Only one member of the tribe remains alive. His name is Squanto, and he also has quite a story.

As a young man, Squanto and twenty other local Indians were captured by an Englishman named Thomas Hunt, who lured them aboard his ship and clapped them in chains. Destined to be sold into slavery in Spain, they endured six weeks trapped in the hold, living on raw fish and stale bread.

Squanto is enslaved in Spain but ransomed by a group of monks. Squanto soon finds himself in London, the servant of John Slaney, a wealthy merchant who owns land in the New World. The Indian learns English and eventually convinces the landowner that he can be useful if allowed to return to Massachusetts. Slaney agrees.

It takes five years, but Squanto finally finds his way home, only to discover illness has killed his tribe. To survive, he becomes a translator for the newly arrived Englishmen. William Bradford will call him a "special instrument sent of God."

So it is that Squanto will become the most important friend of the Puritan settlement.*

✢ ✢ ✢

Samoset and Squanto set off a chain of events. In a gesture of goodwill, the Indians return tools stolen from the English. Then, treaties are made. The settlers negotiate an agreement that neither the English nor Wampanoag tribe will "injure or do hurt" to the other. Squanto is ordered to stay with the settlers and teach them the Indian ways of survival.

After so much death and deprecation, there is now hope. Squanto is about forty years old and a gifted communicator. In clear English, he instructs the settlers how to hunt and trap game,

---

* The plague extended from 1614 to 1619.

where the fish and eels are feeding, and the best fields to plant corn, squash, beans, potatoes, and even pumpkins. Bury dead fish in the soil, he says, to help the crops grow. Rotate seeds to keep soil healthy. He points out which wild berries and nuts are safe to eat and which plants will make them sick. When settlers explore the lands beyond Plymouth, he is their guide. When they negotiate trading agreements with other tribes, he is the interpreter. What the Puritans do not know is that Squanto is ambitious. To gain power within the Indian community, he is exaggerating his relationship with Plymouth. Squanto claims the Puritans keep their fatal diseases in storage pits. He warns other Indians that if they do not do as he tells them, he will ask the English to release the plague upon them.*

Despite this deception, the relationship between the Indian community and Puritans has grown strong. Plymouth has survived its first winter. It put stakes in the ground and is beginning to harvest crops.

William Bradford, now thirty-one years old, is appointed governor. Bradford is of average size and has a pleasant face, set off by a trimmed beard. He was sick throughout much of his childhood. So rather than working, he reads the Bible. The governor is considered a thoughtful man, admired for his tact and forbearance. Bradford and his wife, Dorothy, arrived together on the *Mayflower*, leaving their three-year-old son, John, behind in England. The boy will eventually come to the New World.

✦ ✦ ✦

There are new worries. And they have to do with personalities. Captain Myles Standish is a skilled military leader who provides security and confidence. However, he is known to have a quick

---

* Squanto will die a sudden and unexplained death from a simple illness while traveling with Governor William Bradford in 1622. Samoset will live until 1653, dying in what is now Bristol, Maine, of unknown causes.

temper and too easily resorts to violence. When the colony is threatened by Indians from the Massachusetts tribe, he arranges a meeting with their leader, Pecksuot. But rather than negotiating, Standish grabs the Indian's knife and stabs him to death. He then returns to Plymouth carrying the head of another warrior he has killed. That cements his reputation as a brutal man.

The other powerful leader in Plymouth is John Alden, who has taken a prominent role in building houses and fortifications. Alden is among the most popular men in the settlement. Although he is younger than the other leaders, his opinions are respected and his advice sought. Alden and Standish get along but are opposite in their view of life. That rivalry will soon surface.

✣ ✣ ✣

Despite the positive turn of events at Plymouth, there is still death. Susanna White was pregnant when the *Mayflower* left England and gives birth to the first English child born in the new colony— her son Peregrine is born November 20, just as the ship reaches American shores. But her joy is tempered weeks later when her husband, William White, suddenly dies of unknown causes. Susanna is left to fend for her five-year-old son, Resolved, and baby Peregrine.

The name Peregrine is auspicious. It means "to come from far away" and is often used to describe those on a religious pilgrimage. Governor Bradford often uses the term *pilgrim* to describe those in their midst who once made the trip from England to Holland. And Edward Winslow, in his journal about the *Mayflower* passengers, refers to the Plymouth colonists as pilgrims. Over the course of the next century, that word will become synonymous with these colonists.

In fact, Winslow, an adviser to Governor Bradford, also loses his spouse, Elizabeth. By May, the widower Winslow and the widow White decide to marry. Such rapid nuptials are not unusual, for love is a luxury in desolate places. Men and women have clearly defined roles and often marry for convenience. It is believed there are only two religious sacraments that must be observed: baptism and communion. The actual marriage ceremony is a civil matter. And there is no celebration: no music, no dancing, no laughter. At the nuptials, the Puritans recite psalms.

But even the pilgrims believe in consummating a marriage. Edward Winslow and Susanna White will go on to have five children.

✥ ✥ ✥

The first harvest goes well.

To celebrate, the English invite the Wampanoag to join them in a feast. Governor Bradford writes, "Amongst other recreations we exercised our arms, many of the Indians coming amongst us, and amongst the rest their greatest king, Massasoit, with some ninety men, whom for three days we entertained and feasted."

Bradford watches warily as games of chance and skill are played. Indians dance around campfires. Wild turkey, venison, duck, and shellfish are served. Beer and wine flow freely. It is truly an unexpected spectacle. The stoic settlers, who follow a strict religious code emphasizing modesty and virtue, mingling with the almost completely naked Indians. The English watch the Indians' painted, tattooed faces reflected in the fires as they whoop and holler and let loose their joy. Yet a mutual respect now exists between them. Both sides are surviving in a brutal new world.*

✥ ✥ ✥

---

* The harvest celebration is not named at the time but will eventually be called the first Thanksgiving. It is not known what time of year this feast took place, but it was likely sometime between late October and mid-November. President Franklin Roosevelt proclaimed Thanksgiving a national holiday in 1941.

Winter is coming once again. And the settlers understand the incredible hardship those months will bring. As they are preparing their homes, something very strange occurs: a ship appears off the coast. No one knows from where it has come. The settlement is not expecting supplies. The fear is this is a French ship—arriving to stop English expansion in America. Myles Standish puts the colony on alert. Men and boys are given guns and Indian allies notified.

As the mystery ship floats far offshore, some believe Standish actually *wants* a fight. And he may get his wish.

Finally, the ship makes way—sailing directly into Plymouth Harbor. As it comes closer, it shows the Union Jack! The ship is the *Fortune*, sent by London merchants. It is carrying thirty-seven passengers.

There is a reason the ship lay quietly. The *Fortune*'s crew and passengers are terrified of what they might find. The *Mayflower* had returned to England with dire news about the colony, so the arrivals are being very cautious.

The new settlers are mostly lusty young men who recover quickly from the long voyage. While Plymouth is thriving, there are not many women in the colony. In fact, there are four or five men for every available woman. Competition is fierce and eventually gives rise to one of the great romantic stories of history.

According to the poet Henry Wadsworth Longfellow, young John Alden is smitten by the lovely Priscilla Mullins but lacks the courage to reveal his attraction. Myles Standish, recently widowed, is also interested in Priscilla. So the soldier asks his rival, Alden, to present his marriage proposal to her. As chronicled by Longfellow, she rejects Standish and reveals her feelings for the young Alden. Eventually, John Alden and Priscilla Mullins become the third couple to be married in Plymouth. In their case, they marry for love.*

---

* The writer Henry Wadsworth Longfellow is a direct descendant of John and Priscilla. He based his massively popular 1858 poem "The Courtship of Miles Standish" on a family history.

The Plymouth Colony soon welcomes more arrivals. Ships are now leaving England nearly every month for the New World. The economic success of the Puritans has spurred both merchants and individuals looking for a better life to cross the Atlantic.

But many do not understand what they are sailing into. Every aspect of life in Plymouth is now based on Scripture. For Puritans, the purpose of the law is to ensure proper morality. The legal system is set up mostly to punish sinners. It includes a ten-shilling fine for "those who profaned the Sabbath." Moral failings are often treated as harshly as is larceny. Adultery, for example, is punished by a public whipping, and guilty parties are required to sew the red letters *AD* to their upper garments. Blasphemers are forced to wear a red *B*, and those who are drunk in public affix a red *D* to their clothing.

Sentences include spending time in the stocks, being burned on the shoulder, and even banishment. Capital punishment, the death penalty, might be imposed for several crimes, including treason, willful murder, sodomy, bestiality, and "Solemn Compaction or conversing with the 'divell' by way of witchcraft conjuracion."*

All of the moral laws quickly create tension between the Puritans and the Strangers. Hard feelings permeate Plymouth. The Strangers want no part of a Bible-based justice system. For them, life is to be enjoyed. For example, Puritans do not celebrate Christmas and Easter. These religious holidays are not mentioned in Scripture—so they are treated as normal working days. Strangers strenuously object to this. Also, services are held twice on Sunday, through the morning and most of the afternoon. All Puritan families must attend.

---

* Stocks, or pillories, are wooden boards placed horizontally and hinged on one side. Matching half-circles are cut in the adjoining boards to restrain a felon's hands, feet, and occasionally neck, preventing him or her from moving. This was a method of public humiliation that was often accompanied by other citizens throwing trash and spoiled food at the convicted individual.

The Strangers do not. Most of them follow traditional Christian practices and reject the Puritan approach. So, as Christmas draws near, the Strangers make it clear to Governor Bradford they are not going to work on that day.

Bradford initially respects their decision. On Christmas morning, he goes to labor with the Puritans in the fields. However, the governor is surprised when he returns for the noon meal to see a public celebration. Strangers are playing games in the streets, "some pitching the bar, and some at stool ball and such like sports." For Bradford this is too much. He is infuriated. If the Strangers really want to show their devotion to Jesus, he believes they should do so in the quiet of their homes: "There should not be gaming or reveling in the streets."

Bradford takes action. He works with Myles Standish to seize all gaming equipment and forbids such displays in the future. This disrupts the entire community and will eventually lead to a serious fissure.

The Strangers want out of Plymouth. They want freedom in this New World.

It will soon become a devil of a problem.

Chapter Three

A trap is in motion.

The Reverend John Lyford and his wife arrive in Plymouth. He is an ordained Puritan minister—the first one in the colony. Lyford is sent to the New World by English merchants who are providing financial support. These businessmen want stability and efficiency, and some of them do not trust how Plymouth is being run. Lyford is not coming to Plymouth to help the Puritans but is being forced on them by the merchants, who seek to overthrow colonial Plymouth leadership for their gain. The settlement is not yet profitable, and investors are hesitant to provide additional funds. Some of them have even withdrawn their original investment.

Pastor Lyford is a shadowy figure. He has confessed to many "corruptions" during a spell in Ireland. He is also an ambitious man. And Governor William Bradford does not trust him. It doesn't take long for hostilities to break out. Lyford soon loses authority in Plymouth—so he moves to a new colony called Nantasket, almost thirty miles away.

Yet Lyford is not finished with Plymouth.

William Bradford suspects the pastor is actively undermining the original colony. Bradford also learns that Lyford fled Ireland after being accused of rape, and his own wife admits he still "meddles" with their servants.

Someone has been sending letters critical of Plymouth's leadership to the merchants in London. The missives describe the colony as "intolerant." The Puritans are accused of being "contentious, cruel and hard-hearted." It is obviously an effort to convince the London backers to install new leadership.

Governor William Bradford knows there is danger in Lyford's subterfuge. So he secretly arranges a rendezvous with Captain William Pierce, whose ship is carrying mail from Massachusetts back to London. Pierce stops at sea as soon as the ship is over the horizon from Plymouth. Governor Bradford is rowed out and climbs onboard. There he finds a number of letters written to the London merchants by Lyford and another settler, a merchant named "Mad Jack" Oldham. The missives are full of false accusations. Bradford takes some of the correspondence with him when he returns to land. He will defeat his enemies at their own game.

✛ ✛ ✛

The governor waits for the perfect moment to spring his trap.

It comes weeks later. At the crowded Sunday meetinghouse, Bradford suddenly confronts Lyford and Oldham, who are in attendance. These men are "evil, profane and perverse," he shouts.

Lyford is outraged. "Lies," he says. The minister denies having anything to do with the written accusations. As that denial echoes through the public house, Bradford dramatically produces letters in Lyford's own hand. He then reads the most damning portions out loud.

Lyford "is struck mute."

The newly arrived minister is permanently expelled from Plymouth. So is "Mad Jack" Oldham. But before the conniving thirty-year-old can leave the colony, he is put through the "gauntlet," where settlers hit him with the butt end of their muskets.

Being a minister, Pastor Lyford is spared that painful humiliation.

✛ ✛ ✛

A blood feud has been created. In response, Plymouth becomes even *more* intolerant—and self-sufficient. Bradford eliminates food shortages by having Puritans switch from communal to private farming. They are motivated to work longer and grow more food, knowing it will feed their families, and, perhaps, make them money. Women had previously stayed home to raise the children but now work in the fields to increase crop yield.

All this new prosperity only increases the awareness that outsiders are not welcome. Those who "sin" are treated brutally. As a result, about a quarter of all Plymouth residents decide to leave. Most are Strangers who came here to make a new life and do not care about religious tenets. Some of them return to England; others spread throughout the colony. One of those dissidents, Roger Conant, joins Lyford and Oldham in Nantasket.[*]

The thirty-two-year-old Conant is an interesting character. He has come to America for opportunity, not religion. It's immediately obvious to him he doesn't fit in Plymouth. After a brief stay in Nantasket, Conant and his family make the long journey sixty-five miles north to Cape Ann.

The Cape Ann Colony is a farming, fishing, and salt-making settlement established by non-Puritans in 1623. Fewer than thirty people live there. It has not been successful, so plans are made to move the colony farther inland. Roger Conant leads a small group desperately searching for a good place to farm. There is nothing but woods away from the coast, so Conant and his party settle in abandoned wigwams left empty by a nomadic band of Indians.

---

[*] John Lyford eventually sails to Virginia, where he dies in 1632 at the age of forty-two.

Eventually, the new settlement is named Naumkeag. In London, the New Council for New England, chartered to maintain order in the New World, takes charge of Naumkeag. In 1628, Puritan John Endicott along with about fifty planters and servants arrive to impose order on the new colony.

Endicott is a man of quick temper and religious views that might be considered extreme, even for Puritans. He seeks to establish a dress code in the colony, women forced to dress even more modestly and men ordered to keep their hair short. Backed by the mandate of the merchant company that has sent him to the New World to produce a profit, the newcomer also decides to change the colony's name.

No longer will it be called Naumkeag.

Instead, Endicott prefers the name "Salem."

It has similar roots to the Hebrew "shalom," a word meaning "peace."

But peace will not be coming to Salem for a very long time.

✤ ✤ ✤

It is hectic in the New World. The fact that Plymouth is not yet profitable puts enormous pressure on the townspeople. Hundreds of settlers are arriving up and down the East Coast of America—sent by investors hoping to grab a share of the riches. Some settlements fail. But others succeed, inspiring more investment and more settlers. It's like a game of musical chairs—without music and with rickety stools rather than chairs.

Back in London, King Charles I grants John Endicott even more power in the form of a royal charter transforming several settlements into a single larger community known as the Massachusetts Bay Colony. The king gives it a seal—a friendly Indian holding an arrow pointing down: the signal for peace.

The English flag is now firmly planted in New England. But King Charles chooses not to interfere with how the new entity interprets religious law. He allows the Massachusetts Bay Colony to impose strict Puritan practices.

However, when it comes to money, the sovereign always has the final say. London merchants are pressuring King Charles to put strict business procedures into place. More colonists are needed to work the land and hunt for furs. So, in 1630, a massive eleven-ship fleet brings wealthy lawyer John Winthrop and an estimated seven hundred to one thousand new settlers to Massachusetts. Ironically, among these vessels is a ship known as the *Mayflower*—though not the same vessel that brought the Puritans to the New World a decade earlier.*

In time, Winthrop will become one of the most influential religious figures in American history, seeing no differentiation between church and state. He will stipulate that the one true faith of the Massachusetts Bay Colony is that of the Puritans.

But money is what brought him across the Atlantic. Winthrop has been elected governor of the new colony by its shareholders. These wealthy men live in London, yet they dictate what will happen here. Thus, John Winthrop becomes more powerful than Plymouth governor William Bradford. Surprisingly, Bradford welcomes him to New England, referring to Winthrop as "my much honored and beloved friend."

John Winthrop is forty-four years old, born into wealth, a stern man with piercing brown eyes. He is a tough businessman, intent on providing profits. But equally important, he believes the colony must be a "city on a hill," a shining example to the world of Puritan values.

Massachusetts Bay and Plymouth are now both ruled by strict religious law. Under Winthrop, Puritan leadership imposes even more draconian punishment on anyone who strays. For example, in the new town of Salem, failing to honor the Sabbath or committing

---

* The fate of the original *Mayflower* is unknown. There is some evidence it was broken up in the mid-1620s and its timber sold to construct a barn.

blasphemy are both serious crimes. There is no appeal process. Male church members in Salem decide guilt or innocence.

✢ ✢ ✢

Back in Plymouth, William Bradford has a problem: more dissent has arisen. A young minister named Roger Williams, who arrives in the same fleet as Winthrop in 1630, wants no part of the harsh governance.

Williams is a man of great confidence who graduated from Cambridge only four years earlier. After settling in Plymouth, he begins openly challenging Puritan legal and theological doctrine. He claims the civil court has no right to prosecute violations of church law. Williams tells parishioners, "The distinction between the church and the world must always be kept clear, otherwise the wilderness of the world will invade the garden of the church."

Roger Williams also objects to the way the colony treats Native Americans, publicly questioning the validity of treaties that do not include payments to Indians for their lands. He even decides to live with them "in their filthy smoke holes to gain their tongue."[*]

Governor Bradford is clearly worried about Williams. "He fell into some strange opinions which caused some controversy between the church and him," Bradford writes.

Action is taken. In 1635, Roger Williams is brought before the General Court. He is accused of sedition and heresy. Williams refuses to recant and is convicted of spreading "diverse, new, and dangerous opinions." The sentence: forced banishment from Plymouth Colony for three years.

Suspecting he is in even greater danger from his Puritan brethren, Roger Williams strikes out during a blizzard. Throughout the harsh winter, he is given food and shelter by Native Americans.

---

[*] Williams was referring in general to the Wampanoag and Narragansett tribes. Eventually, he became a close friend of Wampanoag chief Massasoit, a relationship that will save his life.

Eventually, Williams purchases land from the Narragansett and establishes a new settlement known as Providence Plantations, located in the present-day Rhode Island.

Providence is everything Salem is not. It is run by majority vote and is the first place in the New World where there is separation of church and state. But while Roger Williams is now safe from religious persecution and can live the life he chooses, towns like Plymouth and Salem continue adding restrictions. Yet this is also a time of prosperity. The pursuit of wealth suppresses religious tension—for now.

✢ ✢ ✢

Up north, Massachusetts Bay is flourishing. So many "New Planters" are arriving it cannot possibly absorb them all. So Governor Winthrop orders them to scatter throughout New England. New settlements are founded in Charlestown, Cambridge, Roxbury, Medford—and a bustling waterfront town with a deep harbor named Boston. Founded in 1630, Boston quickly becomes one of the most important ports in America.*

✢ ✢ ✢

Alongside the settlers, there are now approximately seventy thousand Native Americans in New England. Trade is profitable for both the Indians and the Puritans. The first Bible printed in the colonies is a translation into Algonquin as the Puritans seek to convert Indians to Christianity. But it does not work. Instead, some of the settlers are quietly becoming intrigued by tribal cultures, consulting shamans, listening to tales of witchcraft and ghosts, and investigating spiritual healing.

For their part, the Native Americans are less worried about

---

* One of Bill O'Reilly's ancestors, Simon Hoyte, signed a charter for Charlestown, which is now a Boston suburb, home to Bunker Hill.

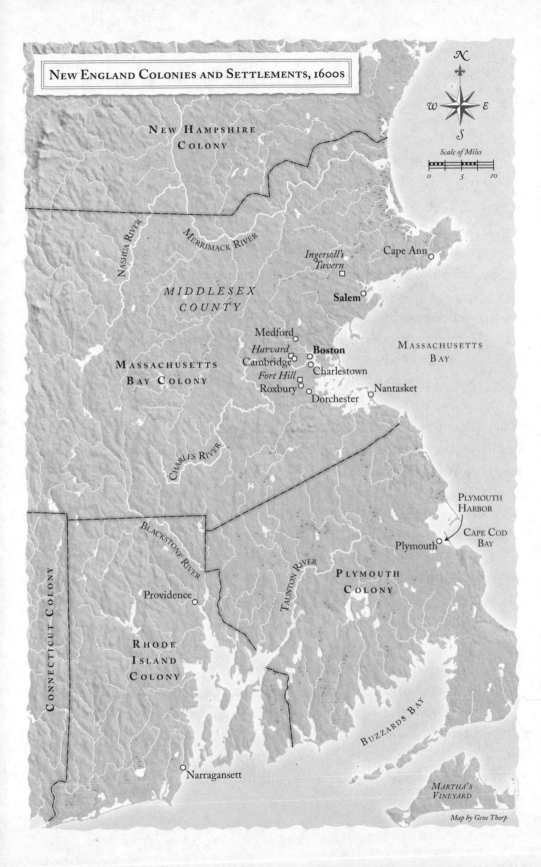

NEW ENGLAND COLONIES AND SETTLEMENTS, 1600s

N
W E
S

Scale of Miles

0   5   10

NEW HAMPSHIRE
COLONY

NASHUA RIVER

MERRIMACK RIVER

*Ingersoll's
Tavern*

Cape Ann

MIDDLESEX
COUNTY

Salem

MASSACHUSETTS
BAY COLONY

Medford

Harvard
Cambridge
Boston

MASSACHUSETTS
BAY

Fort Hill
Roxbury

Charlestown

Nantasket

Dorchester

CHARLES RIVER

PLYMOUTH
HARBOR

CAPE COD
BAY

BLACKSTONE RIVER

Plymouth

CONNECTICUT COLONY

TAUNTON RIVER

PLYMOUTH
COLONY

Providence

RHODE
ISLAND
COLONY

BUZZARDS BAY

Narragansett

MARTHA'S
VINEYARD

Map by Gene Thorp

faith than they are about the large number of immigrants settling on their land. Their fears prove correct as fate turns against them. The new settlers bring diseases from England, afflictions against which the tribes have no natural immunity. The Indians are ravaged by disease, primarily smallpox. The Puritans, however, do not think they have brought the plague—they believe it comes from God. A clergyman named Increase Mather will write, "About this time the Indians began to be quarrelsome, touching the bounds of the land which they had sold to the English, but God ended the controversy by sending the smallpox amongst the Indians."

Excepting Roger Williams's Providence, all the New England settlements, including Salem, are now theocracies. Reverend John Cotton, who preaches in Boston, writes, "Liberty of conscience is for those who truly fear the Lord. A fundamental task of the state is the establishment of pure religion."

Governor John Winthrop goes even further, stating that citizens should not have free will to rule themselves: "A democracy is, amongst civil nations, accounted the meanest and worst of all forms of government."

Thus, every aspect of life in New England is governed by the church. Women have to wear gowns that touch the floor and are forbidden to wear lace. Married women have no legal rights. All forms of gambling are outlawed. Celebrating Christmas or Easter is punished with a five-shilling fine. Adultery can bring death. Displays of affection are not allowed in public: a sea captain returning after years away is seen kissing his wife—and then both are sentenced to several hours in the stocks.

And so it is that towns like Salem evolve into hotbeds of rabid religiosity. There is no dissent. The townspeople do what they are told. Ironically, superstition—which is the opposite of faith—is deeply ingrained in the population.

The Puritan leadership has absolute power.

And, as the adage goes, absolute power corrupts absolutely.

Chapter Four

Bridget Bishop is a troubled rebel.

It is some seventy years since the *Mayflower* spilled forth Puritans onto American soil. Bridget herself came from England in 1664 in the Massachusetts Bay Colony's second generation of immigrants. Her first husband died of an unknown illness just as they arrived in the New World, leaving her the widowed mother of three young children. That's when her troubles began.

Bridget has long followed her own rules, even when they conflict with the harsh Puritan dictates. She wears flashy clothes and is known to speak confidently to men. Her independent attitude earns her few friends among the residents of Salem, who dutifully follow theocratic orders.

Bridget Bishop is an attractive woman with strong features. And available. She soon marries again. That's acceptable; widows are encouraged to remarry. But this is not a loving relationship. Thomas Oliver is much older and has three grown children. He also has a nasty temper, and he abuses his wife. But Oliver is respected by his neighbors, and he works for a time keeping track of newcomers, "what strangers do come or have privily thrust themselves into the town."

Even though wedded, with a new last name, Bridget remains an outlier. The New England colonies are settled now, the wild early days of exploration done. Salem is a tight-knit place. Its residents depend on each other. Everybody plays a role in the health and security of the town. They share each other's secrets. There is little room for nonconformist thought. Especially since there is a new danger threatening the community: the peaceful relationship with the Wampanoags has broken down. The possibility of Indian attacks has drawn the colonists even closer.*

✦ ✦ ✦

In Salem, the law is very clear: the husband has complete control of everything in a marriage—including his wife. But Tom Oliver goes too far. The couple is brought into court for brawling several times. At one hearing, a neighbor testifies she saw "Bridget's face at one time bloody and at other times black and blue."

Bridget fights back—which causes even more trouble. A court gives the couple a choice: ten whiplashes each or pay a fine. They pay.

After another arrest, they are ordered to "stand back-to-back . . . in the public marketplace." They are to be gagged, wearing a printed sign on their caps detailing their offense. This time, Oliver's daughter from another marriage pays his fine, but Bridget is forced to face the public humiliation.

And so it goes.

Bridget Oliver recognizes her precarious position and joins Reverend John Hale's church in nearby Beverly, attending services faithfully. But she just isn't like everybody else. Rather than dressing in an acceptably conservative manner, Bridget uses colorful

---

* By 1671, Native American raiding parties are attacking homesteads and villages. Tribes accuse the colonists of breaking agreements. America's first major Indian conflict, King Philip's War, begins in 1675. Homesteads are attacked. Dozens of towns are damaged or destroyed. It takes three years and hundreds of casualties to defeat the Indians.

patches to repair her worn clothing. And she insists on wearing a "red paragon bodice," an upper-body garment, in public.

It's all too much. She becomes a target for the anger and frustrations of the townspeople. Rumors begin spreading: Bridget Oliver is a witch.

✤ ✤ ✤

That is a dangerous accusation. Most people accept the existence of powers they can't see; if there is a God, there must also be a Devil. And it is witches and warlocks that do his bidding in the world. There are laws. England's Witchcraft Act of 1604 ruled that a witch who commits a minor offense could be imprisoned for a year; the penalty for committing a second act is death. Massachusetts Bay's "1641 Body of Liberties" includes the biblical admonition "If any man or woman be a witch, that is, hath or consulteth with a familiar spirit, they shall be put to death."*

Such executions begin in 1647. They start in the Connecticut Colony, adjacent to Massachusetts Bay. Thirty-seven women are tried for witchcraft. Eleven are convicted and hung by the neck until dead. These prosecutions are primitive, tried in small hamlets primarily by hysterical zealots. At this point, Connecticut is not as organized as the Massachusetts Bay Colony. There is no central authority. So atrocities are common, carried out by fanatical people who fear no reprisal for these executions.

✤ ✤ ✤

Now, in Salem, Bridget's life takes the same terrible turn. A hatmaker named Samuel Gray claims her "spirit" was present when

---

* Most European countries treated witchcraft as heresy—defined as a crime against the Church—and the penalty for that was being burned at the stake. But in England and her colonies it was considered a criminal offense—a crime against the government—and the penalty for that was hanging. Contrary to the myth, not a single witch was burned in Salem.

his child died. Another neighbor testifies she paid him for some work he had done—and the money disappeared from his pocket. That same man also says Bridget asked him if his father would mill her grain, "because some folks counted her a witch."

Bridget has no protection. Her husband, Thomas Oliver, dies in 1679. She inherits his small estate—and whispers say she used witchcraft to kill him for it. People in Salem have never forgotten Thomas's accusations: "She was a bad wife . . . the devil had come bodily to her . . . and she sat up all night with the devil."

In February 1680, Bridget is finally arrested—but not for the murder of her husband. She is accused of witchcraft by a slave with the unlikely name Juan, who claims she spooked his team of horses, causing them to drag his wagon into a swamp. The slave also says he encountered her "specter" in his master's barn, but it vanished when he tried to hit it with a pitchfork.*

There is no longer much doubt in Salem that Bridget Oliver is a witch. Human nature is pretty simple: when something not easily explained takes place, people look for a reason. Black magic is as logical as any other cause in New England.

Several other residents accuse Bridget or her "specter." Samuel Shattuck is convinced she has bewitched his son. So he takes steps to break her spell. He sends the boy to scratch Bridget "below the breath" and draw blood, which is believed to neutralize spells. Instead, Bridget hits his son with a shovel—drawing blood. Samuel Shattuck is furious.

✢ ✢ ✢

---

* A specter is a ghost, the spirit of a person. It is an apparition, able to move through solid structures, appear and disappear, and influence events. There is debate about whether spectral evidence, claims by people that they have been visited by these spirits, can be used as evidence in a witchcraft trial. Connecticut had permitted it. It was allowed in Salem too.

Sensing her life is in danger, Bridget Oliver marries Edward Bishop in 1685 and takes his surname. He is a prosperous wood-cutter and she raises chickens. The couple own a pair of very popular taverns. Soon, they tear down the house she shared with Tom Oliver to build a new home. But hidden in the cellar walls of the old house workers find several poppets. These small dolls in human shape are used in magical ceremonies for casting evil spells. Most often they are stored in chimneys, so even though there is no evidence Bridget knew these implements were in her home's foundation, there is shock among the townspeople.

The accusations pile up. Several men claim that Bridget has visited them in their nightmares. She is now fifty-five years old and, in addition to witchcraft, she is charged with theft. The owner of Salem Mill accuses her of stealing a valuable brass fitting. She denies it and the court dismisses the case for lack of evidence.

That does not mollify the mill owner. He soon accuses Bridget of stalking him. As he is walking to his barn, he suddenly is thrown against a stone wall and down an embankment. He looks around—but there is no one there. However, he has no doubt who to blame for his misfortune.

Then life in Salem takes a dark turn.

It is no longer just enemies of Bridget Bishop who feel the Devil's presence.

In January 1692, the daughter and niece of Salem's minister Reverend Samuel Parris are found to be "afflicted." Parris immediately warns the town: they are bewitched, he says.*

Soon there are other "victims." Bridget's own pastor, Reverend Hale, has seen them: "These children were bitten and pinched by invisible agents; their arms, necks, and backs turned this way and

---

* In New England, people who began to act strangely are described as afflicted. If doctors deem there is no logical reason for this strange behavior, it is often attributed to witchcraft.

that way, and returned back again, so as it is impossible for them to do it themselves, beyond the power of any . . . natural disease . . . their limbs wracked and tormented so as to move a heart of stone."

Someone must take the blame.

Thus, Bridget Bishop is living on the edge of disaster.

Chapter Five

Fear descends.

The Indians have again turned hostile. Reports that they are torturing Europeans are terrifying. Inside Salem, the Puritan village is being ripped apart by apprehensions—Indian attack, starvation, winter cold. There is no central authority. There is a shortage of almost everything because of poor harvests. Once friendly neighbors are fighting over property. It is a perfect cauldron for witches and warlocks.*

Seventy-two years have passed since the first settlers landed in Plymouth. They are long gone. The small outposts they founded have grown into crowded towns. Their children and grandchildren are now in charge. John Alden Jr., whose father oversaw the beer supply on the *Mayflower*, is one of the first New England celebrities, distinguishing himself as a merchant and adventurer. He is a charter member of Boston's prestigious Old South Church. When there is a negotiation in the

---

* An essential belief of Puritans is that everything is caused by a divine power. God is the source of all things good. Bad things are the work of the Devil.

Massachusetts Bay Colony, John Alden Jr. is often at the center of the discussion.

Recently, Alden stopped in Salem on his way back from prisoner exchange negotiations with the French in Canada. He does not like what he sees. The town has become a cold, colorless place haunted by religious extremism.

Alden quickly notices that life is dominated by the church. It is a respite from work, a gathering place where the faithful can save their souls. Residents attend mandatory three-hour-long services each Sunday, at which they are lectured about the evils of all pleasure. They also gather in the meetinghouse every Thursday afternoon to hear additional hellfire sermons.

It is an austere life. Quite the opposite from cosmopolitan Boston, just twenty-five miles away. In Salem, religious holidays still do not exist, even after all these years in America. There is no Christmas. No Easter. Daily, adults work on the farms or docks, then go home to simple meals. They eat foods that are readily available: grains, fruits, vegetables, and nuts. Fish are caught and preserved with salt. Wild game is sometimes available, though harder to find as the colonial population grows. Low-alcohol apple cider is the most popular beverage.

The typical home in the town of Salem is two stories high, with a large hearth on the ground floor to provide heat. Food is cooked in the fire as well. There is often a long table and wooden chairs but little other furniture except a sewing wheel. Upstairs, bedrooms are heated by the chimney that runs through the center of the house. The rooms are tight, as Puritans possess little. Windows are few because glass is expensive.

Salemites relieve themselves in chamber pots, which are either dumped into nature or used as fertilizer. In winter, only the fire provides relief from the cold. In summer, there is no respite from the heat, houseflies, mosquitoes, and ants.*

Women wear undershirts, corsets, and long petticoats. Outer clothing consists of a gown or long skirt. Females also wear white linen caps to cover their hair. Their shoes and stockings are no different from men's.

The men of Salem wear a shirt, stockings, garters, breeches, waistcoat, neckcloth, and a knee-length coat. Leather and coarse wool are the most common fabrics. More prosperous individuals favor linen. The tall hat with the broad brim that will become synonymous with Puritan appearance did not become fashionable until 1670 and is already being modified. In time, the habit of buckling three sides of the brim to the upright cap will become known throughout the colonies as the tricorn.

Many children die in infancy. And those who do survive are extremely limited in their daily lives. Young people are expected to do chores and attend school, where they are taught Latin and study a Bible-based curriculum. They are not allowed to play with toys, which are considered a "sinful distraction"—although, with the permission of their parents, the young can sing and play outdoor games like tag. But in reality there isn't much for children to do other than study the Bible and fear the Lord.

Secretly, some of the young girls wonder about the man they will eventually marry. There is one dangerous way to find out: the use of a "Venus glass." It is called that because Venus is the goddess of love and romance. The glass was introduced to the girls by a slave woman from the Caribbean named Tituba. And, in the winter of 1691, it has become a rage among Salem's young females.

---

*The most renowned house in Salem is Captain John Turner's 1668 home. It is made famous almost a century later by writer Nathaniel Hawthorne as *The House of the Seven Gables*. Originally, it is a two-story house with a massive central chimney and large front porch. Within a decade Captain Turner started adding new rooms to transform it into a mansion.

However, any fortune-telling is forbidden in the town because it goes against the word of God. So the children know they are at risk if their parents find out what they are doing.*

Everyone in Salem understands that violating religious law will result in harsh punishment. Women have to cover their heads, arms, and legs in public—even on the hottest days of the summer. Sex is never talked about, and adultery has long carried a potential death sentence. Women who break that law are publicly shamed, sometimes whipped, and told to wear a scarlet *A*. A few adulterers are hanged. By law, the leaders of Salem are allowed to put children born out of wedlock into indentured servitude—and whip the mother.

Men work from dawn to dusk. No one has much free time. The main diversions are taverns, where males are always welcome—but women are not allowed.

✤ ✤ ✤

John Alden Jr. recognizes the harshness of life in Salem. But elements of that restrictive life are also becoming more common in his hometown of Boston. For example, the frightening sermons of Reverend Increase Mather have made him one of the most powerful men in New England. Born in Dorchester, Massachusetts, in 1639, Increase was raised by his father, Reverend Richard Mather, to preach the Puritan gospel. No one does it better or is more respected. After graduating from Harvard as a seventeen-year-old, the kindly-looking Mather eventually becomes president of that college at age forty-five.†

---

* The Venus glass requires suspending egg white in a glass of water. After it takes shape, the girls use their imaginations to predict what sort of man they will marry. If it looks like a fish, they will wed a fisherman. A ship, then a merchant. The worst outcome is a coffin, meaning they will die a spinster.

† Harvard is the first college in America, founded by Puritans in 1636. It is named for Reverend John Harvard, who left his library and half his estate to the school. For the first century of its existence, Harvard was run by Puritans. Its mission was to train ministers.

Increase Mather has no doubt the Devil exists. He has been investigating witchcraft for most of his career. His sermons, which reinforce widely held fears against witches, are published and read throughout the colonies. "Thunder is God's voice," he rails from his Boston pulpit, warning New Englanders against even a brief slip from Puritan orthodoxy.

His most famous sermon, "The Day Trouble Is Near," which he delivers in 1674, warns, "Shouts of anguish will be heard on the mountains, not shouts of joy. . . . Your doom has come to you, O inhabitant of the land. The time has come; the day is near, a day of tumult, and not of joyful shouting on the mountains."

The Puritans understand. He's telling them what they fear most: God is angry because they are not strictly practicing their faith. Those words circulate. Wherever Increase Mather goes to preach, churches are packed. His name is meant to honor God, who "increased" his love for this world by giving mankind his son, Jesus, to save sinners. "Increase" is the literal translation of the name Joseph.

The son of Increase Mather, Cotton, often joins him on the pulpit and also becomes an important voice against witches. Cotton has the glowering countenance of a scold that makes him look older than his thirty years. He has actually surpassed his father as the leading expert on witchcraft. Cotton Mather's popular 1689 book *Memorable Providences* tells the story of a poor Irish immigrant named Ann Glover. Four young children, he writes, accused her of torturing them. Mather details the charges and actually believes them. Predictably, his vivid descriptions about how the four children were harmed terrify the already superstitious New Englanders: "Sometimes they would be deaf, sometimes dumb, and sometimes blind, and often, all this at once."

In 1688, Boston authorities place Ann Glover in prison, where Cotton Mather visits her. He then reports she is having trysts in her cell with the Devil himself. He writes that the young woman is unable to repeat the Lord's Prayer. That's evidence she is a witch. As a result, Ann Glover is hanged in Boston on November 16, 1688.

It matters not that the Irish immigrant spoke only her native Gaelic and was thus unable to recite the Lord's Prayer in English: Cotton Mather is well satisfied. "Very poor, a Roman Catholic and obstinate in idolatry," as he describes her, she has been justifiably punished.

✛ ✛ ✛

The power of the father-son Mathers is especially felt in Salem. As John Alden Jr. discovers, people in the town are petrified and fear dominates daily existence. Indians have already attacked more than fifty New England towns. Salem, so far, has been spared. But that does not lessen the apprehension.

Winter sets in. It is unusually cold. Food is becoming scarce. Salemites know who to blame.

Witches.

And Cotton Mather knows how to deal with that.

Chapter Six

Darkness descends.

A howling wind pounds the door of Reverend Samuel Parris's parsonage. The last embers of a dying fire throw jagged shadows against the walls. In an upstairs bedroom, huddled for warmth under thick blankets, the slave Tituba is whispering stories of witches and demons to Parris's nine-year-old daughter, Betty, and his orphaned eleven-year-old niece, Abigail Williams, who lives with them.

The young girls are enthralled.

Tituba knows the witch landscape. She was also Parris's servant in Boston when Ann Glover was convicted of witchcraft and hanged four years ago. She heard that the Irish washerwoman bewitched four children. Tituba tells Betty and Abigail that the victims had fits and lost control of their bodies.

The girls take it all in. The tortured children are about their same age.

Tituba's almond eyes glisten with reflected flames as she relates what else she has seen: Witches flying through the air on sticks and poles. Witches appearing in her dreams as a hog, a dog, a yellow bird, or a three-foot-tall winged creature. She warns the girls:

They must not repeat a word of what she is telling them. The Devil has threatened to cut off her head if they do.

Betty and Abigail vow to keep silent. They know the Devil is watching. They have learned his tricks from Reverend Parris, who came to Salem two years earlier to reignite a fading Puritan zeal in the village. He preaches strict adherence to traditional principles, denying church membership to anyone not faithfully following his dictates. The reverend even wants locals who do not live in Salem to pay a fee to attend his church. But more than anything else, Parris warns the people of Salem to beware: "The Devil is the grand enemy of the Church."

The minister and his wife, Elizabeth, require the children to strictly follow orders. Betty respects her father but is fascinated by the exotic Tituba. Everything about her is strange and different: her bronze skin, the singsong of her Barbados accent, the things she knows about witches. The girls cuddle closer to Tituba in the cold night, for affection as well as warmth. She has raised them. They trust her.

Tituba is a mysterious presence in Salem. Reverend Parris, who inherited a sugar mill in Barbados, bought her and another slave, John Indian, on that island. He then brought the couple back to Boston and eventually to Salem where they are now ensconced. John Indian also lives in the Parris parsonage and is considered to be Tituba's husband, although there is no formal marriage arrangement. The pair understand their status, which is to do what they are told.

Slavery is legal in New England; the first Africans arrived in Boston from the West Indies in 1638. They were traded for tobacco, cotton, and captured Native Americans. Tituba and John Indian are part of an estimated two hundred African slaves in the region.*

---

* Slavery was abolished in Massachusetts in 1783. A court ruling said slavery was incompatible with the state constitution. However, the ruling did not result in direct emancipation. It was the first state to ban the practice outright.

All slaves must hide their intelligence and anger behind a submissive attitude, or be subject to punishment. But reality is far different. For someone supposedly having no power, Tituba controls the young children. She can lead them where she wants them to go. She can shape them.

Reverend Parris is too busy to realize how much influence his slave has over Betty and Abigail. Indeed, Tituba often sleeps with the children, cooks, cleans, does the laundry, and supervises everything they do.

Meanwhile, John Indian works in the fields, fully aware that Reverend Parris doesn't care about the feelings of his slaves. They are given food and shelter and permitted to attend his church—although they are not allowed to be members. His responsibility is to provide for their physical and moral well-being. What Parris will never give John or Tituba is freedom.

Slaves, of course, carry with them memories, and sometimes a knowledge of the dark arts. On Barbados, an English-controlled island colony, "vodun" is common. It is a religion based on a variety of spirits that circulate around a single god. In some places it is called voodoo and its goal is to bring all lives into harmony.

Voodoo could not be more opposite from the Puritan ethic.

Tituba is a clever woman. She understands she can manipulate the children any time she wants. She also knows what John Indian has told her: Above all, slaves must survive. They do whatever they have to in order to make that happen.

In October 1691, a woman in nearby Middlesex is convicted of witchcraft and imprisoned. Two months later, eleven-year-old Mary Knowlton awakens screaming that something is pricking her with pins—and an elderly woman is soon arrested for bewitching her. Reverend Parris makes sure everybody knows about these nearby cases—including his children.

In early February 1692, the Devil comes to Salem.

✢ ✢ ✢

Betty Parris is sitting quietly by the night fire. Without any warning, as if struck by an invisible force, the nine-year-old goes into convulsions. She starts flailing, her arms flying into the air, her body twisting into bizarre positions. She is hurled onto the floor, screaming in fear, then barking like a dog. There is a pause, and she straightens, a pleading look in her eyes—then it starts again. She shrieks in pain, she whines, then crawls under furniture.

"I've got the fever," young Betty cries.

As quickly as the fit began, it ends. The girl collapses onto the floor, helpless. Tituba rushes to her aid and informs her master, Reverend Parris. Over the next few days, it happens again and again. Then cousin Abigail is afflicted by the same mysterious force. Her fits are more dramatic than Betty's. During one of them, she runs wildly around the house, almost falling into the fireplace. Abigail grabs pieces of burning wood and throws them. Reverend Deodat Lawson, who is visiting the Parris home when this happens, writes, "Stretching up her arms as high as she could, and crying 'Whish, whish' several times."

Word about Betty and Abigail spreads quickly throughout Salem. People are talking, although in hushed, scared whispers.

It could happen to their children.

It could happen to them.

The girls are getting more attention than ever before. Their fits arrive more often. They are being pricked with pins, they complain; they are being pinched. When asked who is doing this to them, they don't answer—instead they begin choking.

Reverend Parris prays for them. Have mercy on my children, he beseeches the Lord.

He consults the village doctor, who tells him there is no medical cure for the behavior. Parris knows his most fervent prayers are not being answered. So he goes to an expert.

Reverend John Hale, the respected minister from nearby Beverly, is asked for his opinion. Hale has spent decades investigating cases of witchcraft. "It is preternatural," he explains. "The hand of Satan is in them." There is only one thing to do: "Sit still and wait upon the Providence of God."

There is a folk remedy, although it is very dangerous. A neighbor, Mary Sibley, tells Tituba and John Indian they have to bake a witch cake so they can discover exactly who is bewitching the children. Tituba follows instructions; the witch cake consists of rye bread mixed with the girls' urine then baked in white ashes. She feeds it to the family dog—hoping the dog will somehow indicate who the witches are. It doesn't work—the dog shows no sign of altering its behavior. But word gets out that Tituba knows all about the world of witchcraft. That spells danger for the slave. Suspicions rise. It is now obvious to some who is bewitching Betty and Abigail:

Tituba.

It doesn't take long for the children to identify their tormentor. Betty and Abigail tell Reverend Parris it is, indeed, Tituba's "specter" who is pinching and pricking them with pins. Her spirit follows them around the house, they claim, and she knows what they are doing even when she isn't in the room.

The day after Tituba is named, two other girls in the village, Ann Putnam and Elizabeth Hubbard, are afflicted—and both of them know exactly who is tormenting them. This time it is a nasty, sometimes homeless elderly woman named Sarah Good. Ann and Elizabeth continue their accusation, also naming Sarah Osborne as a witch. The sickly woman is scorned by the village for marrying her much younger indentured servant. The new charges are not hard for town officials to believe.

On March 1, 1692, constables arrest Sarah Good, Sarah Osborne, and Tituba and bring them in for questioning.

The hearing is simply to discover if there is sufficient evidence to charge the three accused women with witchcraft. The proceedings are to take place at Ingersoll's Tavern, the most popular gathering spot in Salem village. But Ingersoll's is too small to hold the large crowd of people who want to attend—so the hearing is moved next door to the dark, decrepit Sunday meetinghouse.

Magistrates John Hathorne and Jonathan Corwin conduct the proceedings. The four bewitched young girls are present to identify their tormentors. Before the hearing begins, the three accused witches are searched for telltale witches' birthmarks. None are found.*

Good and Osborne are questioned first. Both of them deny they are witches, although they do accuse each other of practicing witchcraft. When Sarah Good says she has done nothing wrong, the afflicted girls immediately become "dreadfully tortured and tormented for a short space of time." They fall to the floor and writhe side-by-side, screaming gibberish in shrill voices.†

Spectators are stunned. Yet this is exactly what they have come to see. Most have heard about these fits, but nothing adequately describes seeing it in person. Few people believe the girls are faking it.

Sarah Good's husband testifies. No, he doesn't think his wife is a witch. Yet he doesn't much like her, and has no problem saying so. "She is an enemy to all good," he says.

Tituba is next.

The slave stands to face her accusers. She remembers her "husband"—the law does not recognize slave marriages—John Indian's oft-repeated advice: the first duty of a slave is to survive.

---

* Hathorne and Corwin were not "justices" as such; they were both merchants who served as magistrates—in terms of the Salem witchcraft trials, it might be preferred to refer to them as judges, although it's not clear that they carried that title.

† The description, as well as additional quotes, is taken from the notes compiled by thirty-seven-year-old tailor Ezekiel Cheever Jr., who is charged by the court to take notes by hand.

She knows she has to be clever if she wants to live. At this point there is little question about Tituba's guilt. But in the world of witchcraft trials, escaping the hangman's noose is assured if the accused confesses.

"Why do you hurt these children?" Hathorne begins.

"I do not hurt them."

Then who does hurt them?

"The Devil, for ought I know."

And then Tituba stuns the packed meetinghouse She tells them what they want to hear: she is indeed a witch.

"The Devil," Tituba boldly states, "came to me and bid me serve him."

A gasp fills the room. There is no longer any doubt about what is happening in Salem. The Devil is here. People glance around nervously. They look at their neighbors in a new way, trying to recall strange things people have done. And they remember who came to them in their dreams.

Tituba doesn't hold back. She makes herself valuable. The authorities want to believe Sarah Good and Sarah Osborne are witches. She confirms it. She tells them she has seen four women hurting the children: "Goody Osburn [sic] and Sarah Good and I do not know who the other two were." She explains that it was Osborne and Good who gave her orders to inflict harm: "Hurt the children or they do worse to me."*

Tituba continues to tell vivid stories. She describes flying through the air on a stick. She says a yellow bird offered "pretty things" if she served the Devil. No, she has not told any of this to her "master" because she is afraid he would cut off her head if she was a witch.

There isn't a sound in the room as she gives her testimony. Even

---

* The term *Goody* is used to identify a married woman, generally of low status. It is slang for *goodwife*. A wealthy or upper-class woman would be addressed as *Mistress*.

the four afflicted girls sit quietly. No one has ever seen anything like this. Very few witches ever plead guilty.

At the end of her testimony, Tituba suddenly covers her eyes with her hands and complains, "I am blind now. I cannot see."

No one is surprised. The Devil is angry she is revealing his secrets.

The hearing is adjourned. Tituba's testimony has created a sensation.

One day later, Tituba is brought back for more interrogation. Word has spread that a witch is confessing. She has met the Devil. Far more ominous, she knows there are other witches in the village.

The crowd is even larger than before. People fill every seat and squeeze into vacant spaces. Body heat warms the freezing-cold meetinghouse. There has never been such revealing testimony.

Tituba actually feels empowered. It is an incredible feeling for a slave. Two days ago, she was a piece of property. Suddenly, she has the power of life and death over the people who have looked down on her for years. Strong men fear her. When Tituba looks at them, they turn away.

She continues to embellish. The Devil offered her a deal, telling the slave she must "serve him for six years and he would give me many fine things."

He wanted her to "do hurt to Betty," but she resisted. "I would not hurt Betty. I love Betty."

The questioning continues: Did she see the Devil's book? Oh yes, the Devil showed it to her. She signed it in her own blood and saw other signatures. There are nine witches, Tituba says—more than anyone suspected.

The only names she remembers seeing were Good and Osborne. She can't identify anyone else. All she knows is that some of them live in Boston, others are right here in Salem.

Tituba's testimony is not always consistent. Sometimes her

descriptions change. In later hearings nine witches will become dozens.*

By the time Tituba finishes testifying, Salem has declared war on witches. She has spread a wide net, telling the village that it isn't just females who are in league with the Devil—she has also seen well-dressed men seeking the evil one's company. She doesn't know who these men are. They could be anybody.

It is chilling. Salem has no choice: the town *has to* investigate every accusation, make arrests, conduct trials, and, if necessary, execute the witches. But what to do with Tituba? Once a witch confesses, the Devil usually leaves her. That's why confessed witches are not punished. "The truth" frees them.

Tituba has saved herself. If she had denied what everybody believes is true, she probably would be executed. Instead, she is imprisoned.

From the relative safety of her cell, Tituba watches as the terror she has unleashed takes control of Salem. Reverend Parris embraces her confession. This is exactly what he has been warning for years. The fact that it started in his own household, with his own children, is extremely strong evidence that the Devil is trying to stop *him*. For more than a year there have been people in the village who have tried to get the pastor removed. They refused to pay his salary—they wouldn't even provide wood for his winter fires. Now he knows why. The motive for fighting him becomes clear when Mary Warren becomes the next person afflicted.

The twenty-year-old Mary is a plain young woman with diminished prospects. Life has been hard. Both her parents died and left her nothing. She is a servant, working for John and Elizabeth

---

* Because the new English Royal charter is not yet in force, there is no established legal procedure to follow other than common law. There is no record that accused people or witnesses were sworn in before testifying. But all of the testimony was recorded by hand, providing a record of the proceedings.

Proctor. She watches the first hearings from the meetinghouse gallery, sitting with the other servants.

✢ ✢ ✢

A pattern repeats itself. Mary Warren is another of Salem's marginal people. No one cares what happens to her. Her employer, John Proctor, is a wealthy fifty-nine-year-old farmer and tavern owner. He has been married three times and fathered eighteen children. He works the land while his wife, Elizabeth, runs a tavern. John is a big man with a temper. He is the leader of the group trying to rid the village of Reverend Parris. But now, his servant seems to be possessed by the Devil. And Parris is poised to use that against John Proctor.

The tavern owner doesn't believe any of the witch accusations. It's all nonsense. He has no patience for little girls whining about being terrorized by invisible people. There are others in the village who feel the same way, but most of them are afraid to speak up. Nobody wants to attract attention to themselves.

Mary Warren is sitting at her sewing wheel when the affliction strikes her. She says she is picked up and twisted. Her whole body contorts. She writhes in pain and screams for help.

John Proctor will have none of it. He tells Mary if she doesn't cease this spectacle he will "thrash her." Her fits stop. She admits to Proctor that she faked her symptoms—and accuses the afflicted girls of doing the same thing.

The response from the girls is almost immediate: Mary Warren is a witch! She is doing the work of the Devil by casting doubt. She is detained and questioned. Once again, people crowd into the meetinghouse. They want to know the truth.

Mary's accusers sit only a few feet away from her. The hearing starts calmly. She is asked, "You were a little while ago an afflicted person. Now you are an afflicter: How comes this to pass?"

"I look up to God," she replies, her eyes downcast in respect. "And take it to be a great mercy of God."

In an instant the girls "are grievously afflicted." Others also suffer fits—including Tituba's "husband," John Indian. He falls into a seizure. He rolls on the floor, pleading for help.*

Mary Warren seizes the opportunity. Just as she is about to confess, she is "attacked" by the specters of John and Elizabeth Proctor, her employers. The court records that her senses are taken away from her. She can't see, hear, or speak. The fit lasts for several minutes. It is the most astonishing hearing yet.

There is no use further questioning Mary. Every time she tries to respond she is incomprehensible. The hearing ends with no charges against her.

Yet.

The scene has been set. It is Reverend Parris against John and Elizabeth Proctor. And someone will die.

Witch hysteria is now full-blown. All of New England is beginning to hear about it. It replaces the Indian raids as a primary source of apprehension.

Tituba is kept in prison for thirteen months. According to Puritan law, a prisoner has to pay the costs of the jailing. But the slave has no money. Finally, someone pays for her release, and she disappears along with her "husband," John Indian. They have successfully employed the slave code: they have survived.

Others will not be as fortunate.†

---

* John Indian attends numerous hearings where he has fits. He doesn't name any witches, but other afflicted people include him in their testimony. The slave never reveals why he has involved himself in the witch trials. But some have speculated he is bitter over Tituba's imprisonment.

† Tituba then disappears from the historical record. Nothing is known about her after 1693.

Chapter Seven

The Devil is in the details.

It is a cool late spring morning as Thomas Newton, thirty-one years old, ponders life and death. Four years ago, Newton arrived in the colonies in response to an appeal that honest lawyers were needed in the New World.

He is an ambitious man and quickly becomes attorney general of New York. His most important qualification is that he is one of the few British-trained lawyers in America. Newton knows how the legal system is supposed to function. And he is tough.

In New York, he successfully prosecutes several Dutch men for treason. They attempted to overthrow the king's chosen governor. Two of them are convicted and hanged, but, by English law, that was not the end of their ordeal. "Their bodys Cutt downe to the Earth and Their Bowells be taken out and they being Alive, burnt before their faces; that their heads shall be struck off and their Bodys Cutt in four parts."

Newton's relentlessness comes to the attention of the Puritan preacher Increase Mather, who learns the young man may be in danger as followers of the executed Dutchmen are seeking revenge.

Mather then recruits Newton to come to Salem.

The timing is perfect. More than one hundred suspected witches are locked behind bars, waiting to be tried. Thomas Newton will select the first case.

That choice is vitally important. It will set the tone for all the trials to come. No witch can be allowed to escape. However, picking the initial person is not an easy task. "I fear we shall not this week try all [of them]," Newton writes, "by reason the trials will be tedious and the afflicted persons cannot readily give their testimonies, being struck dumb and senseless . . . at the name of the accused."

✛ ✛ ✛

Bridget Bishop senses it is *her* they are coming for.

It's just a matter of time. The outrageous, three-times-married, sixty-year-old Salem resident has heard the stories. Witches are at play. Arrests are being made.

So it is that on April 18, 1692, Bridget Bishop hears a loud banging on her front door. The constable, holding his staff of office, tells her she is being arrested for the "sundry practice of witchcraft." She is accused by four young girls of having her "specter" inflict hurt on them. He shows her the arrest warrant and orders, "Come with us."

Bridget takes a deep breath. There is nothing she can do. She is innocent, but no one cares. She has to submit to the process. Who knows how long it will be before she is home again? The aging woman's arrest is popular with the people in Salem. All witch arrests are. It is a troubled time. The area is suffering economically in comparison with the rest of Massachusetts Bay.

In addition, the Indian threat is real and terrifying. In order to pay for the militia to protect residents, taxes have been raised in Salem. But perhaps worst of all is that young people are straying from the traditional Puritan lifestyle.

It is clear why: witches.

The response is obvious: get rid of them.

✛ ✛ ✛

On the morning of April 19, Bridget Bishop is taken from her cell, her hands tied behind her back. She is carted standing up through the village to the Town House, where the grand jury will hear her preliminary testimony in her case. This will determine whether or not she stands trial. As Bridget approaches the two-story-high brick building, she glances at the old meetinghouse—seconds later a nail-studded board comes crashing down.

The guards look at each other nervously. Everyone knows what that means. The Devil is watching.

✛ ✛ ✛

The lower floor of the Town House is used as a grammar school. The fire department stores its equipment there. Town meetings are held on the second floor, where the eighteen-member grand jury is seated. Bridget Bishop is accused of several counts: "Wickedly and feloniously hath used Practised and Exercised at and within the township of Salem . . . wicked Arts." As a result, her accusers are "hurt, tortured, Afflicted, Pined, Consumed wasted & Tormented."

Bridget is actually the fourth accused witch brought before this grand jury. Two previous prisoners, Mary Warren and Abigail Hobbs, have confessed. The only man so far arrested, Giles Corey, pleads innocent. It has been a long morning, but the courtroom is still packed. However, Bridget is not intimidated. Asked to make her plea, she says in a firm voice, "I am innocent. I know nothing of it. I have done no witchcraft."

But four witnesses disagree. They say Bridget is tormenting them.

"I never did hurt them in my life," she says as she looks at the four young girls. "I never did see these persons before. I am as innocent as the child unborn."

In an instant, her four accusers are screeching in pain, their heads twisting and turning in unnatural positions. Only when Bridget looks away does the "torture" end.*

When order is restored, lawyer John Hathorne says, "They say you bewitched your first husband to death."

She replies, "If it please your worship I know nothing of it."

This is too much for accuser Ann Putnam, who screams at her, "She calls the Devil her God."

"Tell us the truth," Hathorne demands. "How come these people who are tormented charge you with doing it?"

"I am not come here to say I am a Witch," she responds. "To take my life away."

Seventeen-year-old Mary Walcott testifies that her brother struck at Bridget's "specter" with his sword—and Mary heard the fabric ripping. Court officials carefully examine the coat Bridget is wearing—they find a swatch of cloth hanging loose, as if it has been torn. "A rent that seems to answer what was alleged was found," the court is told.

"I am no witch," Bridget repeats.

"Have you not to do with familiar spirits?"

"I have no familiarity with the Devil."

"How is it then that your appearance [specter] doth hurt these?"

"I know nothing of it. I am innocent to a Witch. I know not what a Witch is."

✢ ✢ ✢

The grand jury does not believe her. Judge Hathorne tries to trap her. "How can you know, you are no witch, and yet not know what a witch is?"

The accused stands straight and tall. "I am clear: if I were any such person, you would know it."

---

* The descriptions of the hearing are taken from court records, which exist to this day at the Peabody Essex Museum in Salem.

It is clearly a threat. A low murmur ripples through the courtroom. "You may threaten," Hathorne warns, "but you can do no more than you are permitted."

Another accuser stands and asks her, "How come [your apparition] came into my bedchamber one morning and asked me if I had any curtains to sell?"

"I am innocent," she pleads. "I know nothing of it." In frustration, Bridget opens her eyes wide and looks to heaven.

Instantly, almost as if they are connected, the young victims' eyes roll back in their heads. Their cries bellow through the courtroom. Ezekiel Cheever has been writing down the proceedings with his quill. At the end of his notes he adds, "I have also . . . taken notice that all her actions have great influence upon the afflicted persons and that [they] have been tortured by her."

The grand jury hearing ends. Bridget knows she has very little hope of acquittal. The town has been after her for years. However, it is punishment that concerns her. She thinks back to 1680, the last time she was tried for witchcraft. She hadn't been punished. But this time there is a different feeling in Salem. Fear and anger are aimed at her.

The court decides there is enough evidence to try Bridget Bishop for "sundry acts of witchcraft."

Bridget is taken back to her cell to await her formal trial. Outside, Salem is gripped by anticipation.

✢ ✢ ✢

Bridget Bishop languishes in a dirty jail cell for six weeks, barely given enough food and water to survive. She well understands her plight. Her husband, Edward, has abandoned her, fleeing the area. She has no legal advocate.

Worst of all, anti-witch hysteria is building.

✢ ✢ ✢

In the meantime, there has been a power change in the Massa-chusetts Bay Colony. William Phips is the newly appointed royal governor. Like Thomas Newton, Phips is a disciple of the powerful preacher Increase Mather. He was appointed governor by King William and Queen Mary, at the behest of Mather. The powerful job is his reward for delivering wealth to the Crown.

Williams Phips, a largely uneducated man, made his fortune as a treasure hunter. He is one of the New World's first homegrown heroes, a man of action, not books. He has little interest in prose-cuting witches.

In 1687, Phips recovered a great treasure from a sunken Spanish ship, the *Conception*, in the Caribbean. The bounty of silver, gold, and jewelry was substantial. Phips sent a portion of the wealth to the king. In return, he is knighted—one of the first men in the colonies to receive that honor.

In May 1692, William Phips returns to New England from London as the royal governor. He lives in Boston but is well aware that a growing number of people are being accused of witchcraft in Salem. He also knows there is a sense of panic in the colony. More than 125 people have now been arrested and imprisoned for witchcraft in Salem and Boston. Every day neighbors are turning on each other as more people are accused. The jails in Salem and Boston are overflowing. Phips has to get the situation under con-trol. He turns to his mentor, Increase Mather, for advice.

To meet the threat, on May 27, Governor Phips makes the un-usual legal choice of creating the Court of Oyer and Terminer—a phrase meaning to "hear and determine" the witchcraft cases. Normally, such a commission only hears cases of treason and fel-ony. A judge and grand jury will sit to listen to evidence before making this decision. At Increase Mather's suggestion, Phips ap-points Thomas Newton chief prosecutor. Most of the jurists will be successful Puritan merchants.

The prosecution is allowed several different ways of showing proof of witchcraft, including the introduction of "spectral evidence." Of course, there is no possible way of refuting such claims because the accused is not allowed to present any defense.

Lieutenant Governor William Stoughton will hear the cases, heading the nine-judge Court of Oyer and Terminer. Stoughton lives in Dorchester, just outside Boston. He is an arrogant, intimidating man with no fear of witches. As a Puritan, he knows God protects the righteous. For three decades he has prospered and become a wealthy landowner and merchant. Stoughton has nothing material to gain by accepting the role as the chief witch hunter. He takes the position to protect the people of New England from this terrible threat. But there is a risk.

The Devil is a dangerous adversary to anyone who opposes him.

✣ ✣ ✣

Bridget Bishop will finally stand trial.

On June 2 at ten o'clock in the morning, the Salem witch court is called to order. Before witnesses are introduced, Doctor William Griggs physically searches several accused women for the "devil's mark." They find one on Bridget—a "preternatural excrescence of flesh between the pudendum and anus much like teats and not usual in evidence." Barton examines her again in three hours—the mark has disappeared! The thought can't be avoided: Has the Devil removed the evidence?

Bridget is brought upstairs. Her five accusers are present. She looks at them and, immediately, they are thrown into convulsions. None of the twelve jurors can possibly ignore the spectacle.

The courtroom is silent as the evidence is presented. There's a lot of it, and it is damning.

One of the afflicted girls, teenaged Susannah Sheldon, says Bridget's spirit admitted to her that she had killed four women. Another young victim sits with her hands folded and describes calmly how Bridget took her from her spinning wheel to the river and threatened to drown her if she didn't sign the "Devil's book."

The gruesome testimony continues. A thirty-two-year-old tailor, John Louder, says Bridget's specter came at night and beat him on his chest. When he confronted her in person, Louder testifies, the Devil "sent black pigs and a talking, flying monkey with the face of a man to threaten him."

"Not true!" Bridget cries. "I don't even know this person."

Judge Stoughton is appalled. "How can that be when your orchards are next to each other? And the two of you have had many arguments?"

✢ ✢ ✢

The verdict is guilty. No one is surprised.

Since the medieval reign of the Holy Roman Empire and its *Constitutio Criminalis Carolina* code of law, the proper method of executing a witch has been burning at the stake. It is estimated that fifty thousand such killings have been conducted this way in Germany, Scotland, France, England, and Scandinavia since the fifteenth century. Yet a new English law stipulates that hanging is now the legal style of execution.

Judge Stoughton issues the sentence. "Whereby [the accusers'] bodies were hurt, afflicted, pined [*sic*], consumed, wasted and tormented," even if they looked healthy to spectators, Bridget Bishop, alias Oliver, is ordered "hanged by the neck until she is dead."

Until that moment, Bridget still had hope. Since 1647, eighty people have been accused of witchcraft in the colonies but only thirteen have been executed. Bridget will be number fourteen.

✢ ✢ ✢

Midmorning on June 10, the bedraggled Bridget Bishop is taken from her cell and put on a cart. As she is drawn through Salem, people stop whatever they are doing to look at her. There is hate in their eyes. Her journey is one very long mile. She is taken to a rise visible from much of the town, which will soon become known as Gallows Hill. A small crowd follows the wagon. Among them are several of the afflicted girls and Reverend Hale, who is holding a Bible.

The summit is too high to pull the cart all the way to the top. So at the bottom of the ridge, at a rocky outcropping that will become known as Proctor's Ledge, Bridget's hands are tied behind her back. There is no room to build a gallows, so a tree will suffice. Her dirty petticoats are fastened tightly around her legs, for modesty. Reverend Hale lowers his head and prays loudly. The fact that he would pray for a witch disgusts several people, and they will tell him so later.

Sheriff George Corwin reads out the sentence: death. One last time, Bridget pleads her innocence, begging for help. The last thing she sees before the burlap sack is placed over her head is the pious and bearded Reverend Hale, a fifty-six-year-old pastor grasping his Bible as if it were a weapon.

It is a beautiful spring morning. The sun is shining, a sign of God's approval. A ladder is put below the thick branch of an old oak tree. Two men lift Bridget onto it. She feels the noose as it is placed over her head, then tightened around her neck.

Suddenly, the ladder is kicked out from beneath her. Bridget slowly strangles, kicking out hard with her legs. Then she is still.*

The crowd approves. They are safer now.

But in reality, no one is safe in Salem.

---

* There is no record of what happened to Bridget Bishop's body. The ground beneath what will become known as Proctor's Ledge was too rocky to serve as a burial site. In legend, victims were buried in shallow graves and at least three of them were later recovered by their families and reburied near their homes. A memorial was unveiled at Proctor's Ledge in 2016. There is also a memorial at Charter Street Cemetery, which was dedicated in conjunction with the Witch Trials Tercentenary in 1992.

✢ ✢ ✢

In Boston, Governor William Phips does not like what he is hearing about witches. He quickly leaves Massachusetts and travels north to Maine to fight rebellious Indians, leaving his wife alone. That decision will prove disastrous.

Back in Salem there is a new controversy. It is much easier to convict someone of witchcraft if "spectral evidence" is allowed, but there is debate about this. The powerful Increase Mather is opposed to the admission of spectral evidence: "To take away the Life of any one, meerly because of a Spectre or Devil, if a bewitched or possessed person does accuse them, will bring a Guilt of Innocent Blood on the Land."

But his son, Cotton Mather, defies his father—advocating the use of spectral evidence. He convenes a group of twelve ministers to give an opinion. They fall in line with him. Spectral evidence should be permitted in a witch trial. For some of the accused, that decision seals their doom.

✢ ✢ ✢

Cotton Mather is very pleased. But not everyone feels that way. One witchcraft trial judge, Nathaniel Saltonstall, resigns in disgust. The first witch execution, that of Bridget Bishop, has rattled Saltonstall. But soon rumors spread that he has another reason for stepping down: several of the afflicted claim to have seen his specter with known witches. The judge says nothing and continues to reside in the area as the accusations die down. No action is taken against him.

Nathaniel Saltonstall is fortunate.

The gallows of Salem are only beginning to be put to use.

Chapter Eight

Rebecca Nurse is next.

The frail seventy-one-year-old English-born resident of Salem stands trial this morning for witchcraft. She will plead not guilty.

And she stands a very good chance of winning her case.

✜ ✜ ✜

Rebecca's problems began three months ago in March, as twelve-year-old Ann Putnam awakens at first light.

She will claim that she sees a witch standing over her, a diabolical smile on her face. There is fire in her eyes. She is dressed in nightclothes and carrying a red book—the Devil's book.

Ann recognizes the specter. It is Rebecca Nurse, whom she has known most of her life. The last person anyone would suspect of being a witch. Nurse angrily thrusts the red book at her. Sign it! she demands. Sign away your soul.

Instead, Ann closes her eyes and begins reciting Scripture, her faith the only weapon against the Devil.

The battle for her soul rages for two hours. Rebecca Nurse promises greater rewards if she signs. Ann refuses.

Morning finally arrives. The specter disappears. Ann Putnam is saved.

But she does not forget.

✣ ✣ ✣

At the same time, Rebecca Nurse is resting in her own bed. She has been sick in her house for a week. Her husband, Francis, tends to her. Rebecca has no idea what is coming. She simply wants to feel better.

✣ ✣ ✣

Salem is stunned when Ann Putnam's accusations are delivered to the court. In the past, those accused of being witches have been outcasts—poor or socially marginal. They are known to be difficult and cause problems. The village will be better off without them.

But Rebecca Nurse and her husband are well respected. They are wealthy, pious people who regularly attend church services. They have lived in the community for nearly five decades. They have helped it grow, shaped its values. Rebecca is a gentle woman, admired for her compassion and decency.

Ann Putnam's accusation sends a warning: if a good person like Rebecca Nurse can fall prey to the Devil, no one is safe.

But beneath the surface there are worldly issues: Francis Nurse is a member of the five-man committee trying to get rid of Reverend Parris. Francis is also involved in a property dispute with the Putnam family. Clearly, things have become political.

Around town, the accuser's mother, also named Ann Putnam, is respected but considered "fragile." Three years earlier her sister and three of her children passed away. Her wealthy father, George Carr, also died, leaving his entire estate to her brothers. Then Ann's infant daughter died. It is too much, people whispered, and has left her troubled in the mind.

Rebecca Nurse learns she is accused only when four friends visit her bedside. She is bewildered. "As to this thing," she says, "I am as Innocent as the child unborn, but surely, what sine hath god found out in me unrepented of that he should Lay such an Affliction upon me In my old age?"*

In late March, Rebecca is arrested and carried out of her house to answer the accusation. Once again, the meetinghouse is packed with spectators. This is Salem's first witchcraft trial of a respectable person.

It is almost stunning. When Rebecca married Francis only about a thousand people lived in Salem—fewer than one hundred of them on farms outside the town proper. In the ensuing years, Salem and nearby Boston have become two of the economic engines of the colonies. It is the most populous area in America, a sophisticated center of trade, commerce, and immigration. When one of New England's first newspapers, *Publick Occurrences*, begins publishing in 1690, more than two thousand people reside in Salem, about five hundred on farms.

Francis and Rebecca Nurse have played an important role in the area's growth, becoming founders and active members of the Puritan church.

A conviction will prove everyone is in jeopardy, even the most faithful. But an acquittal will cast doubt on those who deliver "spectral" testimony.

The hysteria surrounding Rebecca Nurse spreads.

She is now accused by several others, including Ann Putnam's daughter and Abigail Williams, who has fallen under the spell of Tituba. These girls attend the hearings and mimic every move

---

* This response was submitted to the court in a deposition filed by the people who visited her on March 24, 1692: Israel Porter, Elizabeth Porter, Daniel Andrews, and Nurse's brother-in-law Peter Cloyce. Eventually, the wealthy Andrews is accused and flees to safety. Cloyce's wife, Sarah, is also accused but survives. Elizabeth Porter was Israel Porter's wife. Daniel Andrews was later accused of witchcraft and fled Salem only to return later after the trials ended. He was not tried.

Rebecca makes. She spreads her arms; the girls fly to the floor. When she tilts her head to the side, one of the girls' necks bends sharply—and another one cries out to straighten Nurse's head before the girl's neck is broken.

Rebecca Nurse is sternly ordered to stand quiet even though she is ill. At times, a constable holds her hands together.*

Judge John Hathorne is relentless in his pursuit of the Devil. Some wonder about the source of his zealotry. Maybe he really is fighting evil. But, by statute, the property of a convicted witch is seized to pay for lodging in jail and the trial. Hathorne and other court officers are well paid for their services.

Rebecca Nurse knows a confession may save her life. Witches who admit dealing with the Devil almost always receive clemency. They are no longer a danger. The Devil abandons them. But Rebecca refuses, swearing, "I can say before my eternal father I am innocent. . . . I have not been able to get out of doors these eight or nine days."

Ironically, Rebecca *does* believe witches exist. Like many residents of Salem, she is unsure as to whether or not an evil spirit can take control of her body, using her as a vessel to afflict others.

That presents a difficult question: If the Devil creates a specter in the image of an innocent person, is that individual responsible for crimes committed by the specter? Judge Stoughton resolves the problem. He rules that the Devil cannot take on someone's appearance unless that person gives permission. Stoughton's judgment is based on no legal precedents. It is simply his belief.

Rebecca Nurse's trial begins on June 30. Bridget Bishop was hung in Salem just three weeks ago, so Rebecca and her husband know her life is at stake.

---

* Law enforcement in New England is based on the English system, in which a constable would follow the court's directives. That includes making arrests, serving warrants, and keeping order in the courtroom.

✣ ✣ ✣

The jury consists of twelve men. By law, they all must be members of the church. Rebecca Nurse has little chance. According to English law, accused persons are guilty until proven innocent. They are not allowed to be represented by a lawyer nor to present a defense. Witnesses appear and are questioned by the prosecutors and the judges. No one is allowed to act formally on Rebecca's behalf.*

But there is unrest in Salem. Some are outraged about the trial. Unlike the public response to most of the other accused witches, people are supporting Rebecca Nurse. Among them is John Putnam's brother, Nathaniel. His property borders the Nurses' land, and there have been quarrels over where the boundary lines are drawn. However, when Rebecca is accused, Nathaniel Putnam makes a strong witness for her. This shocks some of the onlookers. Nathaniel is on record as believing in witches and that they must be punished. He, himself, has accused two women of being disciples of the Devil and provided evidence against two others. So his doubts about Rebecca Nurse make an impact on the court.

Nathaniel Putnam stands before the judges, holding a hat in his hands, speaking calmly. "What I have observed of her human frailty is excepted," he says. "Her life and conversation had been according to her profession [of her Puritan faith] and she hath brought up a great family of children and educated them well."

As for the property feud, "I have known her to differ with her neighbors, but I never knew or heard of any did accuse of what she is now charged with."

That complicates things. As Judge Stoughton suggests, if Rebecca Nurse is actually innocent, the "afflicted" children are murderers. The jury must decide who to believe.

---

* The University of Chicago Library website explains this in the following: "The colony created the Court of Oyer and Terminer especially for the witchcraft trials. The law did not then use the principle of 'innocent until proven guilty'—if you made it to trial, the law presumed guilt. If the colony imprisoned you, you had to pay for your stay."

In the middle of the testimony, one of the afflicted, thirty-six-year-old Sarah Bibber, suddenly cries out in pain, shouting that Nurse's specter has jabbed her with pins. She lifts her skirt to show marks left just below her knee.

Immediately, Rebecca's daughter-in-law Sarah responds: "I saw Goodwife Bibber pull pins out of her [clothes] . . . then she cried out and said Goody Nurse pricked her."

The courtroom erupts. An afflicted woman has been accused of lying. If true, it means there is deceit, which might cast doubt on previous accusations.

The judges calm the courtroom. Then they allow accuser Bibber's claims to be entered into the record.

Rebecca Nurse's trial lasts several hours. Thirty-one witnesses testify or provide depositions attesting to her good character. But several people stand against her. Among the final witnesses are confessed witches Deliverance Hobbs and her teenaged stepdaughter, Abigail. Naming witches and testifying against them guarantees *their* survival.

Rebecca has been imprisoned with them. So she is surprised to see Deliverance and Abigail brought into the courtroom. "What? Do these persons give in evidence against me now?" she asks. "They used to come among us."

Deliverance Hobbs testifies she had seen the defendant at a witches' "gathering."

The jury deliberates briefly. Foreman Captain Thomas Fisk, a soldier who had led Salem's militia to victory in King Philip's War, pronounces the verdict: NOT GUILTY!

The courtroom is stunned. No one expected this decision. Even before Rebecca Nurse could thank the Lord, the afflicted girls react. They scream, writhe in pain, their limbs twisted. They shriek and howl. Within seconds, other afflicted girls standing outside the courtroom respond the same way.

Judge Stoughton is surprised by the verdict. After calming the courtroom, he speaks directly to the jury. Perhaps, he asks, they did not fully understand that Rebecca Nurse had referred to a confessed witch as "one of us." Is that not a confession, he wonders.

The jurors are confused. They stay their verdict and question her: What did she mean by that?

But Rebecca Nurse stands mute, completely confused by events. Seconds pass. Everyone in the courtroom waits for her response. She says nothing in her defense.

Her silence is taken as evidence.

The jury immediately reconsiders its verdict: GUILTY!

Rebecca is removed from the courtroom and taken back to her dingy cell. Later, she is asked by her family why she didn't respond. She was confused, she says. She thought she had been acquitted. And besides, because of her poor hearing, she didn't understand the question in the noisy courtroom. When asked, jury foreman Fisk explains the consequences of that. "I could not tell how to take her words . . . till she had a further opportunity to put Sense upon them, if she would take it.

"But [she] made no reply, nor interpretation; whereupon these words were to me a principle evidence against her."

Stoughton pronounces her sentence: death by hanging.

Rebecca appeals, explaining, "My saying that Goodwife Hobbs and her daughter were of 'our Company;' but I intended . . . they were Prisoners with us. And I being hard of hearing, and full of grief . . . had no opportunity to declare what I intended when I said they were of our company."

Too late. Salem has turned against Rebecca. She is doomed.

✤ ✤ ✤

On Thursday, July 3, 1692, Rebecca Nurse is brought in chains to the church. It is a sorrowful sight. Since its founding twenty years earlier, she has been an upstanding member of the congregation. No longer. She stands there as Reverend Nicholas Noyes asks the congregation if a convicted witch should remain a member of their church.

The vote is unanimous. She is excommunicated.

For her, this punishment is as painful as her death sentence. She will never be allowed to take communion. Her soul is condemned to hell.

Still, her husband, Francis Nurse, fights for her life. They have been married almost five decades. He spends all his time gathering statements attesting to his wife's good character and travels to Boston to present his petitions to Governor Phips. This is a mistake, he pleads. She's an old woman, hard of hearing; she didn't hear the judge's questions. She recognized the Hobbs woman from prison, not from a gathering of witches.

Governor William Phips has just returned from the Maine frontier and hears the petition. Phips is easily persuaded. He is fighting a brutal war against a local Indian tribe—he has no time to battle "spirits." He agrees to grant a reprieve. It looks like Rebecca Nurse's life is saved.

Phips's ruling arrives in Salem before Francis Nurse can even get home. The "afflicted" respond with grand seizures. Their own lives are in jeopardy, they fear. If the witch is freed, she might take revenge against them.

A group of unnamed "Salem gentlemen" ride quickly to Boston, twenty-five miles away, to meet with Phips. He is dealing with many serious problems and has little interest in getting further involved in this situation.

Using the technique of Pontius Pilate, the governor throws up his hands, then rescinds his decision.

Rebecca Nurse's sentence is reinstated.

✦ ✦ ✦

Saturday, July 19, is an oppressively hot day in New England. Five witches, Rebecca among them, are to be hanged this morning. It is the largest execution yet and has attracted the biggest crowd.

The condemned women are carted through Salem, with a

procession of villagers falling in line behind them. Francis Nurse and several members of his family join the procession. They walk slowly to the top of the rise above town.

Reverend Noyes stands near the witches, begging the convicted to confess so they can die with truth on their lips. None of them do. Rebecca Nurse is quiet and dignified as a hood is slipped over her head.

Noyes turns to Sarah Good, telling her to confess so she does not die a liar. "I am not a witch," Good says firmly.

Reverend Noyes calls her a liar.

"You are a liar!" Sarah shouts loud enough to be heard by the crowd. The spectators are shocked. All the other witches have died in peace with God. But Good is furious at this injustice. "I am no more a witch than you are a wizard. And if you take away my life, God will give you blood to drink."

Those are her last recorded words. It is a curse from Revelations.

Each of the condemned is hung separately. One by one, they are put upon a tall ladder, which extends to a tree limb. Once on the ladder, a noose is put around each one's neck and the ladder is kicked away. The victim drops quickly and dies from a broken neck. Then the body is removed and thrown into a cart. The same procedure is followed for the next four people.

The five convicted witches are dispatched within thirty minutes—then dumped in a shallow grave.

That very afternoon, new accusations are made.

✛ ✛ ✛

Ironically, Sarah Good's curse will be recalled twenty-five years later, when Reverend Noyes is suddenly struck by a brain hemorrhage, causing him to cough up blood, which eventually chokes him to death.

✛ ✛ ✛

There are now six corpses, including Bridget Bishop, on the Salem witch ledger. The town is somber, afraid, and depressed. All are suspect.

As Rebecca Nurse's situation demonstrates, the hangman's noose does not discriminate.

Chapter Nine

It has been a cold winter in Massachusetts.

John Proctor is in the central room of his Salem farm home. Morning light is shafting through the small windows. His twenty-year-old servant girl, Mary Warren, sits across the room at her spinning wheel. Last week, Mary had a visit from seventeen-year-old Elizabeth Hubbard, an afflicted young woman. With excitement, Elizabeth told Mary about the turmoil taking place in Salem village.

Days later, Mary feels the Devil.

She stops weaving, staring into the shadows. She sees an apparition, a neighbor. She reaches toward it, pulling it onto her lap.

John Proctor notices her behavior. He is aware of all the craziness in the village, and it isn't welcome in his house. "It's nobody," he says firmly.

Mary tells him she sees his specter.

"It's my shadow," he says. He has warned her before, "You are all possessed with the Devil. It is nothing but my shape." If this nonsense keeps up, he threatens, he will have to "thrash" the Devil out of her. That's the best way to deal with all this, he has boasted to others. One trip to the whipping post would end the spectacle.

Apparently, Proctor has hit Mary Warren before. In Salem, this is an acceptable way of dealing with miscreant servants and slaves.

Mary returns to her spinning wheel. In the past Proctor's threats silenced her. Not this time.

✛ ✛ ✛

Many in Salem are deeply disturbed by the witch hunt. But they are afraid, not wanting to attract attention. John Proctor is different—he loudly asserts the entire thing is a fraud.

Proctor is a large man, tall, broad-shouldered, and stout. He and his family live just outside the village and attend the town church. Like Francis Nurse, Proctor's decision not to support the village parsonage infuriates the Putnam family and Reverend Parris.

John Proctor has been married three times, burying two wives, and has eighteen children. He settles near Salem in 1666, renting seven hundred acres of farmland and opening a tavern on Ipswich Road, the dirt path separating the town and the village. By Salem law, Proctor can serve only nonresidents, so his tavern becomes a popular stopping place for passersby, who often bring the latest news from Boston.

In 1678, Proctor was accused by neighbor Giles Corey and several other men of serving "cider and strong water to an Indian." Corey testified the man got so drunk he passed out cold on the floor. Proctor is fined a small amount.

But it is actually Proctor's third wife, Elizabeth, who runs the tavern. She is a robust woman with a tainted past. Her grandmother Ann is a Quaker and a midwife, two reasons Salemites distrust her. Ann's ability to heal people and safely deliver babies is so unusual that the nearby town of Lynn tries her for practicing witchcraft. She is acquitted but remains suspect.

Elizabeth also has another curious connection to witchcraft: she is related by marriage to the executed witch Rebecca Nurse.

✛ ✛ ✛

The servant Mary Warren has had a rough life. Both her parents are dead, and at an age when most young women are preparing for marriage, she is stuck working for low wages. She is looking for a way out. Against John Proctor's wishes, Mary testifies against Rebecca Nurse. Proctor is furious. Once again, he threatens to beat her. But Mary Warren will not cease and desist.

People are beginning to believe that John Proctor is a danger to the community. He has influence. Many consider him the leader of the movement to get rid of Reverend Parris. He is a big target.

Several of the afflicted young girls claim his wife, Elizabeth, is tormenting them. The accusations are backed by Proctor's enemies, including Reverend Parris. But John Proctor refuses to be silenced. Rather than hanging so-called witches, he tells anyone who will listen, it is the people behind this farce who should be hanged.

It is a fatal mistake.

On April 4, 1692, Proctor is arrested. The primary evidence is given by Abigail Williams, who says his specter attacked her. One week later, John and Elizabeth Proctor are questioned in court. They proclaim their innocence. Abigail Williams cries out that she sees his specter and says that he is "going to hurt" Sarah Bibber, one of the accusers. At that point, Bibber immediately drops to the floor and begins convulsing.

Although Elizabeth Proctor is pregnant, she and her husband are imprisoned. This is a big step. Until now, only females have been accused.

The Proctors' property is seized by the sheriff, including all household goods and cattle.

Spectators pack the meetinghouse for every hearing. People squeeze together on the windowsills, blocking the light and making the courtroom even darker.

At Elizabeth Proctor's hearing, the girls break into fits. Abigail Williams screams that John Proctor's specter is in the courthouse. She can see him. He's threatening to hurt her if she accuses his wife. The other girls join in. They claim to see him too. One of them even claims Proctor is sitting in the judge's lap.

Mary Warren is not among the accusers—at least not yet. Instead, she cares for the five Proctor children, left alone when their parents are thrown in prison. Her silence infuriates the other girls—until they realize that she, too, is a witch.

Facing that lethal accusation, it takes Mary three weeks to admit that John Proctor's specter forced her to sign the witches' book. She is a witch, she confesses. Among the first people she names is Elizabeth Proctor, swearing that she "hath often tortured me most grievously by biting me and choking me and pinching me and pressing my stomach till the blood came out of my mouth."*

✤ ✤ ✤

The witch hunt expands. Whole families are ripped apart. In addition to John and Elizabeth Proctor, three of his children, two of Elizabeth's relatives, and three more distant relations are arrested. The Devil must be stopped if Salem is to be saved. All opposition to Reverend Parris is now eliminated, and he attends most of the hearings, adding the authority of the Puritan Church to the proceedings.

Many people have known John Proctor for decades. They understand he can be difficult, but they also believe he is honest and fair. No one has ever seen him have anything to do with the occult. More than fifty people, including some of the wealthiest members of the community, file petitions, telling the court the Proctors are upstanding people and should be spared. The petitioners suggest

---

* Mary Warren's role changes several times, from afflicted to accused to accuser. Eventually she identifies more than twenty people as witches and testifies in numerous trials. Her lies save her. It is not known what happens to her after the trial's end.

that the Devil is behind the accusations, citing that Satan once used a specter to become the prophet Samuel.

John Proctor can't believe this is happening to his family. He is a good Christian. He writes to Reverend Increase Mather, still presiding over Boston's prestigious North Church, appealing for mercy. He asks the reverend to move the trials to Boston, where he might be fairly judged. He knows he has no chance if he is tried in Salem. "Our innocent blood will be shed" because "the People . . . being so much inraged and incensed against us by the Delusion of the Devil, which we can term no other, by reason we know in our own Consciences, we are all Innocent Persons."*

"Help us," Proctor begs Increase Mather. "They have already taken all our property, but they won't be satisfied until they have [our] blood."

The letter does no good. The powerful Mather will not intervene.

On August 2, the Proctors are tried. Among the evidence is Reverend Parris's handwritten statement swearing he had been told that John Proctor threatened to whip the Devil out of Mary Warren. Also, when asked about the poor afflicted children, Parris accuses Proctor of saying, "Hang them, hang them."

Instead, it is John and Elizabeth Proctor who are sentenced to hang.

Elizabeth's execution is postponed because she is pregnant—although she must stay in prison.

On August 19, John Proctor and four others—including the former Salem minister George Burroughs, who had preceded Parris—are put on a horse-drawn cart and taken one mile to Proctor's Ledge, near Gallows Hill, to be hung. The night before, in his dark prison cell, John Proctor writes a new will. He leaves his

---

* Proctor's letter is written on July 23, two weeks before his trial. In addition to requesting his trial be moved, he also asks for new judges—knowing his fate is sealed with Stoughton and the others on the bench.

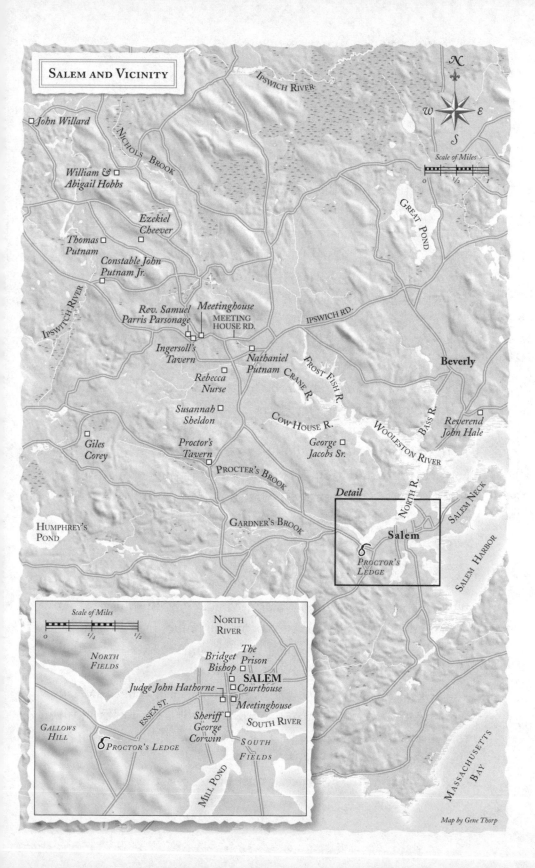

condemned wife out of it, believing she will also be executed. He wants to make sure his children get as much of his property as possible.

John Proctor and Reverend Burroughs are the first men sentenced to death. It is the biggest turnout for an execution thus far. People fall in behind the cart and walk solemnly up the hill to the hanging tree.

They get what they came to see.

✤ ✤ ✤

The execution of Reverend Burroughs, forty-two, is a sensation. He lived a strict Puritan life in Salem for years before moving north to Maine. In fact, after being accused by twelve-year-old Ann Putnam, authorities had to travel sixty-six miles to arrest him.

While he is being transported to the gallows, a huge thunderstorm erupts. Many people believe it is the Devil's attempt to free him.

Increase and Cotton Mather take special interest in his case. Increase actually rides from Boston to attend Reverend Burroughs's trial. Cotton Mather warns everyone that Burroughs had betrayed the Lord in exchange "for the promise of being a King in Satan's kingdom."

Convicting a minister requires substantial evidence, so thirty people testify against Burroughs. One of them is Mercy Lewis, who had escaped an Indian raid in Maine with Burroughs years earlier and then became a servant in his home. "Mr. Burroughs carried me up to an exceeding high mountain," she says, "and showed me all the kingdoms of the earth and told me that he would give them all to me if I would write in his book and if I would not—he would throw me down and break my neck: but I told him they were none of his to give and I would not write if he threw me down on 100 pitchforks."

After hearing the evidence against Burroughs, Increase Mather writes, "Had I been one of his judges, I could not have acquitted him."

Cotton Mather is front and center at the execution of the five "convicted" witches.

While all proclaim their innocence, they ask Reverend Mather to pray with them. He does. As George Burroughs stands on the ladder, the rope around his neck, he prays so diligently many people start crying. It is his final sermon and perhaps his greatest. "He gained the admiration of all present," a spectator wrote; his words struck "like that would be produced by thunderbolts." They knew him when he served the community. Many of them like him and wonder how they could have been fooled so completely. But they cannot forgive him.

Then Burroughs does something unexpected. In clear tones, he recites the Lord's Prayer. The spectators are stunned: witches cannot do that. The Devil doesn't allow it. One of the witnesses, Samuel Sewell, writes that the reverend's perfect recitation "did much move unthinking persons."*

There is a murmur in the crowd—folks beginning to question if somehow a mistake has been made. People were so upset, said one spectator, "there was fear that it seemed to some that the spectators would hinder the execution." The afflicted girls speak up: they see the Devil standing near Burroughs, dictating the correct words of the Lord's Prayer.

On horseback, twenty-nine-year-old Cotton Mather has been watching closely as the executions unfold. He's pleased death day has finally come. But the prayer causes everything to stop. The spectators turn to him. He understands their confusion but says, "The Devil has often been transformed into an angel of light. Satan is a cunning enemy."

The crowd is appeased. The nooses tighten.

---

* Forty-year-old Samuel Sewell was one of the nine judges appointed by Phips to the Court of Oyer and Terminer to hear witch cases.

✤ ✤ ✤

The bodies are taken down and buried in a single unmarked grave. It is done so quickly, rumors circulate, that parts of Burroughs's body poke up out of the shallow ditch.

Elizabeth Proctor is spared. She remains in prison until winter, awaiting the birth of her child. By the time John Proctor III is born in January 1693, the witch fervor has somewhat quieted. However, Judge William Stoughton will not relent. He makes a last-minute effort to have Elizabeth executed—but fails. She is eventually released.

Ironically, having been convicted, she is still considered a witch. All of her property is gone. It takes more than a decade before a portion of it is restored.

✤ ✤ ✤

There have now been eleven accused of being witches executed in Salem. All citizens live in fear they could be next. Well, almost all.

For Increase and Cotton Mather, the witch executions are bringing fame and prosperity. They are absolutely happy to be doing the Lord's work.

Chapter Ten

No one is more powerful in New England than Reverend Increase Mather.

Except, perhaps, his son, Reverend Cotton Mather.

Together they are the voice of God. They are very clear about it: God approves of hanging witches.

It takes courageous men to lead the fight against demons. The most powerful weapons are the spoken and written word as well as meaningful prayer. Increase and Cotton Mather accept this challenge. Together, they use the strength of the pulpit to make New Englanders aware that witches have arrived—and they must be found and destroyed.

Salem was settled in 1626 in order to give glory to God. "It is the 'city upon a hill, a shining light for all to see.'" Nothing has changed in sixty-six years. Among all the ministers in New England, it is the Mathers who are closest to the deity. It is his wishes they channel.

The Mather saga began in Boston in 1635. The family patriarch, Reverend Richard Mather, flees England to escape religious persecution. He immediately establishes himself as an expert on Puritan doctrine. In 1640, he collaborates on *The Whole Book of*

Psalms Faithfully Translated into English, commonly known as the Bay Pslam Book. It is the first book published in North America.

Richard's son, Increase, enters Harvard College in 1651 as a twelve-year-old and thirty-four years later becomes the school's first Massachusetts-born president. Increase Mather's ability to understand and interpret the lessons of the Lord, as recorded in the Bible, make him one of the best-known men in the colonies.

When he becomes minister of the North Church in 1664, Boston is an increasingly important city of almost three thousand residents, with "streets many and large, paved with pebble stone" and houses of "brick, stone and lime, handsomely contrived."

Increase Mather lives in a comfortable home on North Square with his wife, Maria, who is also his stepsister. Their house is conveniently only steps away from the church. Increase spends most of his time working in his den, saying, "I have loved no place on earth more." He keeps a library of almost one thousand books. While preaching and leading Harvard, he becomes the most prolific author in New England, which brings him fame, prestige, and wealth.

Increase Mather is a lean and somber man. His face is oval, and his features are soft. He is almost handsome. His appearance serves to reinforce the belief that he is a common man with an uncommon intellect. People travel long distances to hear his sermons.

Increase is not a hellfire preacher. He does not threaten people who stray with eternal damnation. Instead, he instructs. "He spoke with a grave and wise deliberation," wrote his son. "But on some subjects his voice would rise . . . that the Hearers would be struck with an Awe, like what would be produced on the Fall of Thunderbolts."*

The elder Mather is a shrewd man who doesn't want to push

---

* Hellfire-and-brimstone preaching refers to loud, raucous, threatening sermons using vivid biblical references of eternal damnation to frighten parishioners into obedience.

the Puritan faithful too far. So his sermons comfort but also warn what might happen if people sin. One widely circulated sermon proclaims "The Day of Trouble Is Near." The tract laments rising materialism: "As we now begin to espouse a Worldly Interest, and so to chuse a new God, therefore no wonder that War [with the Indians] is like to be in the gates . . . if thou hast but one Tear in thy Eyes, if thou hast but one prayer in thy heart, spend it now."

Reverend Mather is also a champion of strict rules. In his essay "An Arrow Against Profane and Promiscuous Dancing," Mather denounces "mixt" dances, wondering, "Is this a time for Jigs and Galiards?" He rails against "Stage-Plays," maypoles, drinking, gambling, and pagan Christmas celebrations.

People love him. He is their teacher and guide to heaven. Ministers tend to all aspects of life, and, unlike politicians, they are trusted. Citizens turn to Increase Mather for advice on both religious and secular matters.

The reverend is so greatly respected that when King Charles II revokes the Massachusetts Bay Colony's charter in 1684, Mather travels to England to negotiate a new one. The results are better than anyone expected. The Crown grants increased self-governing powers and the right to elect a legislature, and unites Massachusetts Bay and Plymouth. This success makes Increase Mather even more powerful.

So when Mather tells people that witches are real and actually living among them—they know it is true.

Witches exist. They are here in New England. In Salem. Their specters are not bound by natural laws; they can fly, they can pass through walls, they can inflict pain—and they can commit murder.

The appearance of witches in New England, Increase Mather explains, is caused by a decline in religion. It is God's way of expressing His unhappiness with the increased emphasis on commerce, possessions, and individual achievement.

The reverend approaches the subject of witchcraft as a warrior and scholar. While some people question the existence of super-natural beings, the majority of New Englanders believe witches are very dangerous. Mather's 1684 essay "Illustrious Providences" re-lates several stories of witchcraft as well as his own practical knowl-edge. In it, he rejects many of the folk tests for finding witches as superstitious and unscientific. For example, he writes that some people believe "water refuseth to receive witches into its bosom," so suspected witches can be tested by being cast into water. If they sink, they are innocent. As a man of science, Mather dismisses this as "having no foundation in nature, nor in Scripture . . . the Bodies of witches have not lost their natural properties."

✛ ✛ ✛

As the number of executed witches grows, it is obvious control has been lost. Now, there's nothing Increase Mather can do to stop the hangings even if he wanted to—which he doesn't. However, he finally delivers a sermon urging New Englanders to "attend to his or her own soul," which is taken as a message to focus on personal issues rather than witches.

No one listens.*

The only witch trial Increase Mather actually attends is that of Reverend George Burroughs, who may have once substituted for him on the pulpit at North Church. When Burroughs is found guilty, Mather doesn't say a word. His silence is interpreted as approval.

His son, Cotton, seconds the motion and attends Burroughs's hanging—calming the large crowd when objections are raised.

Cotton Mather is far more outspoken in support of the witch hunt than his father. Cotton is twenty-nine years old when the trials begin, the eldest of Mather's children. In 1674, at age eleven, he becomes the youngest entering student in Harvard's history.

---

* It is widely believed Increase Mather feared that someday the witch hangings might be found to be illegitimate, even immoral. Knowing that, he tempers his message for history.

He is following the path laid down by his father. He is a brilliant young boy and intends to go much further.

Religious fervor is the theme of Cotton's life. As an eight-year-old, the child reads fifteen biblical chapters every day. He writes, "In my early youth, while others were playing in the streets, I was preaching to large assemblies, and I was Honored with great respect among the people of God."

Unlike his father, who is known for his "silver tongue," Cotton Mather stammers. That disability sets him apart and shapes his personality. For a time, it causes him to consider medicine as a career. But with discipline, he overcomes the impediment by teaching himself to speak slowly and deliberately. In 1685, he joins his father as co-preacher of the prestigious North Church.

Although he never equals his father's accomplishments as a colony leader nor becomes president of Harvard, Cotton surpasses him in the campaign against witches. No one fights the Devil harder than Reverend Cotton Mather! In his book *Memorable Providences*, Cotton alerts New Englanders that witches have arrived. His story of the Goodwin children bewitched by Goody Ann Glover creates a great stir. He tells readers what to watch out for, warning that witches could appear as their specters. That they can fly. That they gather at night in meadows to meet with the Devil. And in their supernatural shape, they do the work of the Devil.

The book terrifies Salem—and makes Mather the leading expert on witches.

Cotton Mather fathers fifteen children by the first two of his three wives. Life expectancy in the colonies at that time is about sixty-five years—much higher than in England. However, Mather's first two wives die young. His third spouse, Lydia Lee, whom he describes as "one that shines forever with a Thousand Lovelinesses," slowly goes insane. The cause is not known, although he claims, "She has been attacked by an evil spirit."

The tragedy of Cotton Mather's life is that only six of his fifteen offspring live to maturity. The harsh New England climate too often causes disease and death. Three of his children die from measles. Another is accidently smothered by a nanny keeping her warm. Mather finds some solace, he says, in the fact that God had told him they would all go to heaven.

Cotton Mather also has money problems, supporting all the children and his three sisters on a minister's salary. So he begins to write. And write. And write. All told, Mather publishes more books and essays than any other person in American history.

And it isn't all theology. The reverend also writes about history, science, and even verse. His knowledge of science is so respected he is one of the first Americans invited to join London's Royal Society for Improving Natural Knowledge—a prestigious organization chartered in 1660 to advance experimental science.

Incredibly, Cotton Mather could write in seven languages, and even learned the Iroquois dialect. In these areas he far outpaces his father. He is credited with some four hundred published works.

In his personal appearance, Cotton Mather is meticulous. His shoulder-length hair is well groomed, even after a horseback ride. He wears expensive clothing and the finest boots made in England. The austerity of his father is lost on Cotton.

He also indulges in fine food and drink and, as the years pass, becomes quite corpulent. That doesn't seem to bother any of his three wives, two of whom turn out children at an astonishing rate.

But above all, Cotton Mather is obsessed with fighting the Devil.

Whenever the witch call comes, Mather responds.

In one case, a woman named Martha Carrier defends herself against accusations, calling her child accusers crazy. The powerful Mather responds by describing Goody Carrier as "a Rampant hag" and "the Queen of Hell."

She is executed on August 19, 1692.

However, there is a problem developing. As more witches are hanged, the governor of Massachusetts Bay, William Phips, is becoming uneasy. He doubts that witnesses really see "supernatural" beings in their visions and dreams. Phips does not believe in "spectral evidence." So he asks Cotton Mather and several other ministers for guidance. People will live or die depending on what they say. If the governor tells the courts to ignore spectral evidence, the witch trials will soon end.

That would be the worst thing that could happen to Cotton Mather.

The clerics confer and Mather writes the report. Among the dozen people who sign it is his father. The ministers now oppose relying solely on spectral evidence to condemn witches. But, at the same time, the clerics support the ongoing witch hunt, urging "the speedy and vigorous prosecution of such as have rendered themselves obnoxious, according to the direction given in the laws of God."

Governor Phips is satisfied. The trials continue.

Privately, there is growing tension between Increase and Cotton Mather. The father knows the son is ambitious and wants to become a co-minister of the North Church. Increase is against it but is forced to agree because the congregation strongly supports his son.

Another source of friction is that Increase Mather has finally come to the conclusion that spectral evidence is morally wrong. "It would be better for ten witches to go free," he writes, "than for one innocent person to be condemned." But he does not publicly criticize his son, who has now become the most feared witch hunter in North America.

However, that description has a downside. Respected English-born writer Robert Calef ridicules Mather's participation in the witch trials. Calef's attack on Cotton in his book *More Wonders of the Invisible World* is so harsh that no one in Boston will print it, so it is published in London in 1700. Long after the trials, Robert Calef directly blames Cotton Mather for the witch executions and general hysteria in Salem.

Rather than responding to the charges made in Calef's book, Mather calls him a "follower of Satan," citing a passage from Exodus: "Thou Shalt Not Speak Evil of the Ruler of Thy People."

Among the readers of Cotton Mather is a teenager named Benjamin Franklin. Born in Boston in 1706, Franklin certainly is aware of the events in Salem. He is considered a young man of great promise and pseudonymously contributes articles to his brother's newspaper. Among them are parodies of Cotton Mather's writing. But the more Franklin learns about Mather, the more intrigued he becomes.

In 1722, sixteen-year-old Ben Franklin arranges a meeting with the reverend at Mather's home. Years later Franklin remembers their conversation as enjoyable and productive. "He condescended to entertain me," Franklin wrote, "with some pleasant and instructive conversation."

As he is leaving Cotton Mather's house, the minister suddenly issues a stark warning: "Stoop! Stoop! Stoop!" But Franklin does not pay attention—and bangs his head against a low beam.

"Let this be a caution to you," Mather advises, "not always to hold your head so high. Stoop, young man, stoop, as you go through the world—and you'll miss many hard thumps."

Young Benjamin Franklin gets the message: remain humble. But he does not realize at the time how much Reverend Cotton Mather will influence him and his country in the years to come.

✣ ✣ ✣

Back in Salem, the evil continues. There is no end to the pattern of accusation and execution.

And, incredibly, things are about to get even worse.

Chapter Eleven

Margaret Jacobs is terrified.

Watching from a window, the sixteen-year-old sees men make their way down the gently sloping meadow and cross the Cow House River. They are leading an empty cart. The men barely wet their boots—a long drought has left the river only inches deep. She recognizes one of them, the small, burly constable, John Putnam. "They're here, Grandpa," she says, with fear in her voice.

Her grandfather, eighty-three-year-old George Jacobs, hobbles over to the window on his two canes. His eyesight is failing but he can see four men approaching. He lays a reassuring hand on Margaret's shoulder but says nothing. They are innocent of any crime.

Margaret reaches up, covering his hand with her own. She is shivering.

Behind them, the family's twenty-year-old servant, Sarah Churchill, stands excitedly, hands clasped on her apron. She has a bemused smile on her face. She has been waiting for this day. "Bitch-witch," the old man had called her. "Bitch-witch," more than once. Now he would learn his lesson.

Just yesterday, four members of the Jacobs family found out they are accused of witchcraft. In response, Margaret's father,

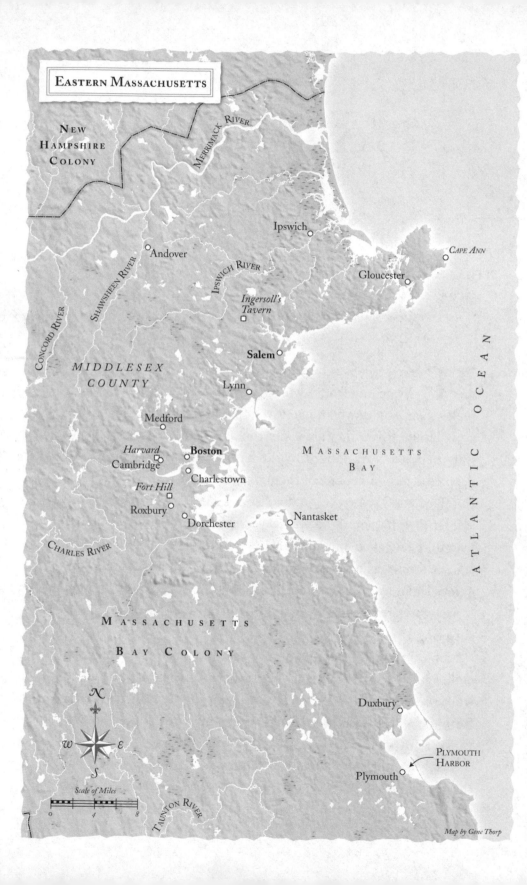

EASTERN MASSACHUSETTS

NEW
HAMPSHIRE
COLONY

MERRIMACK RIVER

Ipswich

Cape Ann

Andover

IPSWICH RIVER

Gloucester

SHAWSHEEN RIVER

Ingersoll's
Tavern

CONCORD RIVER

Salem

MIDDLESEX
COUNTY

Lynn

Medford

ATLANTIC OCEAN

Harvard
Cambridge

Boston

Charlestown

MASSACHUSETTS
BAY

Fort Hill
Roxbury

Dorchester

Nantasket

CHARLES RIVER

MASSACHUSETTS

BAY COLONY

N

W   E

S

Duxbury

Scale of Miles

0   4   8

PLYMOUTH
HARBOR

TAUNTON RIVER

Plymouth

Map by Gene Thorp

George Jacobs Jr., and her uncle, Daniel Andrew, flee in the night. They tell no one where they are going—leaving young Margaret and old George to fend for themselves.

George Jr. also leaves behind his mentally ill wife, Rebecca, and their four other children. Rebecca's mother acknowledges her daughter is "crazed, distracted, and broken in her mind." Her husband believes no one would harm a damaged woman and young children. It is him they want—so he vanishes.

Now, there is a knock on the door. In that instant, life changes for Margaret and her grandfather. The officers immediately arrest Jacobs and the girl. The old man is lifted into a cart. Margaret then joins him for the trip to jail. Days later, Constable John Putnam will return to the farm to arrest the delusional wife, Rebecca Jacobs, and seize her husband's property. He takes everything, from the food in the pantry to her wedding ring. As Rebecca is led away, the remaining four children run after their mother until they can no longer keep up.*

✤ ✤ ✤

George Jacobs Sr. is a cantankerous old man. He settled in Salem with his second wife in 1658 and eventually amassed a large amount of land. He has always been a loner, rarely attending church services. Most of his neighbors keep their distance, wary of his "salty tongue" and his temper. They remember his trial years ago for beating his indentured servant to death—even though he was acquitted of the charge.

So no one is surprised when he is accused of witchcraft. The family has always been troublesome. Not young Margaret, though. She has never bothered anyone. But now, people wonder if she has inherited some of her mother's "distraction."

The teenager has grown up on the family farm, doing her chores

---

* The four Jacobs children are separated and taken in by neighbors.

and helping raise her younger siblings. She is a simple, hardworking girl, and there hasn't been time—or need—for education. The Jacobses are not religious, they don't read the Bible, so Margaret is barely literate.

Like other girls her age, she daydreams that one day she will be married and raise a family of her own. But that is a long way out, as she is locked in a Salem cell where men she does not know are asking her frightening questions. Is she a witch? Are there witches in her family? She can't think. She is cold and scared—and alone.

The interrogators continue: You're lying! they insist. Tell the truth!

Margaret wants it all to stop. But there is only one way to make that happen. She must confess. Gradually, Margaret begins to falter. She can save her own life by admitting she is a witch and accusing others. These men interrogating her will help do that.

Salem citizens have learned that confessing your dealings with the Devil will save your life. The widow Dorcas Hoar is found guilty of witchcraft and sentenced to hang. But after she confesses and names others, she is given a reprieve. Several more people follow that strategy and live. The message is clear: the court wants admissions of guilt.*

The law does not recognize the concept of innocent until proven guilty. Margaret Jacobs does not understand the law but realizes she is likely to be hanged if she does not confess to being a witch. For her, it is lie or die. And she chooses the former.

✢ ✢ ✢

---

* The concept of confessing guilt can be traced back to the fourth century BC, when ancient Greek and Roman courts asked defendants if they were innocent or guilty. People who pled guilty generally received a reduced sentence. It has been part of English law since at least 1164. "Plea bargaining," confessing in exchange for a reduced sentence, was used for the first time in America in Salem but did not become common until 1832, when defendants in Boston began making deals. Today, in the United States, it is a staple of the criminal justice system.

Margaret breaks down. She is a witch, she admits. When the court informs her that the family servant, Sarah Churchill, has accused her grandfather, she agrees it is true. Yes, she has seen him perform diabolical feats. Yes, he has signed the Devil's book.

But at his own hearing on May 14, George Jacobs refuses to confess. Instead, he makes fun of the accusation, telling the court, "You tax [takes] me for a wizard, you may as well tax [take] me for a buzzard. I have done no harm."

George Jacobs remains chained in his cell through the summer, as does his granddaughter. As his trial approaches, Jacobs knows the hangman's noose awaits. When he is inspected by authorities, "witches marks" are found on his body. Ordered by Judge Hathorne to recite the Lord's Prayer, he stumbles, leaving out entire sentences. His fate is obvious: "Hang me or burn me," he tells the court. Six people testify against him, including his granddaughter. On August 5, 1692, the eighty-three-year-old is convicted and sentenced to death.

Margaret is distraught. Her testimony has condemned her grandfather, whom she loves. So she makes a courageous choice—to save him she takes back her own confession, as well as her accusations. Nothing I said is true, she claims. I am not a witch. I did not see any others. Her reason, she says, is pure: "The Lord, charging it to my conscience, made me in so much horror, that I could not contain myself before I had denied my confession, which I did, though I saw nothing but death before me; choosing rather death with a quiet conscience, than to live in such horror, which I could not suffer."

Upon saying that, Margaret has put her own life in jeopardy. Now she will be tried.

And it is too late to save her grandfather. George Jacobs Sr. is going to die.

✦ ✦ ✦

Two days before her grandfather is to be executed, Margaret is granted the right to visit him. Three months in chains have weakened him. There is death in his eyes.

Forgive me, Margaret begs. I had no choice. I was confused, frightened. I thought we would be safe.

The old man looks at his granddaughter, the young girl who betrayed him to save herself—then found the courage to recant. Offering her own life to save him. George and Margaret are only permitted a few minutes together, not enough time to say what they want.

Jacobs remembers his religious teachings. He understands and accepts his granddaughter did what was necessary to survive. He even includes her in his will, leaving her £10, two cows, and four sheep.

They embrace each other for the last time.

On August 19, 1692, the eighty-three-year-old Jacobs Sr. is hanged by the neck until dead.

✛ ✛ ✛

Margaret survives the winter. Her trial is postponed, and by the time it is rescheduled Governor Phips has paused the executions. In January 1693, she officially takes back her confession, telling the court, "They told me, if I would not confess, I should be put down into the dungeon and would be hanged, but if I would confess, I should have my life . . . with my own vile wicked heart, to save my life; made me make the confession I did, which . . . is altogether false and untrue."

Margaret remains imprisoned in Salem for several more months, unable to pay her court fees. Eventually, her father and uncle return from Maine, where they had been hiding. All charges are dropped against the Jacobs family—thanks to Governor Phips. Incredibly, the family stays in the Salem area, where Margaret marries and eventually gives birth to seven children.

✢ ✢ ✢

The Gospel according to John is clear: "If we confess our sins, He is faithful and just to forgive us our sins and to cleanse us from all unrighteousness."

But in Salem, "forgiveness" is harsh. It is permissible to torture an accused person until he or she admits the "truth." In the English legal system, witchcraft is considered *a crimen exceptum*—a criminal act so exceptional that extreme measures can be used to combat it.

The Salem court takes pride in its method of extracting a confession. It does not resort to the old European methods of inflicting pain with medieval devices. There are no "iron maidens" or finger screws.*

Instead, the accused are chained in small, damp, rat-and-lice-infested cells for months. They spend much of their time in darkness. The Salem jail is near the North River, and during the highest tides the water in the cells is ankle high. Unless prisoners can afford straw for bedding, they sleep on hard wood. They aren't given sufficient food and sometimes are deprived of drinking water.

If those conditions are not harsh enough to force a confession, other methods are used. Prisoners are tied to chairs for long periods or made to stand for hours with their arms outstretched. They are locked in cells so small they can't sit down. Their feet are hogtied to their neck and they are hung upside down until blood flows from their nose and eyes. They are poked and pricked with pins, sometimes in intimate places.

But all that will stop with an admission of guilt.

✢ ✢ ✢

---

* The iron maiden is a torture device rumored to have been used in medieval times. It is a human-sized hinged box with stakes on the inside, so when it swings closed the victim inside the box is impaled.

Salem sheriff George Corwin is profiting from the witch hysteria and has his eyes on eighty-one-year-old Giles Corey's farm, a large holding a few miles south of town. If Corey were to be convicted of witchcraft, his property would fall under the power of Corwin. Thus, things begin to unfold.

Corey's third wife, Martha, is arrested in late March 1692. The sixty-two-year-old woman attracted attention to herself by criticizing the court and the young accusers. Although known for her piety and a respected member of the church, she makes the mistake of admitting she does not believe in witches and warlocks. When the first accusations are made, she tries to persuade her husband not to attend the witch hearing. It's too dangerous to be there, she warns him.

When he insists on going, she hides his saddle.

Giles Corey is furious. A woman has no right to stop her husband. He manages to get to the meetinghouse. There, he publicly complains about his wife, telling people she believes the afflicted are lying and the judges are corrupt.

Days later, Martha Corey is accused. People in Salem are reminded of her scandalous past: Two decades earlier, she gave birth to an illegitimate mixed-race child, who now lives with her and Giles. It is widely suspected his father is Native American. But Martha has spent her life repenting that sin and has been forgiven.

Initially, her husband actually supports the allegations. People who know them are not surprised. It is rumored to be an unhappy marriage. They are known to bicker. Giles testifies against her, claiming that among other crimes she has often tried to stop him from praying.

A husband admitting his wife is a witch is unusual, but no one is surprised when Giles Corey does it. He is a nasty old man with few friends. Several of his neighbors still believe he got away with the murder of an indentured servant. But then the saga of the Coreys takes another turn.

Giles is also arrested and charged with witchcraft. The accusation is ridiculous. He knows he isn't a witch. But he also knows there is no way out.

"I never had no hand in witchcraft, in my life."

The usual four or five young girls attend the hearing. They mimic Corey's movements. According to the court transcript, after his hands are tied, he "drew in his cheeks, and the cheeks of some of the afflicted were suckt in."

Giles Corey remains in jail throughout the summer. His trial is scheduled to begin in early September. The brutal heat is rough on the elderly man, but rather than weakening him it hardens his decision: he will never confess to something he hasn't done.

He knows he has little hope of being acquitted. No one who has pleaded not guilty has been spared. He is also aware Sheriff Corwin has taken his property.

So Corey devises a clever plan to thwart Corwin.

While in prison he draws up a will: "I am very weak in body, but in perfect memory," he writes, then deeds all his property, "lands, meadow, housing, movables and immovables, money," to his two sons-in-law.

Corey's trial begins in mid-September. Asked how he pleads, he looks at the judges and says nothing. The law requires a defendant to state his plea—guilty or not guilty—before a trial can begin. As long as the defendant remains silent, the court cannot proceed.

The judges ask him again. But the old man does not reply.

The judges know how to deal with this. According to English law, a defendant who refuses to plead has to be brought into court three times—and each time be warned about the consequences. Corey's continued silence forces the judges to invoke *peine forte* *et dure*, a "strong and forceful punishment." The punishment of pressing to death has rarely, if ever, been used in the colonies.*

On September 17, jailers take Giles Corey to a field next to the Salem jail. He is nearly naked. He lies on the ground and boards are placed on his chest. One by one, large rocks are placed on top of the wood, pressing down on Corey.

More weight is added. Each time, he is given an opportunity to plead. He remains silent.

A full day and night pass. Corey is denied food and given just enough water to keep him alive.

A second day goes by. More stones are added. It is a remarkable display of will, especially by such an elderly man. At one point his swollen tongue protrudes from his mouth.

Sheriff Corwin pokes it back inside with a stick.

On the third day, as an official gets ready to add yet another rock, Corey again is asked how he pleads. His response is simple: "More weight."

Giles Corey dies that day without pleading. As he intended, all his property remains in his family.

✢ ✢ ✢

Three days after Corey dies, his wife, Martha Corey, is taken to what will become known as Proctor's Ledge with seven other convicted witches. Along the route the cart holding the prisoners gets stuck in mud, and it takes some time to be freed. It is generally agreed that this is the work of the Devil, trying to stop the executions.

Author Robert Calef witnesses Martha's death: although she has been excommunicated, "Martha Corey, wife to Giles Corey,

---

* The right to torture a defendant refusing to plead was made legal by the Statute of Westminster in 1275. Originally it meant a defendant was imprisoned and starved until making a plea or dying. In 1406, the penalty became being "pressed," or crushed with weights—stones placed on boards—until there is an outcome.

KILLING THE WITCHES — 109

protesting her innocency, concluded her life with an eminent prayer upon the ladder."

It is a gruesome sight. Eight human beings hanged within an hour. And some in Salem may have had enough. People don't like watching an old man die in agony. Nor his wife hanging from a tree. The whispering begins: maybe this has gone too far.

To counter the rising dissent, twelve-year-old Ann Putnam, one of the afflicted girls, testifies that a specter appears and tells her Giles Corey killed him many years ago. Villagers are reminded that Corey deserves no sympathy.

✤ ✤ ✤

Back in Boston, Cotton Mather knows discontent over the witch executions is a danger to his control. From his pulpit, he claims that Ann Putnam's statement is proof that specters exist because the incident she mentioned happened years before she was born. The only way she could have learned about it was being told by a specter.

✤ ✤ ✤

The executions in Salem have reached critical mass. In London, tales of brutality and legal malfeasance have reached King William and Queen Mary—who become concerned. Soon, the monarchs' displeasure reaches the most powerful man in New England— Governor William Phips. But the governor has a dilemma. In order to stop the witch trials, he will have to go up against Cotton Mather and other influential Puritan clerics. That could present a danger to Phips. The governor's decision will soon come—but in a very unexpected way.*

---

* Since the *Mayflower* arrived in Massachusetts, there have been nine rulers: Kings James I, Charles I, Charles II, James II, William III, and Queen Mary II. Queen Ann ascended to the throne in 1702. The anti-royalist Oliver Cromwell and Richard Cromwell also reigned, though as lord protector instead of king.

Chapter Twelve

A powerful man has been incarcerated. John Alden Jr. sits in a dirty cell awaiting his fate. He has been there four long months. Torches and candles barely illuminate dark, damp stone passages. Locked behind cell doors topped with iron spikes are murderers, pirates, rebels, debtors, Quakers, slaves—and accused witches. Incredibly, the respected Alden, whose parents, John and Priscilla, came over on the *Mayflower*, stands accused of witchcraft.

It is a situation beyond Alden's comprehension, and he knows he could be executed at any time. Thus, arrangements have been made to save him. A key turns softly, his cell door swings open, and several men enter. One of them unlocks his leg chains. Moments later, John Alden Jr. is on a horse, escaping the hangman's noose.*

✢ ✢ ✢

A few months earlier, in May, John Alden stopped in Salem on his way back from Quebec, where he negotiated the release of British

---

* Boston's first jail, located on Prison Lane, opened in 1635. It is surrounded by stone walls three feet thick. One inmate writes, "If there is any such thing as a hell upon earth, I think this place is the nearest resemblance of any I can conceive of." Among prisoners held there was the notorious pirate Captain Kidd.

prisoners captured fighting the French. Alden knows few people in town, but they know him. He is famous throughout the colony.

He intends to rest there only a brief time before resuming his journey to Boston. Word quickly spreads that he is at the inn. That piques the interest of Mercy Lewis and several other afflicted girls. They have become celebrities in Salem and are now more militant than ever before.

The problem is they have never seen and cannot identify John Alden. Nevertheless, the girls take their concerns to the court. Alden is soon arrested on charges of witchcraft.

Salem's jail is so packed with witch suspects that Alden is moved in chains to Boston.

His arrest stuns New England. There must be some mistake. Alden is almost seventy and a member in good standing of the Puritan Church. His father fought alongside Myles Standish and served several terms as deputy governor of Massachusetts Bay. John Alden Sr. also signed the Mayflower Compact—and when he dies in 1687 at age eighty-nine, he is among New England's most revered men.

John Alden Jr. is one of ten children. Like his father, he has spent his life respecting the Crown while building a new country. Living in Boston for three decades, he has gained recognition as a courageous naval commander, a successful merchant, and an Indian fighter. He and his wife, Elizabeth, have twelve children. No one doubts his piety and courage.

At first, Alden refuses to take his arrest seriously. He has fought cunning enemies in combat on land and sea and survived. Now, he is facing several apparently delusional children.

But Alden makes a mistake by underestimating them.*

At his hearing in Salem on May 31, Alden denies the accusations.

---

* No one knows exactly why Alden is accused. Some people believe he was named because he is too friendly with Indians, but more likely the girls wanted to accuse a famous person in order to get even more attention.

Standing on a chair, he watches the proceedings and then bellows, "Those Wenches being present, who plaid their jugling tricks, falling down, crying out, and staring in Peoples Faces."

When Alden closes his hands, the girls hit the floor and curl up. Judge Stoughton tells a marshal to hold the defendant's hands open.

As with other accused witches, John Alden cannot believe this is happening. None of it makes sense. Court officers take Captain Alden, his official rank, outside into the sunlight so the afflicted girls can get a better look at him. The court wants the accusers to be sure it was Alden's specter that tormented them. The girls circle him. One of them shouts, "There stands Alden . . . a bold fellow. He sells powder and shot to the Indians and French and lies with the Indian squaws and has Indian papooses."

The girls continue dancing around him, hurling accusations. Alden is speechless.

After a few days, constables take John Alden back to Boston bound in leg irons. He is one of several hundred men and women accused of witchcraft being held in four different New England prisons. As weeks pass, reality sinks in: John Alden knows he may be executed.

In fact, nine witches are sentenced to be hung in the next weeks. Alden doesn't intend to be the tenth.

On a moonless night in mid-September, John Alden slips out of the Boston jail with the help of paid confederates. They provide a horse, and he rides through the night, hiding by day. He races thirty-four miles to the settlement at Duxbury, where he grew up. Some members of his family still live there.

They welcome him, although no one has been told about his situation. Asked why he has come, Alden responds coldly, "I am flying from the Devil."

He is safe—temporarily. The jails are bursting with accused witches, with more arrested every day. So there is no one available to organize a search for John Alden. But it is too dangerous for him to stay in Duxbury. The witch hysteria has spread beyond Salem to almost every New England town, and because of his fame many people know what he looks like.

He can't hide anywhere in Massachusetts. So he seeks sanctuary far away—in New York City.

It is a long journey, more than two hundred miles, and takes several weeks. But Alden will be safe there. New York is a rapidly growing port city, almost as big as Boston. It has become a haven for people fleeing the witch trials. Unlike New England, which was founded as a Puritan refuge, New York is a secular economic center. The Dutch, who once dominated the city and whose influence is still felt, oppose witch hunts. In fact, practicing witchcraft isn't even considered a crime in New York. While some believe witches exist, prosecutions are rare.*

John Alden remains secure in New York for several months but knows there is a warrant out for him. A proud man, he wants to clear his name. In April 1693, after the trials have paused, he returns to Boston and Governor Phips absolves him of all crimes by proclamation.

Other accused witches also escape. When the sun rises, they are gone from the jails. None of them could have done it without help.

✢ ✢ ✢

By the end of September 1692, Salem has executed nineteen witches. This does not include Giles Corey, who was executed without entering a plea. The number of "afflicted" men and women continues to

---

*The few people actually tried in New York are acquitted. But one of them, known as the Witch of Esperance, is later shot to death by superstitious neighbors unhappy with the verdict. A spoon is melted down to make a silver bullet, and it is fired through her kitchen window. She is buried upside down under a tree, so her soul cannot escape and take revenge.

grow, as it has become obvious that just about all accusations—no matter how absurd—will be taken seriously.

Some accusers are exploiting the witch hunt to get even with people they don't like. Others are using it to settle business or financial disputes.

The fact that convicted witches forfeit their property has made wealthy people enticing targets.

But even after a powerful and admired man like John Alden is arrested, some still refuse to acknowledge the lethal danger.

Captain Nathaniel Cary is a very successful shipbuilder in Charlestown, a settlement northwest of Boston. He and his wife, Elizabeth, are respected and wealthy churchgoers. An ancestor, George Cary, had sailed around the world with Sir Francis Drake, setting foot on the Pacific Coast about 1578. Nathaniel's father settled in Plymouth in 1634. The Carys have five children and live in a stately home.

Few in New England are as secure as the Cary family.

Or so they think.

The Carys are shocked when Elizabeth is accused. She does not know any of the afflicted young girls, nor has she been in Salem for a long time. A whispered word to one of the accusing girls is sufficient. The Carys know Elizabeth is not a witch and naively have confidence in the legal system. They agree to answer the charges and voluntarily make the half-day sail to Salem Town.

Since none of the accusers has ever seen Elizabeth Cary, they can't identify her. The Carys believe that fact will quickly prove her innocence.

But nothing in their lives could have prepared them for what is going to happen next.

Nathaniel and Elizabeth stop at Ingersoll's Ordinary, a popular tavern, the main gathering place in Salem. The afflicted girls are informed and immediately go to the tavern and fall into fits. They mimic each of her movements, screaming in anguish. Authorities rush to the scene and a hearing takes place right there in the ale house.

Captain Cary is stunned at the way his wife is treated. "She was forced to stand with her arms outstretched," he writes. "I did request that I might hold one of her hands but it was denied me. Then she desired me to wipe the tears from her eyes and the sweat from her face, which I did. Then she desired she might lean herself on me, saying she should faint. Justice Hathorne replied she had strength enough to torment these persons, and she should have strength enough to stand."

Prosecutors order the "touch test." Forcefully turning Elizabeth's head so she cannot look at the accusers. Suddenly, one of the girls yanks her down onto the floor.

Nathaniel Cary is furious. "You are inhuman!" he shouts. "God will take vengeance on you!"

The court ignores him. One of the girls testifies Elizabeth's specter admitted to murdering a young child. This evidence is accepted by the court. Prosecutors see with their own eyes how Elizabeth is torturing the poor girls.

Elizabeth Cary is arrested and taken to jail in Boston. Her legs are chained in eight-pound irons.

Nathaniel Cary is well connected. He knows influential people. But they refuse to help him. Everybody is frightened. No one wants to be accused.

While his wife languishes in jail, Captain Cary goes back to Salem. He wants to witness a witch trial, "to see how things were managed," but, "finding that the spectral evidence was there received . . . I did easily perceive which way the rest would go."

In Boston, accused people who can afford to pay a fee are allowed to spend their days in the jail-keeper's house instead of a cell. That's where Nathaniel gives Elizabeth the bad news: "if she were carried to Salem to be tried, I feared she would never return."

There is only one option: escape.

Money makes the difference. Captain Cary arranges for Elizabeth to be transferred to the less secure prison in Cambridge. They know him there. Some of the people in Cambridge are against the trials, although they are afraid to say it. Among them are the respected minister Samuel Willard and his son John.

Young John makes all the arrangements. On a late September night, Elizabeth Cary escapes.

The husband and wife ride as fast as they can. They don't know if anybody is chasing them. They push hard, taking only two days to travel the seventy-five miles to "Road Island."

But it is not far enough. Before they can get settled, they learn they are being hunted.

So they ride to the safety of New York City. There, Elizabeth Cary is welcomed by New York colonial governor Benjamin Fletcher, who has opened the city to the oppressed—as long as they bring money with them.

Back in Cambridge, constable John Willard is arrested for assisting Elizabeth's escape. After a trial, he is found innocent.

✤ ✤ ✤

As the witch hysteria spreads, people have to decide whether to stay in Salem or run for their lives. Not everyone is wealthy enough to escape to New York. However, there are other options. Thomas Danforth is serving as acting governor when the trials begin. He is a wealthy man, owning almost fifteen thousand acres of land southwest of Boston. Danforth has been involved in the colony's government for decades. He is considered tough but fair. He attends one of the first witch trials in Salem and is shocked by the spectacle.

Thomas Danforth respects the law. So he is greatly disappointed when Judge Stoughton not only allows the introduction

of spectral evidence but convicts people because of it. The law is being terribly misused, Danforth believes.

He watches helplessly as innocent people are arrested—and hanged. Danforth begins working quietly to save some of the accused, allowing anyone who can reach his vast property to hide there.

✦ ✦ ✦

Sarah Bridges Cloyce is one of those who hides out in the Danforth estate. She is the youngest sister of executed witches Rebecca Nurse and Mary Eastey. Sarah is a dissident—she becomes a target by storming out of Reverend Parris's church during his sermon affirming the witch trials. She slams the door behind her. That is a huge mistake.

Days later, she is accused of witchcraft. Almost immediately she is imprisoned in Boston's jail.

Tom Danforth watches all this with disgust. He knows Sarah's family does not have enough money to buy her freedom, so he manages to get her transferred to the less secure jail in Ipswich.

There, Sarah's husband, Peter, is allowed to visit her. They both know she has little time left. They also understand several other accused witches have already escaped from Ipswich—one of them twice—but they have all been quickly recaptured. They have to act fast.

Sarah's escape is successful. Jailers cooperate. No doubt, cash changes hands.

Peter and Sarah cannot afford to go to New York, so they must find another sanctuary. They move at night, as much as possible staying off the main road, the Old Connecticut Path. They actually walk fifty miles to reach Tom Danforth's property. It is covered with forests and caves, even hollowed tree trunks that provide good places to hide.

Sarah Cloyce shelters there through the hard winter. The comfortable life she once knew is finished. Now all that matters is survival. She lives in fear constables will come searching for her. She moves her hiding place often. The many "witch caves" on Danforth's land provide protection. Her husband is an experienced woodsman. He knows what to do. The cave entrance is blocked; holes are stuffed with snow and leaves. A small fire provides some warmth. Her family brings her food, blankets, and warm clothes.

So many people fleeing the trials are living in Danforth's forests that they become known as "Salem's End." Thomas Danforth does not supervise the fugitives, nor do they gather together. No one knows who can be trusted.

Sarah Cloyce survives.

The horror of Salem continues. A former constable, John Willard, is arrested in early May. That puts him in severe jeopardy. When a warrant is issued for his arrest, he flees to land he owns forty miles away. But that is not nearly far enough. Constable John Putnam Jr. apprehends him as he works in a meadow and brings him back to Salem.

During Willard's trial, Judge Hathorne declares, "That you were fled from Authority . . . is an acknowledgment of guilt."

John Willard is hanged. The death toll continues to mount.*

---

* The constable John Willard who was hung for a witch was a different person than the John Willard previously discussed—that Willard was the son of the Reverend Samuel Willard who had also opposed the Salem witchcraft trials. John Willard, the minister's son, helped Elizabeth Cary escape. He was arrested and tried, found not guilty—but he wasn't tried for witchcraft. The constable John Willard was tried and executed for witchcraft.

Chapter Thirteen

The stone-gray sky sends an ominous message.

A harsh wind is blowing through the village, bringing a sting of winter. Crisp brown and yellow leaves are swirling to the dry ground. The witch hunter Thomas Putnam pulls his coat together for warmth as he bends into the wind, walking rapidly down Meeting House Road toward the courthouse. His shoulders are hunched protectively, his Puritan hat pulled down tight. He clutches two furled depositions from his afflicted daughter, Ann. He has spent much of the night writing them by the flickering light of candlewood.

Demons have been at work again; he knows it is up to him to stop them. It is his great burden.

There are few people on the road. Salemites now avoid straying from their homes unless it is absolutely necessary or if there is a hearing. The court sessions are important—avoiding them can be mistaken for disapproval.

Passersby nod in recognition to Tom Putnam but no longer stop to speak to him. No one wants to draw his attention. Everybody knows what happens to his enemies.

A thick layer of paranoia covers Salem village. The arrests and the hangings have taken a great toll. Families have been ripped apart. Parents are wary around their own children. Friendships have ended.

Past deeds have been remembered and taken on different, darker meanings. Casual words are now used as weapons.

Anyone who has not seen the afflicted girls act out has certainly heard about it. But it is the executions that haunt Salem. These were their friends and neighbors. People they drank beer and cider with, people whose barns they helped raise. But that is long gone. Now, they are lifeless bodies dangling at the end of a rope.

Travelers on their way to Boston no longer stop in Salem. Local farmers stay out of the village as much as possible. Inns and shops are nearly empty. At night, people huddle close to their own fires. There is too much risk. Even church pews remain half-empty for Reverend Parris's Sunday services.

Only the witch trials themselves draw a crowd.

No one understands the change in Salem better than forty-year-old Thomas Putnam. He is the center of this maelstrom. Three generations of Putnams have lived and prospered here. Like his forebears, Tom is a good Puritan, and that makes him a strong supporter of Reverend Samuel Parris.

However, the affluent farmer's life until now has been filled with disappointment. Tom Putnam has never achieved the status he expected. His father was a popular selectman, a town leader, but his son has not risen above constable. His older, wealthier uncle, sixty-one-year-old Nathaniel, is well respected and constantly asked for advice.

No one seeks Tom Putnam's counsel. Now, Putnam's bitterness has turned to revenge. An accusation from him can end your life.

Putnam controls the four primary accusers: his twelve-year-old daughter, Ann; seventeen-year-old servant Mercy Lewis; eleven-year-old neighbor Abigail Williams; and another seventeen-year-old, Mary Walcott. The girls are too young to draft legal statements, so Putnam does it for them. When Governor Phips creates the Court of Oyer and Terminer to hear the cases, Putnam volunteers: "it [is] our duty to inform your Honors of what we conceive you have not Heard, which are high and dreadful . . . to prepare you, that you may be a terror to evil-doers."

Judges Hathorne and Jonathan Corwin welcome his assistance. From the beginning of spring 1692, into the winter, no one is more zealous about hunting down witches than Thomas Putnam. In fact, he personally accuses forty-three people—twelve of them are executed while two others die in prison awaiting trial.

Putnam's power in Salem is immense. People who once dismissed him now fear him. He has no official position, but he is everywhere. When court is in session, he can be relied on to be there. When an afflicted person wants to make an accusation, he will take it down. If there is a witch in sight, Tom Putnam will crush that person.

But the afflicted girls are the true source of the injustice. They make accusations and identify witches; they are bewitched themselves. For these nine girls, it is the most exciting time of their young lives. Their days are a continuing round of drama.

Putnam's daughter, Ann, is the leader. She is a lively child, smart and quick. She testifies against sixty-two witches, more than anyone else. More than two hundred accused witches have been arrested. Seventeen of them are executed.

But Ann is now paying a heavy price. The specter attacks on *her* step up. She says she is in constant pain. She fights back by identifying even more witches. Her father proudly records her statements and takes them to the court.

It is an incredible experience for a twelve-year-old. Within weeks of her first accusations, everybody in the village knows who she is. When she walks down the road, people point her out. Her father, who until now has been preoccupied with his farm and business, lavishes attention on her. Rather than being stuck in a schoolroom or at home doing chores, Ann Putnam has become a star.

Best of all, no one seriously challenges her. One of the first persons she accuses of being a witch is four-year-old Dorothy Good. Ann also names Dorothy's mother, Sarah Good, "a forlorn, friendless, and forsaken creature," a beggar whose presence annoys the village.

Little Dorothy thinks it's a game—until she is chained in prison. Her young age does not stop the jailing; a witch is a witch. As the constable takes her away, an observer notes, "The child looked hail, as well as other children." But, after being locked up for several weeks and being questioned continually, Dorothy confesses. Her mother is a witch, she tells prosecutors; she gave her a snake—a witch's tool. The snake bit her—she shows them a red mark on her finger. That testimony is enough to convict Sarah Good, who is hanged shortly thereafter.

The four-year-old remains chained in Boston for nine months. Her father finally raises the money to pay her prison fees and she is released. She has turned five in jail. She has survived, but the experience has driven her insane. The little girl is changed forever; she will never function normally.

Often, twelve-year-old Ann Putnam and her mother testify together. When people find out the Putnams will be appearing at a hearing, the meeting room is packed with excited spectators. It is the most astonishing show they have ever seen.

Some other children get the message. Whatever happens to Ann begins happening to them. For example, seventeen-year-old Mary Walcott, Ann's stepcousin, joins the afflicted group and testifies against more than thirty people. Sixteen of them are executed.

The Salem girls' reputation quickly spreads throughout New England. In July, they are invited to Andover, fifteen miles to the northwest, to help identify witches. Ann and Mary Walcott find numerous suspects but are unable to identify those who are "attacking" them because they don't know the names of people living in that town.*

Eventually, sixty-seven witches are arrested in Andover—more than Salem. But just three are hanged as political complications arise with the executions. Andover does not have the same fervor for death as Salem.

A month later Ann Putnam and other afflicted girls visit Gloucester, an oceanside town north of Salem. More witches are discovered and arrested. Wherever the girls go, they are feared.

Cotton Mather watches all this with satisfaction. Personally, he makes no accusations—that's not his job. He never encounters a specter. His responsibility is to support the girls. In his typically stern language, he convinces New England that these children are telling the truth. They are being attacked by the Devil. Even though their words can be lethal, they must be believed.

Mather knows this from his own experience. In 1688, he alerts Boston that the Devil is on the attack. When the four children of mason John Goodwin burst into fits for no obvious reason, he writes in his widely read book *Memorable Provinces*, "They were cut with Knives and struck with Blows that they could not bear. Their necks would be broken . . . their Heads would be twisted almost round."

Mather's gruesome tales spread throughout the colony, bringing him more notoriety and wealth. In the book, he vividly describes the Goodwin children's fits, including having nails driven into them.

---

* Until the early seventeenth century, children under fourteen were not considered credible witnesses. King James changed the law in the early 1600s, writing, "Children, women and liars can be witnesses over high treason against God." In 1612, in Lancaster, England, nine-year-old Jennet Device told a court, "My mother is a witch. . . . She would have him [her half-brother] help her to kill." As a result of her testimony, her grandmother, mother, half brother, and several neighbors are hung. The court clerk turns his notes into a bestselling book for magistrates, which is read and cited by the Salem judges as the reason young children are allowed to testify against witches.

Of course, it is Cotton Mather's job to save the children.

Massachusetts Bay Colony is the first place in America to pass laws forcing parents to teach their children to read and write. But minors are mostly considered valuable assets. As soon as they are capable, usually about twelve years old, they are put to work at home or at a trade. Families are large; Tom and Ann Putnam have twelve children. Governor Phips is one of *twenty-six* children—that means more young workers. Minors are often treated harshly. Survival is a constant struggle, and there is little room for sentimentality. New Englanders follow the admonition "spare the rod, spoil the child."

Inevitably, some children turn on their parents.

✢ ✢ ✢

After that, many parents begin looking differently at their own children. Sometimes with abject fear.

Confessed witches are often confined together in a Boston cell, where they have nothing to do but talk to each other. They quickly figure out that if they accuse others, they may avoid the noose. So the incarcerated witches provide a steady stream of new names. One of these prisoners is fourteen-year-old Abigail Hobbs; she is the youngest person to be sentenced to death.

A lot of people are pleased by Hobbs's conviction. The teenager is out of control; she's a "wild child," a bad influence on other children. She is disrespectful to her parents; she mocks their Puritan values—once she threw water on her mother and yelled that she was baptizing her.

Realizing she is in grave danger, Abigail apologizes for her behavior from her Boston cell: "I have seen sights and been scared. I have been very wicked. I hope I shall be better."

More is required if she is to live. So, almost immediately, Abigail Hobbs accuses her stepmother and father. Deliverance Hobbs confesses, but William Hobbs does not. He can't believe his daughter would betray him like this. The Hobbs family are questioned separately: Deliverance admits her daughter and her husband are bewitched. Again, William Hobbs denies everything. "My soul is clear," he says. Asked if his only child is a witch, he hesitates, then shakes his head and replies, "I do not know."

Three members of the Hobbs family are convicted of witchcraft. But because of the huge backlog of cases, they are never executed. William Hobbs disappears, leaving his wife and daughter. History does not record what happens to them.

By the winter of 1692, Salem is completely devastated. Nineteen "witches" have already been executed. Scores remain in prison awaiting their probable executions.

However, the Devil has not been defeated. In fact, it looks as if he is growing stronger.

Chapter Fourteen

It is twenty-seven years before the Salem horror unfolds.

Fifteen-year-old William Phips tends to his flock of sheep on a bright summer day. He is one of twenty-one brothers and four sisters. All help on the family farm, which is precariously located in Indian country. The Abenaki are hostile to the English; therefore, all must be on guard for an attack at any moment.

William and his brothers and sisters have little diversion from labor. Among the most popular entertainments is fortune-telling, but that is banned by the Puritan culture. However, the children partake, and William Phips is told he will have a bright future.

✦ ✦ ✦

1692. The shepherd boy is now the royal governor of Massachusetts Bay. William Phips stands on a crowded, noisy dock in Boston Harbor. He has just returned from the Maine frontier, where his soldiers built a great stone fort to stop French and Indian raiding parties. It has been a frustrating expedition; the fortifications were erected but men were lost. Now, Phips is greeted with terrible news.

Incredibly, his wife, Dame Mary Phips, is accused of being a witch. She has been detained in Boston.

Phips is furious. He demands to know who her accuser is. The name is whispered, but it is not for the public. The governor has been in the wilderness nearly two months. He has been out of touch with Salem. But in that brief time, he realizes, the New World has gone mad.

The jails in Boston and Salem are filled beyond capacity with accused witches. As many as two hundred people are chained in cells, waiting to be tried.

But worst of all, in his absence, the Devil has entered his own home.

✤ ✤ ✤

Later, alone in his office, Phips tries to calm himself. He should not be surprised; he understands that. This is a turbulent time and his marriage to Mary has always been fodder for rumors. Some wonder how a tall, corpulent man like William Phips could have attracted a wealthy, beautiful widow such as Mary.

Others are jealous that Phips was fortunate enough to discover a sunken Spanish treasure in the Caribbean—which led to the British Crown granting him title and power.

But William Phips has a secret. When he was a younger man he consulted a fortune-teller. On his voyage to the Caribbean, some on the ship believed Phips knew the area of the Spanish wreck. It was a coincidence, of course. No ordinary person could possibly ascertain where the ship had gone down. But it is rumored that after finding the treasure, William Phips gifted an old soothsayer £200.

Consulting a fortune-teller was a pleasant game when Phips was growing up. But that would not happen now. Soothsaying and predictions are proof of witchcraft. So the governor keeps his story quiet.

To make matters worse, Dame Mary Phips has public connections to the occult. Witchcraft is believed to spread in families, like a fever, and a relative of hers in Falmouth, Massachusetts, has been accused of sorcery.

The governor and Dame Mary live differently. They have no children—some witches are believed to be barren—but keep two servants in their home: a black slave and a white Catholic girl Phips captured when he besieged a town in Jamaica two years earlier.

As he sits at his desk, the afternoon has turned into night. Phips knows what he has to do. He has tried hard to stay out of the witch fight. He handed the power to deal with it to the Mathers and to Deputy Governor William Stoughton. But obviously, with his wife now accused, that has to change.

William Phips is "an honest man," writes Salem yeoman Joseph Hutchinson. "But by a series of fortunate incidents rather than by any uncommon talents, he rose from the lowest condition in life to be the first man in his country."

Everybody in New England knows his story. Phips was born and raised on the Maine border. When he was eighteen, he moved to Boston and was apprenticed as a ship's carpenter. There he met and eventually married a wealthy widow, Mary Spencer Hull. She is five years older than him and considered to be among the prettiest women in New England. Mary's late shipbuilding husband left her well off. Phips was given control of that business.

William Phips and Mary Hull both grew up in coastal Maine. Their families knew each other. They share a background; it is natural they should be friends. But marriage? William was barely literate and most comfortable in the wilderness; Mary was educated and gained sophistication from her first husband. She knew how to navigate Boston society.

Captain Phips is a roughhewn individual. He is a natural leader, but solving problems is not his greatest skill, so as governor he appoints others to do that for him. And there are many ambitious men in New England happy to fill those positions. When Phips hands them the power, they use it in his name. Sometimes, the governor doesn't even know what his underlings are doing.

Thus, when Phips returns from Maine to find the Salem witch trials totally out of control, he is angered. Salem is in the midst of "a most horrible witchcraft or possession of devils," Phips writes to the king's Privy Council. The prisons are filling rapidly. Fear has paralyzed the colony.

✜ ✜ ✜

Cotton Mather has emerged as the moral leader of the witch conflict. Phips has a strong relationship with his father, Increase Mather. The governor knows it is the elder Mather who convinced King William to give him his position, and he's grateful for it. So he trusts and respects Increase Mather and relies on his advice.

Governor Phips well understands the survival of the colony may be at stake. The French and Indians in alliance are a real threat, and they are moving south. Their successful raids in Maine have caused hundreds of refugees to crowd into Boston and Salem. That is a serious problem. The continuing drought has reduced the harvest, and it is going to be hard to feed everyone. The king has made matters even worse by raising taxes. Phips is frustrated—he does not have time to focus on witch trials. But all that changes when he finds his wife accused.

It was Mary Phips herself who spurred the witch situation while her husband was away in Maine because of fighting between colonists and Indians. First Lady of the Massachusetts colony, she receives a plea for clemency from an imprisoned witch and signs a release warrant.

It is a whim—she has no legal right to do so. But the Boston jailer John Arnold obeys. Mary Phips is the governor's wife, and she knows what power she has. He lets the prisoner go.

For that act of mercy, he is fired by English authorities in London. Mary knows the risks that come with helping an alleged witch.

People brave enough to stand up to the court are often accused themselves. Witches help witches, the court believes. Not long after, Mary is charged with witchcraft, although she is not imprisoned. She remains in the marital home.

The first thing William Phips does after landing in Boston is to ensure the safety of his wife. She is fine, she tells him. But he sees she is shaken.

The fact that a person as pure and pious as Mary is cried out as a witch leads him to a dreadful conclusion: other completely innocent people must also have been accused.

After securing his wife's release, Phips contemplates the possibility that his career may be over. If innocent New Englanders have been executed solely on the basis of children's fabricated visions, there is a good chance the Crown will revoke the new charter and his government will collapse.

However, Phips also believes there is a change in public sentiment. When he departed for Maine, most people supported the witch trials. But the numerous arrests and gruesome hangings of their friends and neighbors have caused some to question whether justice is being done.

Phips consults Increase and Cotton Mather. It is well established the father believes more than spectral evidence is necessary for a witch conviction. But his son disagrees. The governor reads Increase Mather's manuscript *Cases of Conscience Concerning Evil Spirits Personating Men*, which makes a strong argument for ending the trials.

However, Chief Judge Stoughton remains defiant: his court has done only what is absolutely necessary. Either you believe witches exist and are a grave danger or you do not. When you find a witch, you don't allow any quarter.

To save the colony, the trials must continue, Stoughton insists.

Days after returning to Boston, Governor Phips begins to fight for his own survival. He writes to London, officially informing the

Crown of the events that have taken place in Salem and around New England.*

What has happened is not his fault, he insists in his letter: "When I first arrived I found this Province miserably harassed with a most horrible witchcraft or possession of Devill." He goes on to claim that he relied on others to deal with the witch frenzy: "The loud cries and clamors of the friends of the afflicted people with the advice of the Deputy Governor and many others prevailed with mee to give a Commission of Oyer and Terminer for discovering what witchcraft might be at the bottom or whether it were not a possession. The chief Judge in this Commission was the Deputy Governor and the rest were persons of the best prudence and figure that could then be pitched upon.

"I was almost the whole time of the proceeding abroad in the service of Their Majesties in the Eastern part of the County and depended upon the Judgment of the Court as to a right method of proceeding in cases of Witchcraft."

Then the crusher: Phips suggests that innocent people may have been executed because of the accusations.

✤ ✤ ✤

After alerting the Crown, William Phips takes action. He forces the court to drop witch charges against his wife. Then, he temporarily suspends the arrests of *all* accused witches—releasing many of them from prison. Finally, to protect his reputation, he bans all publications about the witch hunt.

Some critics consider Phips's ban the first act of government censorship in America.

The governor allows one exception to the ban: with his permission, Cotton Mather publishes *The Wonders of the Invisible World*,

---

* The Connecticut witch trials, taking place between 1647 and 1663, were responsible for eleven executions. In February 2023, 375 years after those hangings, the state of Connecticut formally pardoned the accused.

his defense of the trials and the judges—emphasizing in the book five convictions and executions that did not rely solely on spectral evidence. In a desperate attempt to justify his own actions, Mather writes, "An army of devils is horribly woke in upon the place, which is . . . the first born of English settlements."

✤ ✤ ✤

On October 29, Phips officially shuts down the witch court for good. He is trying to maintain a delicate balance, keeping the support of both those who believe New England is bewitched and others who are convinced this is a terrible misuse of justice.

To replace the court, the governor creates another judicial body, the Superior Court of Judicature. He does that because pressure is put on him by the Mathers, who are desperately trying to save their own reputations.

The new court convenes for the first session—fittingly, in Salem—in January 1693. It is specifically prohibited from considering spectral evidence in witch cases.

Nevertheless, the fanatical Judge Stoughton goes behind Phips's back and orders eight graves dug in anticipation of more hangings.

When Phips finds out, he is enraged, overrides Stoughton, and cancels all executions.

That sets up bad blood between the governor and the judge. Stoughton is confident the Mathers will back him.

But the clerics have their own problems. Now, they want to retreat. When Stoughton realizes this, he quietly resumes his place on the new court—but with much less militancy.

More witch trials are held, but there will be no more hangings.

However, the Devil in Salem is still on the loose. There is coming a new wave of accusations—a furious wave.

Against the accusers.

Chapter Fifteen

Payback is not always assured.

Because English law allows the trials and executions of alleged witches, there is no organized investigation of the Salem witch accusers. Governor Phips stopped the trials and incarcerations but did little else to hold those who persecuted people accountable. The militia was not assigned to Salem, and no central authority looked into the atrocities that happened there.

The reign of terror ends abruptly for the Salem girls. After Governor Phips halts the Salem and Boston trials in September 1692, civic leaders in Gloucester ask the afflicted young women to expose witches in their village.

The girls name three people but are stunned when none are arrested. While riding in a cart taking them back to Salem, an interesting thing happens: as the girls cross a stone bridge over the Ipswich River, they pass an old woman and immediately dissolve into fits. A month earlier this might have been a death sentence for the harmless lady. Yet the elderly woman simply keeps on walking with no interference.

The end has come. Few pay attention to the girls any longer— yet they are never confronted over their deadly accusations.

✦ ✦ ✦

However, a few individuals do pay a price, beginning with Reverend **Samuel Parris**—the first Salem resident to profit from the witch hunts.

In 1689, Parris became Salem's only ordained minister. He was hired for the sum of sixty-six English pounds per year, free firewood for his home and church, a barn, and two acres of land. But his dogmatic and confrontational behavior soon turned the town against him. In fact, the original contract was rescinded and there was a movement to fire Parris.

All of that changed when Parris's nine-year-old daughter Betty began barking and screaming loudly when she heard someone praying the "Our Father." Parris quickly began promoting the presence of witches in Salem, and most criticism of him stopped out of fear the reverend and his daughter would accuse the dissenters—which, of course, they did.

After the jailing of two hundred suspected witches and Governor Phips's order of release, Parris now struggles to retain his hold on Salem. He fails.

He is forced out of his ministry and, in order to survive, accepts a preaching job in remote Stow, Massachusetts. But with his witch-hunting past following him, he is fired there as well. He dies alone in 1720.

As for **Betty Parris**, she leaves Salem with her father and eventually marries, bearing four children. She will die in Concord, Massachusetts, on March 21, 1760, her witch hunt and trial participation largely forgotten.

✦ ✦ ✦

Thomas Putnam Jr. was a bitter man long before the witch trials. His father died in 1686, leaving a significant estate to a son born from a second marriage, but nothing to Thomas. His wife, **Ann**

Carr Putnam, was similarly disinherited by her father, who left his considerable fortune to her brothers. Both Tom and the often-anxious Ann struggle to feed their twelve children and constantly need money. They both sue to get those wills overturned but are unsuccessful.

Thomas's indignation grows worse when his half brother, Joseph, marries into the Porter family, with whom Putnam has a long-standing feud. Such animosity is not unusual for the belligerent farmer, who has many enemies throughout Salem. His active participation in the Devil hunts was Thomas Putnam's cruel but ultimately successful method for damaging these rivals. He never left Salem, dying there of an unknown illness on May 24, 1699. The same sickness led Ann Putnam to follow her husband in death just two weeks later.

Their daughter, also named **Ann**, was among the first three Salem girls to become "afflicted." Just twelve years old when the trials begin in 1692, she teams with Elizabeth Parris and Abigail Williams to accuse others. Servant Mercy Lewis of the Putnam household soon joins them. Ann Putnam makes a specialty of accusing those who quarrel with her family or disagree with Reverend Parris. Her name appears four hundred times in court documents, and she is responsible for the hanging of eleven individuals. She dies unmarried in 1716 at the age of thirty-seven, though not before confessing in 1706 that she lied on the stand during the witch trials.

✛ ✛ ✛

Seventeen-year-old **Mercy Lewis** is a primary accuser. In fact, throughout the brutal summer of 1692, she testifies against dozens of innocent people. After the witch trials cease, Lewis becomes pregnant out of wedlock and is banished from Salem. Her fate remains unknown.

✛ ✛ ✛

Sarah Churchill, accuser of George Jacobs and his granddaughter Margaret, barely eludes the gallows herself by confessing to be a witch. Sarah is twenty-five. Seventeen years after the trials in 1709, she is back in jail, charged with premarital fornication, another banishment offense. She also disappears from the historical record.

✤ ✤ ✤

Orphan **Elizabeth Hubbard**, seventeen, is well known to trial-goers for her fits and convulsions. By the time the trials come to an end, she is responsible for testifying against twenty-nine people, leading to thirteen executions and two others dying in jail. Elizabeth Hubbard vanishes after the trials close.

✤ ✤ ✤

Mary Walcott, a cousin to Ann Putnam, is known for being calm on the witness stand. She is a primary accuser. In 1696, she marries Isaac Farrar and moves to Townsend, Massachusetts, where she dies in 1752 at the age of seventy-seven. Mary birthed eight children, and there are no reports of any reprisals taken against her.

✤ ✤ ✤

Mary Warren is among the oldest of the accusers at age twenty-one, though she could have been as young as eighteen. Her birth year is not recorded with certainty. As stated, she worked as a servant in the home of John and Elizabeth Proctor. After being accused of being a witch herself, she is imprisoned but ultimately released, whereupon she disappears.

✤ ✤ ✤

Abigail Williams is just eleven years old when she begins to become afflicted. She testifies in a number of cases leading to executions but runs away from Salem before the witch trials are over. It is reported that she dies in 1697 at the age of sixteen, but this cannot be confirmed.

✤ ✤ ✤

Incredibly, even as the witch trials begin to lose their hold on the province of Massachusetts Bay, the hysteria continues as disturbing decisions are made. Even though Governor Phips stops the trials in October 1692, that same month a young girl in Andover accuses her neighbor's *dog* of trying to bewitch her. Terrified villagers immediately shoot the animal dead.

Many Puritans believe the Devil can be found in any living creature. It is thought by some that oxen, pigs, and cattle can be possessed, helping witches by doing their bidding. Some fanatical Puritans pay close attention to their livestock for just that reason.

Ironically, it is Cotton Mather who eventually clears the slain canine of Devil involvement. Noting that the dog died instantly upon being shot, Reverend Mather declares the animal could not possibly be possessed. If the dog was associated with the Devil, it would not die. Thus, according to Mather, the dog is an innocent victim of the witch frenzy he helped create.

A second dog is actually hanged in Salem after some afflicted girls accuse it of consorting with a witch. This time, Cotton Mather remains silent.

✤ ✤ ✤

High Sheriff George Corwin never prospered from the death of Giles Corey. The old man allowed himself to be pressed to death with stones and boards rather than enter a plea to charges of being a witch. He did that in order to avoid having his family lose their property and possessions. Yet twenty-six-year-old High Sheriff Corwin did not relent, extorting money from Corey's daughter,

Elizabeth, by threatening to find other legal means of taking the land anyway. But Corwin dies of a heart attack at the age of thirty, putting his life of cruelty to an abrupt end.

In short order, another victim of the witch trials, Salem resident Philip English, places a lien on Corwin's corpse. English and his wife, Mary, were accused of witchcraft. English was one of the richest men in Salem. He and his wife fled to New York but returned to Salem after the trials were over. Mr. English sought compensation for lands taken from him by the high sheriff. Only after being paid £60 in silver and jewels did Philip English release the lien. Though some say this is a myth, it is widely believed the Corwin family buried the body of the widely despised sheriff in the basement of their home to avoid desecration.

✢ ✢ ✢

"Hanging John" Hathorne, one of the most aggressive Salem judges, spent the latter years of his life in service to the colonial militia. He died in 1717 at the age of seventy-five and is buried in Salem's Old Point Cemetery. It is worth noting that the author Nathaniel Hawthorne is a descendant of that jurist. Hawthorne changed the spelling of his last name to distance himself from his infamous ancestor.

✢ ✢ ✢

John Alden Jr. withstood the scandal of being accused of witchcraft, even prospering from the experience. Alden's account of the trials was incorporated into Robert Calef's *More Wonders of the Invisible World*, and his innocence was declared by legal proclamation after he spent a year on the run. Alden died in 1702 at the age of seventy-five. His body was buried at the Old South Church in Boston, but the cemetery was dug up for a street widening in 1870 and all bones were removed to an undisclosed location. All that remains is Alden's tombstone, which can be found in the church's south portico.

✦ ✦ ✦

Governor William Phips was largely absent during the trials, spending the summer of 1692 overseeing the construction of new forts in the Maine wilderness. His decision to end the witch persecutions and pardon the convicted was not viewed favorably by Cotton Mather, on whom Phips depended for political support. The governor also underestimated the power of Lieutenant Governor William Stoughton, who began to collude with officials in London to have Phips replaced. Thus, William Phips suddenly found himself under siege and with no political allies. He was recalled to England to answer questions about his behavior in a series of incidents where he was accused of abusing seamen. Suspiciously, the Crown chose William Stoughton to collect evidence against Phips for the hearing. Stoughton, of course, resented the governor for shutting down the trials.

Knowing that his time as governor was likely at an end, William Phips pardoned all in Massachusetts Bay accused of witchcraft before he left for London. And in a last defiant act against the Mathers, Phips deliberately set sail on a Sunday, in violation of strict Puritan doctrine. Just to make sure the colony noticed, Phips ordered the ship's guns fired as the vessel cleared Boston Harbor.

William Phips would never return to Massachusetts.

The governor arrives in London in January 1695. He is immediately arrested, pending his hearing. Though bailed out of jail by a close friend, Phips soon suffers a fatal fever. He dies on February 18, 1695. He is buried at the Church of Saint Mary Woolnoth in London.

As for his wife, **Mary**, she remarries in 1701, six years after the death of her husband. Ironically, her new spouse is Peter Sargeant, one of the eleven judges on the Court of Oyer and Terminer that would have determined her fate as a witch. She passed on January 20, 1705, leaving a large estate. Among those mentioned in her will is Reverend Cotton Mather, who received a small endowment. Her burial location cannot be confirmed, though some accounts record Boston's Granary Burial Ground as her final resting place.

✢ ✢ ✢

The Mathers, father and son, are forever tarnished by the Salem witch trials.

However, at the height of his political power in 1691, **Increase Mather** establishes a close relationship with King William III and Queen Mary II in England, Protestant rulers who have just taken the throne from King James II, a Catholic convert, in the bloodless Glorious Revolution. James had been instrumental in promoting religious freedom in the colonies, which Increase had opposed so violently that he was threatened with an arrest for treason. But under William and Mary, Increase Mather flourishes.

He travels to England, where he is involved in the writing of a new royal charter for Massachusetts that unifies the Massachusetts Bay Colony with the Puritan stronghold of Plymouth seven decades after the *Mayflower*'s arrival.

The witch trials are the first great display of Increase Mather's public celebrity. Yet as the Devil controversy comes to an end in January 1693, with many citizens dismayed by the reign of terror, Increase distances himself from the proceedings. His belief that the accused is innocent until proven guilty and his doubts about spectral evidence are in his favor.

Mather then turns his focus to Harvard, where he has continued as president, fixated on distancing the college from the Crown. King William (Queen Mary died in 1694), however, sought a royal charter for Harvard that would have Mather report to London. The issue appears settled in 1700, but the document is then lost at sea. The order is not revisited. Harvard College's original charter of 1650 remains in force to this day.

But Increase Mather never completely escapes the witch trials. Robert Calef's 1700 book *More Wonders of the Invisible World* blames Increase and Cotton Mather for inflaming the Devil hunts. Increase responds in 1701 by writing a book of his own, accusing Calef of being a follower of Satan. It is rumored that Increase publicly burns Calef's book in Harvard Yard, which would have been the only book burning to ever take place there. Whether or not that is true remains in dispute.

Reverend Increase Mather steps down as president of Harvard in 1701, aged sixty-two. He does not leave of his own volition. Throughout his tenure, he has refused to live near the campus in Cambridge, finding it to be a dreary swamp compared to bustling Boston and cosmopolitan London. His large congregation in the city also demands he remain close to his flock. Instead of Cambridge, he remains in the home he built near the North Church in Boston several years earlier. When given an ultimatum by political enemies within the Harvard Corporation to either move to Cambridge or step down, he chooses to leave.

Of note is that Increase Mather is given a slave named Spaniard as a gift from his son, Cotton, in the late 1690s. The man is originally brought to the New World from West Africa. By 1715, there are more than two thousand African slaves in Massachusetts, up from two hundred in 1676. In his final will, Increase Mather orders that Spaniard be made a "Free Negro"—but only upon Increase's death.

That date comes in August 1723 when Reverend Mather suffers complete bladder failure at the age of eighty-four. He dies three weeks later and is buried in Copp's Hill Burial Ground in Boston's North End. The house Increase built nearby in 1677 remains intact until the early twentieth century. As of this writing, that site near the fabled Old North Church is the location of a 7–11 convenience store.

✛ ✛ ✛

Cotton Mather seeks the presidency of Harvard as his father steps down, but the elders refuse to elect him. The writings of Robert Calef have sullied Cotton's reputation. Harvard historian Samuel Eliot Morison will note centuries later that Calef's writings "tied a tin can to Cotton Mather which has rattled and banged through the pages of superficial and popular historians."

Rebuffed by Harvard, which he now considers too politically liberal, Mather works with Welsh businessman Elihu Yale to make a substantial donation to an orthodox Puritan institution known as the Collegiate School shortly after it is relocated from Saybrook to New Haven, Connecticut. Mather suggests the school change its name to Yale College, which it does.

Yet Cotton Mather's most significant contribution to colonial life was not education or religion but early advocacy for the controversial new method of inoculation to successfully prevent the spread of smallpox. In time, Mather would also be at the forefront of advances in biology, genetics, and the prevention of scurvy. His views on race, in which he considered whites and blacks to be "of one blood" in heaven, did not prevent him from owning slaves.

A young boy in Boston named Benjamin Franklin pays close attention to Mather's scientific and religious work. As Franklin develops his own public presence, he will follow in Mather's scientific footsteps but reject the reverend's belief in "the miseries under which mankind is languishing."

Twice married, Cotton Mather is a widower at the time of his death in 1728, from an asthma attack. He is buried at the Copp's Hill Burial Ground in the North End of Boston. Mather departed this world at age sixty-five.

To the day of his death, the closest Cotton Mather ever comes to apologizing for the witch trials is an admission that "things were carried too far."

✢ ✢ ✢

The people of Salem were devastated by the trials. But with the exception of Judge Samuel Sewall's public contrition, authorities blamed "the trickery of Satan" for the town's participation. In addition, the citizens of Salem took no blame for the hysteria, noting that many of the accused confessed to being witches. Townspeople chose to see the trials as just another series of hardships afflicting the Massachusetts Bay colony, no different from the Indian wars or English taxation.

However, the legacy of Salem becomes one of shame. The area loses business and standing to Boston and is avoided by many who might ordinarily have sought to trade there. The inhabitants of Salem rarely speak of the murders, and their Puritan masters begin to lose influence.

A "specter" hangs over the town.

A series of bad harvests in the years after the trials lead many to believe that God is punishing Salem. On January 14, 1697, the Massachusetts legislature declares a day of fasting to repent for the witch hysteria. Salem would be the last time anyone is accused of witchcraft in New England, and, in 1702, the colony declares all witch trials unlawful. In 1711, the General Court of Massachusetts votes to financially compensate the families of the executed witches. However, it is not until 1957 that Massachusetts publicly apologizes for the trials and executions.

✢ ✢ ✢

By the early eighteenth century, America has now become a far more secular place. However, the old ways of Puritan theology are still widely practiced in the land. That sets up an intense historical and religious conflict that will involve the Founding Fathers, led by Benjamin Franklin, and will help to fuel the American Revolution.

The outcome of this conflict affects every American to this day. It is a struggle somewhat defined by the murders of those accused of being witches in New England—atrocities that have cast a wide spell over the colonies. The power of preachers to unsettle and persuade congregations will have repercussions for established forms of governance; the type of broad influence on religion and society achieved by the Mathers will reverberate in a new generation of religious and political leaders.

The "specter" of those dead accused of witchcraft will continue to haunt colonial America for years to come.

Chapter Sixteen

Apprentice Benjamin Franklin has a secret.

On this raw spring day, twenty-five-year-old James Franklin's *New-England Courant* is publishing a unique editorial written by an anonymous writer. The "epistles," in the author's words, make fun of everything from hoop skirts to the Puritan Church in a warm but sly voice. Usually, the *Courant* runs stories about Boston politics, but that has grown stale. No one knows the real identity of the new author, who mysteriously chooses to slide the editorial under an office door in the dead of night. The only clue is a woman's byline in the name of "Silence Dogood."

The pseudonym hints at trouble. Reverend Cotton Mather is still very much a political force in Boston, yet Silence Dogood is a slap at the reverend. Upon the death of his daughter, Mather preaches a sermon called "The Silent Sufferer"—*Silentiarius* in the Latin.

Thus, Silence.

Mather's previous treatise on Christian behavior, *Bonifacius*, exhorts men and women to "do good."

Dogood.

But nobody figures out the clue. James Franklin, the older brother whom Benjamin Franklin is contractually obligated to serve, publishes the *Courant*. He prints Silence Dogood's saga on

a whim, hoping the article will be a break from the snark and sar-
casm that so often is found in the *Courant*. The story is an instant
hit. That day's edition of the newspaper sells out as Boston begins
buzzing about the true identity of this curious woman Silence.

James Franklin does not know who the woman is but wants to
meet her.

Yet Silence Dogood stands next to James all day, every day.

For the middle-aged widow is actually his brother, Benjamin
Franklin.

✢ ✢ ✢

The deceit begins one year earlier as Boston is hit hard by a smallpox epidemic. Cotton Mather spins his "do good" phrase to defend
those who believe in treating the disease through inoculations and
quarantine. After losing a wife and three children to measles almost a decade earlier, Mather has investigated new research being
done at the Royal Society in London on treating infectious disease
and encouraged Boston physicians to adopt these practices. In an
open letter to the *Boston Gazette* on July 31, 1721, he refers to a
leading proponent of inoculation as a "good genius."

That makes the anti-inoculation James Franklin furious. A
physical man with a temper and a habit of using his fists, the
printer fights back by launching his own newspaper—one that
will harshly criticize Cotton Mather. The first edition of the *New-
England Courant* is one sheet of paper with editorials printed on
both sides. It costs four pennies. The masthead lets it be known
that the *Courant* will be "a jack of all trades" in terms of stories
and subjects—meaning it will take on the religious elite in Boston.

As a man who spent his early training in London, James Franklin
has a touch of the snob. He considers himself an intellectual and does
not appreciate Cotton Mather talking down to simple tradesmen
such as himself. His goal in life is not to run a small print shop but to
edit a major newspaper that compares with London's greatest.

Smallpox seems a good way to build readership. As fear of the disease sweeps through Boston and deaths soar to 130 in September, the *Courant* grows more popular. Some 844 will die between April 1721 and February 1722. James Franklin is a literate man, fond of such writers as Daniel Defoe, whose book *Robinson Crusoe* came out just three years ago. He regularly brings in guest writers to voice an opinion in the *Courant* but also does much of the writing himself. James leans heavily on satire to attack the pro-inoculation believers, even doubting that the epidemic is a disease at all, writing of the "artificial pox."

✣ ✣ ✣

Benjamin Franklin has a different view. He is not anti-inoculation but sides with his brother against Cotton Mather on general principle. At the *Courant*, he sets type, delivers the paper, and runs other errands—everything except writing. It's all part of the nine-year contract with his brother to learn the printing trade. Their father, Josiah, once envisioned Benjamin as a minister, not as a tradesman, and wished him to attend Harvard.

The ministry was once an obvious path for young Ben. The Franklin family's immersion in the church is complete. They attend a Congregationalist service twice a week, with the Sunday sermon often lasting two hours or more. At age five, the boy was reading the Bible, as well as other spiritual books such as *Pilgrim's Progress*. By seven, he was writing poetry, which Josiah proudly sent to relatives back in London. At eight years old, young Benjamin was top of his class at the prestigious Boston Latin School.*

---

* Congregationalist churches are so called for their independence and lack of a governing body. In New England during the eighteenth century, the Puritan teachings of these congregations were heavily influenced by the French theologian John Calvin, a leader of the sixteenth-century Protestant Reformation. Today, the Presbyterian Church is based on Calvin's teachings.

Money problems force Josiah Franklin to end all dreams of Harvard. Benjamin is shattered not to graduate from Boston Latin, but his father is just being practical: the college graduates more ministers than New England can absorb. So Josiah teaches his younger son the trade of chandler—candle making—beginning at the age of ten. Having a trade is vital to financial success in colonial Massachusetts, and the father is only looking out for young Ben, whom he adores.

Josiah Franklin is relentless in his work ethic, demanding that Benjamin pass long days cutting wicks and filling molds. However, his wife, Abiah, insists that her son be allowed time away from the shop. In this way, young Benjamin Franklin grows strong through long days of swimming in the ocean and nearby ponds, adding a physical heft to his intellectual brilliance.

At age twelve, Benjamin Franklin walks away from the candles and into his brother's print shop. He joins the thousands of young people in New England who endure a life of servitude as apprentices. His role as apprentice provides him with a place to sleep, simple clothing, and sparse meals, but little else. He is not allowed to seek other employment and is paid only a small salary.*

And he endures regular abuse. James is often cruel, hitting and slapping Ben over mistakes and petty frustrations. Money is tight. James is soon to marry, assuming the responsibility of feeding a wife in addition to his teenaged brother.

Yet there is one escape for Benjamin Franklin: reading. Among the *Courant*'s contributors is a tanner named Nathaniel Gardner, who enjoys intellectual debate. He gives Benjamin free rein of his considerable library.

The teenager absorbs every word. He even stops going to church on Sunday to make more time for reading, displeasing his parents.

---

* Josiah Franklin was born in England and did an apprenticeship as a candlemaker; therefore it was logical he would direct his sons into the same structure.

Increase Mather was the most influential preacher and minister in seventeenth-century New England.

Cotton Mather, his son, was a prolific author, fiery preacher, and noted witch hunter.

An excerpt of the original document recording Abigail Williams's testimony about witchcraft in Salem.

Excerpt from the testimony of Sarah Bibber, another accuser in Salem.

Arrest warrant for accused witch Sarah Wildes.

Petition for bail from several accused witches who were imprisoned in Boston.

Eighty years after the events in Salem, witchcraft and the power of preachers still influenced the Founding Fathers who were shaping the new American nation.

George Washington

Young Benjamin Franklin

James Madison

John Adams

Thomas Jefferson

Patrick Henry

More than two hundred and fifty years after the events of Salem, a young boy named Ronald Hunkeler underwent exorcisms under the auspices of the Catholic Church. His experiences became the basis for the novel and film *The Exorcist*.

Father William Bowden, who performed one of the exorcisms.

William Peter Blatty, author of *The Exorcist*.

ectator newspaper features articles written under
njamin Franklin spins this into Silence Dogood.
s will relish a jab at Cotton Mather, Ben begins his
mention of an "Educated Minister." Everybody
t is.

ood is clearly an intelligent woman, writing with
ar and a broad vocabulary. Her observations about
re revealing in their insight. Silence seems to know
ig on in town. Her handwriting is impeccable and
aine. At first she seems timid, slowly revealing de-
e thinks a great deal about sex.

anklin is relishing the situation.

✢ ✢ ✢

r is in awe.

hows the Silence Dogood editorial to all his intel-
No one has any idea who the author is. When the
aes the piece on April 2, 1722, it is an immediate

a Franklin writes another. When "Silence" admits
w, eager suitors write the *Courant* proposing mar-
v of the paper soars. Silence is published every two
more explicit. She talks about waterfront prostitu-
ss, and public sex on the Boston Common.

ber of columns, James Franklin finally figures out
ooder" is indeed his brother. He doesn't like it. So
l is silenced for good as James confronts Ben, tell-
amns will stop immediately.

natter of jealousy.

months and fourteen editions, Silence is being
before the state of Massachusetts charges James
He is arrested, jailed, and actually stands trial for
rovocative opinions. Ben then becomes publisher

London's *S*
pen names. B
Knowing Jame
first story wit
knows who th

Silence Do
perfect gramm
life in Boston
everything goi
obviously femi
termination. S

Benjamin F

The *Courant* eventuall
tonians die of smallp
exhausted from the di
Mather's home, James
news. The miscreant v
tion, and the *Courant*

Benjamin Franklin
though he has visited
erend. Benjamin no l
Cotton Mather and l
himself a "thorough d
from memory, pridin
good book. But Franl
Jesus Christ, the pov
preme deity controls

Yet he has not c
during this intellectu
the faith of his childl
cades to come.

But now, in 1722
elite, the teenager is
British newspapers. l
school. So Benjamin
rant in a disguised l
knows James would
Courant.

And his broth
The printer
lectual friends.
Courant publis
success.

So Benjami
to being a wid
riage. Popularit
weeks, growing
tion, drunkenn

After a num
that the "Do C
Silence Dogoo
ing him the co

It's a simple

After seven
retired. But no
with contempt.
the *Courant*'s p

---

* The Library of Congres
 views of certain English
 in Europe toward the la
 influential number of a
 stressed morality and rej
 more than a 'sublime' te

for a time. Ben takes the newspaper in an even more radical direction. But when James is acquitted of all charges in May 1723, their petty animosities return. Ben leaves the *Courant* to continue his apprenticeship elsewhere, only to be denied work at Boston's other four print shops.

Employment is not Ben Franklin's only problem: many now suspect that he is actually Silence Dogood. His strident writing for the *Courant* during James's incarceration is the clue, particularly when it comes to religion. "My indiscreet disputations about religion began to make me pointed at with horror by good people, as an infidel or atheist," he will write in his autobiography.

Franklin decides to make a run for it.

On May 25, 1723, he books passage on a ship bound from Boston to New York. A friend convinces the ship's captain that Franklin has gotten a young woman pregnant and that he must flee to avoid getting married. The captain makes room. Ben sells his library to pay for passage. The coincidence of his escape vessel bearing the same name as a Puritan ship a century before cannot be ignored. Franklin brings just a chest of clothes with him. This is the first time he has ever left Boston.

Yet as he flees his brother James, the seventeen-year-old has not escaped Cotton Mather, nor the legacy of his New England upbringing.*

---

* Benjamin Franklin never moves back to Boston but visits many times. James grew jealous as Ben became more successful, and the two do not reconcile until James Franklin falls into poor health in 1734. The two meet one last time. Ben agrees to raise James's son, James Jr., taking the boy on as an apprentice printer. James Franklin dies on his birthday in 1735 at the age of thirty-eight. Cause of death was an unknown terminal illness. James Jr. serves his apprenticeship in Philadelphia, then returns home to run his late father's print shop. As for Ben's parents, his father, Josiah, dies at age eighty-eight. His mother also dies at eighty-eight. Both enjoyed a good relationship with their son.

Chapter Seventeen

Benjamin Franklin is born again in Philadelphia.

He starts by going to church.

A bedraggled Franklin arrives on a Sunday. He is exhausted. There was no work in New York, where he disembarked from the Boston ship. So he moved on a week ago. A kindly printer named William Bradford suggested the teenager travel to Philadelphia, where his son Andrew runs a printing shop.

By coincidence, the young Bradford has just suffered the death of an employee. Franklin makes the decision to race there before the position can be filled. Believing the journey will be much faster on land, he promptly ships his chest of clothes by sea and begins the long walk across New Jersey. He is young and strong. The prospect of a solitary journey does not intimidate him.

This first test of Ben Franklin's new independence becomes an odyssey. Carrying extra shirts and socks, the teenager marches through bad weather and sleeps in roadside inns. He endures a fever on October 3, two days into the trip. He sweats out the illness by drinking glass after glass of cold water. The next day he travels through torrential rains to Bordentown, only to stay up all night in conversation with Dr. John Browne, a zealous atheist who owns the inn where Franklin is staying. When he arrives in Burlington,

BENJAMIN FRANKLIN'S FLIGHT TO PHILADELPHIA

NEW YORK

N.H.

Boston

MASSACHUSETTS

CONN.   R.I.

HUDSON R.

NEW YORK

PA.   N.J.

Philadelphia

ATLANTIC OCEAN

Sept. 23–27

NEW YORK

TAPPAN ZEE

HUDSON R.

Hackensack

Morristown

NEW JERSEY

APPALACHIAN MOUNTAINS

Newark

Elizabeth Town

New York

LONG ISLAND

RARITAN R.

Perth Amboy

STATEN ISLAND

Oct. 1–2

Raritan Bay

SANDY HOOK

New Brunswick

DELAWARE R.

Hopewell

Princeton

Franklin's route

Oct. 3

MILLSTONE R.

ASSUNPINK CR.

Newtown   Trenton

Oct. 4

PENNSYLVANIA

Oct. 5

Bordentown

DELAWARE RIVER

Burlington

ATLANTIC OCEAN

Oct. 6

Philadelphia

NEW JERSEY

N

W   E

S

Scale of Miles

0   5   10

Map by Gene Thorp

young Ben is relieved to catch a boat traveling down the Delaware River to Philadelphia. He is required to help row. After stopping for a night to make camp on the banks, the vessel pulls up to the Market Street wharf on this Sunday morning.

"I was dirty from my journey," Franklin will recall. "I was fatigued with travelling, rowing, and want of rest, I was very hungry; and my whole stock of cash consisted of a Dutch dollar, and about a shilling in copper. The latter I gave the people of the boat for my passage, who at first refused it, on account of my rowing; but I insisted on their taking it."

Because it is Sunday, the Bradford print shop is closed. Benjamin Franklin buys rolls from a bakery and wanders aimlessly around town, unsure of where to find lodging. He notices a heavy young woman studying him from the porch as he passes a house. "She, standing at the door, saw me, and thought I made, as I certainly did, a most awkward, ridiculous appearance."

Ben Franklin will long remember his first meeting with Deborah Read, who will one day become his common-law wife. She is an Anglican, and on this day soon to leave for services at Christ Church. Deborah's faith and frugal nature are balanced by a temper and talent for profanity. Yet all Ben Franklin sees right now is a woman looking at him with bemusement.

Franklin keeps walking. He realizes he looks like the runaway that he is. Yet there is no place to clean up or sleep. There is also no certainty he will get a job. The independence and freedom of escaping Boston is now being replaced by a growing panic.

Ben Franklin keeps wandering, soon falling in with a well-dressed crowd of people walking in the same direction. Curious as to where they are going, he follows them to a Quaker meeting-house.

The experience is far different from any Puritan service he has ever attended. There is no minister and no sermon. Instead, the room is completely silent for some time. Benjamin Franklin sits in the back, resting on a hard wooden pew. Quakers believe in waiting for the Holy Spirit to speak to members of the congregation individually, inspiring them to rise and share their faith one by one. No clergy member guides them, and women are considered spiritually equal to men. Finally, a church member rises to speak, using the Bible as a reference but also sharing his personal thoughts on faith.

In the back, Benjamin Franklin remains quiet.

The teenager is exhausted. "Being very drowsy through labor and want of rest the preceding night, I fell fast asleep, and continued so till the meeting broke up, when one was kind enough to rouse me."

Franklin will long remember the Quakers' kindness: "This was, therefore, the first house I was in or slept in, in Philadelphia."

Benjamin Franklin soon learns that the City of Brotherly Love is everything Boston is not. This is the place, Franklin will write, where he is delivered "from the poverty and obscurity from which I was born and bred, to a state of affluence and some degree of reputation in the world."*

✢ ✢ ✢

Throughout the colonies, religion remains a major factor. Each region is still defined by its first settlers. In Massachusetts, it is the Puritans. In Maryland, the Catholic majority is being replaced by Protestants. Church of England for Virginia and the Carolinas. The South leans Baptist. And in Pennsylvania, it is the Quakers. Since the year 1700, the number of churchgoers has risen, so that now almost 80 percent of America's population goes to church each Sunday.

Attendance is not always a choice. Mandatory religious services

---

* When William Penn settled the area in 1682, he sought to make peace with the local Lenape Indian tribe. He paid in full for the property rather than take it outright through war. A friendship treaty was also signed. To signify this peaceable transaction, Penn chose the name "Philadelphia," meaning "brotherly love" in Greek.

are enforced by law in many colonies. Not so in Pennsylvania. William Penn, the Quaker who founded the colony in 1681, believes in a separation of church and state. Thus, Pennsylvania becomes the most liberal part of the New World.

A more accepting religious environment is not the only reason Benjamin Franklin soon flourishes in Philadelphia. An ambitious young man, he is now almost insolvent after spending most of his money on dinner and a night's lodging at a tavern known as the Crooked Billet on Water Street. Franklin then wakes up at dawn eager to present himself at the print shop of thirty-seven-year-old Andrew Bradford. Four years ago, Bradford founded Philadelphia's first newspaper, the *American Weekly Mercury*. He also distributes pamphlets critical of the local government, something very attractive to Ben Franklin.

So he makes his way to Second Street, home of Bradford's shop. But Bradford has no work for young Ben, who quickly loses respect for the proprietor. Acting on a tip, Franklin visits another printer in this town of six thousand residents, an eccentric British expatriate named Samuel Keimer. When he arrives at Keimer's shop, Ben repairs the dilapidated printing press and is immediately hired.

They are an energetic pair, the gangly five-foot-nine Franklin and the antiestablishment Keimer, who was actually imprisoned in England for his debts, though there are rumors he was also part of the radical Jacobite movement.* Franklin's work at the print shop is the first paid job of his life, affording him minor pleasures he has never before enjoyed. The business is small, but there is potential for growth.

And that happens. Keimer's shop becomes profitable. Ben develops a reputation as a talented young printer in his own right.

---

*Jacobites sought the return of the Stuart line of succession to the British throne. This is the lineage of James II, a Catholic, sent into exile during the Glorious Revolution of 1688. The name comes from *Jacobus*, Latin for James.

He becomes very social—indulging in evenings of tea tasting. To save money, he becomes a vegetarian, spending his cash on books.

Soon, Benjamin Franklin comes to the attention of the governor of Pennsylvania, Sir William Keith, who suggests Ben open his own print shop—an amazing honor for a young man of seventeen. Governor Keith has just introduced paper money to Pennsylvania, and this represents a lucrative opportunity for Franklin to print this currency from his new shop.

Keith even offers to send Franklin to London to purchase new printing equipment—an incredible opportunity Ben quickly accepts.

"The governor, seeming to like my company, had me frequently to his house, and his setting me up was always mentioned as a fixed thing. I was to take with me letters recommendatory to a number of his friends besides the letter of credit to furnish me the necessary money to purchase the press and types of paper," Franklin will write.

In addition, the teenager also falls in love.

By great coincidence, there is a room available for rent in the home of John Read, father to young Deborah Read, the woman who spied Ben when he arrived in Philadelphia.

Their relationship develops quickly, and Franklin proposes marriage. But that is scuttled by Deborah's mother, who does not feel the teenager can support her daughter. She is also well aware that Deborah is terrified by the thought of sailing across the ocean.

So once again, Benjamin Franklin flees.

✤ ✤ ✤

After a three-week voyage, Franklin arrives in London on Christmas Eve, 1724. The chaotic city of more than six hundred thousand is home to his ancestors, and he immerses himself in attending the theater while continuing to read voraciously. He finds work with two of London's largest print houses as he awaits the letter of credit from Sir William Keith to buy the printing equipment.

A natural flirt, the athletic Franklin enjoys the attention of London women. The many temptations lead him to struggle with the morality of his Puritan upbringing, which still defines him. Expressing himself, he writes a pamphlet: "A Dissertation upon Liberty and Necessity, Pleasure and Pain." Franklin argues that humans lack free will and therefore are not morally responsible for their actions. Eventually, Franklin regrets that point of view because it goes against the morality of Deist thinking.

He will also regret writing to Deborah Read, telling her that he has no intention of leaving London. On August 5, 1724, she marries a British carpenter named John Rogers. At the same time, Benjamin Franklin experiences another setback: Governor Keith is reneging on his promise. There will be no letter of credit forthcoming.

Soon, a broke Benjamin Franklin returns home to Philadelphia after borrowing money for the passage. But he must still pay off the debt from the trip home, forcing him to work for merchant Thomas Denham. Three years after first setting foot in Philadelphia, the now twenty-year-old Franklin is no further advanced in his career than the day he arrived.

Word of Cotton Mather's death in Boston reaches Philadelphia shortly after Franklin returns from London. The witch-hunting minister expires at sixty-five from an asthma attack. But Mather continues to haunt Ben Franklin, who now invents another literary character to challenge his personal demons.

That character is simply named Poor Richard.

Chapter Eighteen

Benjamin Franklin is now a hedonist.

Yet he is mesmerized by a large crowd of the Christian faithful assembling in the streets of Philadelphia. Franklin is still more than a quarter mile from the enthusiastic gathering when he hears the loud voice of a powerful young man preaching to the enthralled crowd. The printer is amazed "to observe the extraordinary influence of his oratory on his hearers, and how much they admired and respected him, notwithstanding his common abuse of them, by assuring them they were half beasts and half devils."

Franklin gets closer, eventually joining the crowd. He studies twenty-four-year-old Reverend George Whitefield, a thickset man with a British accent who wears a white wig as he preaches. Whitefield's evangelism is well known throughout the colonies, at the forefront of what many are calling a spiritual "Great Awakening" in America. Seeing Whitefield's power for himself, Franklin is sure that he is witnessing a transformation in the people around him. "It seemed as if all the world was growing religious," he will later write. "So that one could not walk through town in an evening without hearing psalms being sung in different families of every street."*

Yet Benjamin Franklin remains a nonbeliever.

For now.

✣ ✣ ✣

The successful printer is thirty-three years old. Much has changed about him in the thirteen years since returning from London. His hairline is receding, and his long brown hair shows flecks of gray. Franklin is no longer the slender athlete of his youth, but he still has broad shoulders and a powerful build. He suffers from a chronic disease known as pleurisy, causing sharp chest pain when the lining of his lungs becomes inflamed. Having learned a hard lesson about business from Governor William Keith, Ben Franklin now ranks among the most famous and prosperous men in Philadelphia.†

The rise to success began when Franklin purchased the *Pennsylvania Gazette* from Samuel Keimer a decade ago. The paper provides income and has a recurring enemy in the form of Andrew Bradford, whose print business is suffering as Franklin becomes more well known. Bradford recently served as the postmaster of Philadelphia. During his tenure, he forbade his postal riders from delivering Franklin's *Gazette*. At first, Ben responded by bribing those carriers, ensuring his newspaper got circulated. Later, he successfully schemed to have Andrew

---

* George Whitefield is an ordained Anglican minister but was one of the leaders of a movement within the church known as Calvinistic Methodism. In time, this group would split off to form the Methodist branch of Protestantism.

† Governor William Keith will die penniless in London's Old Bailey prison on November 18, 1749, at the age of eighty. He had to flee America in 1728 to escape creditors. Before Keith departed, he saw Franklin in Philadelphia. "He seemed a little ashamed at seeing me but passed by without saying anything," Franklin will write.

Bradford replaced as postmaster of Philadelphia—by a man named Benjamin Franklin.

The *Gazette* allows Franklin a powerful voice in all things political. The opinions formed over a lifetime of observation and reading are given full vent, though Ben has learned to be more diplomatic in his written attacks, softening the blows with gentle humor.

He has used the *Gazette* to argue for a fire department and lending library in Philadelphia. Franklin has even branched out from local matters to lobby for change at a national level, railing against the cruel taxation of Great Britain's Molasses Act of 1733—which he labels "mortifying." A thorough Anglophile who still misses his freewheeling days in London, this is one of Franklin's first known disagreements with the English Crown.*

From his large print shop and home on Market Street, Ben Franklin has also brought a new version of Silence Dogood to life. Using the pseudonym "Poor Richard"—a pen name he denies as being his own—Franklin publishes an annual almanac that has become a fixture in the American colonies, selling thousands of copies each year. Readers are treated to weather predictions, astronomical observances, as well as pithy reminders such as "a penny saved is a penny earned" and the blunt "fish and visitors stink after three days."

The almanac is so lucrative that Franklin sends five hundred copies to his brother James's widow in New England, allowing her to sell them for profit as a means of staying financially afloat.

✤ ✤ ✤

---

* The Molasses Act was a law that taxed all sugar, molasses, and rum imported from non-British colonies. The act was designed to form a monopoly. Franklin argued against the statute because New England was a large distributor of molasses and rum and would be subject to this tax. Smuggling and the bribing of customs officials caused the act to fail. It would be replaced by the Sugar Act of 1764, which would become an early catalyst for the American Revolution.

The thirteen years since Benjamin Franklin's return from England is a time when Philadelphia almost doubles in population and thrives as one of America's leading seaports. The printer's personal success mirrors that of the city. Ben is now grand master of the local Freemason lodge, serves as clerk of the Pennsylvania General Assembly, and prints Pennsylvania's state currency.

Notably, beginning in 1732, Franklin has been watching the construction of a new Georgian-style structure with a redbrick facade. It will not be completed for two decades, but the towering profile and prominent location on Chestnut Street already makes it a city centerpiece. The Pennsylvania State House, as the building is known, will serve as a legislative meeting place. In the future the structure will become synonymous with the birth of an entire nation—its name changed to Independence Hall.

Benjamin Franklin will also play a prominent role in that transformation.

So it is that Franklin becomes a powerful and wealthy young man, but along with that has come a complicated private life—one that would shock his religious ancestors.

✛ ✛ ✛

Benjamin Franklin and Deborah Read are a couple once more. Her husband ran off in 1728, after being charged with stealing a slave. It is rumored that John Rogers fled to the West Indies, where he was killed. Yet Deborah has no proof of his demise, therefore no death certificate.

But she is sure he is never coming back. So she is receptive when Benjamin Franklin resumes their courtship and begins talking of marriage. But that presents a problem: bigamy.

In Pennsylvania, the penalty for being married to more than one person at the same time is life imprisonment. However, such a sentence is hard to enforce in a territory that borders open wilderness. There is no state prison. Local jails are poorly constructed and prone to easy escapes. If she marries, it is likely that Deborah will be banished. She will be forced to leave Pennsylvania.

As usual, Benjamin Franklin proposes a solution.

He will enter into a common-law marriage with Deborah—that is, a relationship agreed on by both partners but not formally recorded with legal documents. This is a Quaker invention. There is no such thing as common-law marriage in Puritan Massachusetts, except for the slaves' practice of "quasi-marriage." There is only adultery, punished by whipping and even execution.

But not so in Philadelphia. By proposing common-law marriage, Franklin protects Deborah Read from adultery charges—and also prevents her former husband's creditors from coming after her for payment.

But physical attraction and personal fondness are not the only reason Benjamin Franklin proposes marriage to Deborah.

Franklin's busy career makes little time for distractions—like children.

The printer already has a son. William Franklin was born of an affair with an affluent woman whose name is forgotten by history. The child came into the world on February 22, 1730. William has never been baptized, for this would compel the mother to sign her name into the baptismal record and reveal her identity. Ben Franklin keeps the situation quiet but does not deny being the father.

The common-law marriage between Franklin and Deborah is sealed on September 1, 1730, seven months after William's birth. Deborah becomes pregnant soon after. She gives birth to Franklin's second son, Francis, in 1732. But the boy does not live long, dying at age four from smallpox.

As his son's illness takes hold, Benjamin Franklin becomes an advocate for inoculation. He has not forgotten Cotton Mather's long-ago smallpox preventative, even though his brother James was an outspoken opponent. The *Gazette* runs editorials encouraging parents to treat their children for smallpox with a vaccine. This will prove embarrassing to Ben Franklin, for many in Philadelphia will point to Francis's death as a sign that inoculation does not work. He will publicly backpedal when it is learned that he did not inoculate his son.[*]

The death of Francis Folger Franklin deeply affects his father. Ben Franklin also lost his older sister, Sarah, to smallpox a few years prior. Writing of her death, Franklin showed a belief in the afterlife, stating that her family should "be comforted they have enjoyed her so long and that she has passed through the world happily . . . and that she is now secure in rest, in the place provided for the virtuous."

Clearly, spiritual matters occupy Benjamin Franklin's thoughts. Deborah remains a devout Anglican but Franklin's short attempt at being a Presbyterian has come to an end.

So instead of attending church with his wife, he makes up his own list of commandments, to which he rigorously adheres.

They are thirteen in number: temperance, silence, order, resolution, frugality, industry, sincerity, justice, moderation, cleanliness, tranquility, chastity, humility.

Yet as rooted in Puritan beliefs as these traits may be, none of them apply directly to faith in God.

For Benjamin Franklin, one afternoon in Philadelphia makes him reconsider that.

✢ ✢ ✢

"In 1739 arrived among us from Ireland the Reverend Mr. Whitefield, who had made himself remarkable there as an itinerant preacher," Franklin will write in his autobiography.

---

[*] Franklin wrote that he wanted his son to get stronger before inoculating him.

The printer knows of Whitefield from the London newspapers that arrive regularly in the colonies. He is aware that the fervent evangelist draws crowds numbering in the thousands, with one sermon in Britain allegedly drawing an astounding twenty thousand listeners. Franklin finds this ludicrous, thinking it impossible that the voice of one man is strong enough to carry over such a large crowd. So when Whitefield arrives in Philadelphia as part of an extended evangelical journey through the colonies, Franklin reluctantly decides to investigate. He thinks Whitefield might be a charlatan.

Benjamin Franklin bides his time, uninterested in hearing Whitefield speak to small local congregations. Church leaders in Philadelphia are at first enthusiastic about allowing him into their meetinghouses. This does not last long. Whitefield is so charismatic that entire congregations follow him to wherever he might be speaking next, abandoning their normal places of worship.

Whitefield begins giving large open-air sermons, which capture Franklin's attention. He does not agree with all of Whitefield's tenets, such as the gospel of salvation through Christ. Yet he is intrigued that the preacher is doing good works, like opening a large orphanage outside Savannah, Georgia.

As Franklin stands on the edge of the crowd on a cold winter day listening to George Whitefield for the first time, he knows that a collection plate will soon be passed. The skeptic in him thinks Whitefield is attempting to fleece the crowd. He makes a mental list of the currency in his pockets—"a handful of copper money, three or four silver dollars, and five pistoles in gold"—and vows not to donate. "I silently resolved he should get nothing from me."

Then, for the first time in decades, the boy in Benjamin Franklin who once longed to become a minister is revived. Whitehead's words boom over the large crowd. Franklin is taken in by the sincere message of faith: "A wonderful power over the hearts and purses of his hearers, of which I myself was."

The collection plate is passed. Franklin empties his pockets wholly into the dish.

✤ ✤ ✤

Benjamin Franklin sees more than just a preacher in Reverend George Whitefield. The two men meet and soon become business partners, with Franklin securing an arrangement to print Whitefield's sermons. The two develop a deep "civil friendship," in Franklin's words. Whitefield becomes a frequent visitor to the Franklin household, also forming a tight bond with Deborah.

Eventually, Reverend Whitefield becomes one of the most famous religious figures in the world.

Whitefield travels to America seven times over the course of his life. His message of self-determination in religion and civil affairs would resonate throughout the colonies, inspiring rebellion against England. He died on Sunday, September 30, 1770, in Newburyport, Massachusetts, where he is buried under the pulpit of the First Presbyterian Church.

For all his success, George Whitefield never secures Ben Franklin's conversion to Christianity, which will have ramifications for the new experiment in democracy that is coming.

✤ ✤ ✤

As the 1740s unfold, the vast majority of colonists are, unlike Ben Franklin, devoted Christians. But many lack the insight of Jesus and persecute their rivals.

In New England, Puritans have lost their power but not their intolerance. However, the situation is the opposite in the Virginia Colony. A few hundred Puritans migrated there in the 1620s and

1630s. Some are on the run, as are Quakers—a group admired by Franklin.

Unlike mother country England, where the king's church rules, the thirteen colonies are divided by religion, and that will cause a tremendous amount of trouble in the years ahead.*

---

* It seems Benjamin Franklin cannot escape the Mathers, even though they are both dead. On March 1, 1743, Franklin prints and sells one hundred copies of Increase Mather's *Soul Saving Gospel Truths*. In his archives, Bill O'Reilly has the signed receipt.

Chapter Nineteen

JANUARY 30, 1747
WILLIAMSBURG, VIRGINIA
MORNING

Fire races through the Virginia capitol building.

And Governor William Gooch knows precisely who to blame.*

The redbrick building is built in the shape of the letter *H*. Thick, white-paned windows. Round turrets. The first section consumed by fire is in an upstairs room. Smoke and flames poke out through the shingled roof, then spread through the entire structure on this cold winter day. The blaze is too hot to fight. There is nothing to do but watch this celebrated building burn to the ground.

Gooch views the scene through an upstairs window in the nearby governor's mansion. He is certain that it is arson: "apparently the effect of malice and design," the governor will conclude. "I must indeed own it is difficult to comprehend how so flagitious a crime could be committed, or even imagined, by any rational creature."†

But as Lt. Gov. William Gooch well knows, these are irratio-

---

* Formally, Gooch's title was royal lieutenant governor—but in essence, he had the powers of the governor. There were other governors, but for whatever reason they were in England so Gooch had the authority of governor.

† Gooch was wrong about the crime. After investigation, the cause of the fire was ruled to be a faulty chimney.

nal times in Virginia—and religion is the primary cause. He is at the forefront of a pitched spiritual battle that could destroy his colony if he allows it. Virginia has already weathered a witch trial of its own, so there is a precedent for this fear of the Devil. It was 1706 when forty-six-year-old Grace Sherwood was accused of sorcery and thrown into the Lynnhaven River with her hands bound. The accused managed to slip her bonds and return to the surface. The act of not drowning proved her sorcery, and she was then sent to prison for seven years. Many in Virginia know the story of Grace Sherwood. Few have denounced her persecution as being anything but just.

So while most citizens of Williamsburg see a fire, Governor Gooch is witnessing an opportunity—possibly sent by God.

✛ ✛ ✛

Two months after the blaze, on the evening of Saturday, April 1, Lt. Gov. Gooch meets with Virginia's General Assembly. A temporary headquarters has been rented for the citizen legislators, all eager to point the finger of blame for the capitol's destruction.

But as Gooch addresses the group, he shifts his focus from the fire to a metaphor, asking the assembly "as fathers of your country" to fix the "royal fabric" of Virginia.

The legislators understand. "The raging fire," they all agree, was divine intervention: "the wrathful indignation of an incensed God."*

The reason for this furious judgment is the proliferation of non-Anglican preachers throughout the colony. The Anglican Church is the established church of Virginia. Renegade evangelical ministers inspired by Reverend George Whitefield roam the countryside, speaking in churches and in vast open-air meetings, challenging

---

* Those words were placed in the official report of the capitol fire.

Anglican doctrine. Many of these men have no Virginia license to preach, nor credentials showing religious training. But their words are igniting rebellion.

✤ ✤ ✤

Back in Philadelphia, Benjamin Franklin is making enormous sums of money by printing the tracts and books that also inspire religious dissent. He watches the controversy in Virginia with amusement, often commenting about the chaos in his *Gazette*.

But this is no joke to the Virginia General Assembly. Legislators continue to speak about the fire, stating that these "dissenters" implant "a spirit more dangerous to the common welfare, than the furious element, which laid the royal edifice in ashes."

The April 1 session concludes with the lawmakers requesting Gooch take all appropriate measures to stop the evil spread of heresy—to go after the non-Anglican preachers.

✤ ✤ ✤

Although there is no evidence against any evangelical, the fire is a convenient way for Gooch to rid Virginia of religious dissenters. This is not the first time he has tried. Two years earlier, on April 18, 1745, the lieutenant governor encourages the Virginia grand jury to prosecute these wandering ministers for spreading their non-Anglican beliefs. Much to his chagrin, the grand jury declines to do his bidding. England's 1688 Toleration Act specifically protects dissent by those who choose a faith other than Anglican. This does not apply to Catholics.

However, as an Englishman appointed by the Crown, it is Gooch's job to ensure the Church of England remains the one true faith in his colony.

But the fact is the Anglican Church is in trouble.

Religious uniformity has been a way of life in Virginia since

Governor William Berkeley, under orders from King Charles I, demanded strict adherence to the Church of England.

But many Virginians are tired of taking orders from their mother country. The new wave of dissent no longer finds salvation from an earthly king. Already, Puritans have been almost completely driven out of Virginia because of their harsh lifestyle. But Baptists, Methodists, and Presbyterians remain. These sects do not follow strict Church of England tenets, such as infant baptism, nor the belief that only those ordained in the Anglican Church can preach the word of God.

✤ ✤ ✤

Two days after meeting with the Virginia General Assembly, Lt. Gov. Gooch starts his week by issuing a proclamation putting an end to dissenting evangelists. The morning is April 3, 1747. Gooch bars "all itinerant preachers . . . from teaching or holding any meeting in this Colony."

Dissenters will be arrested and jailed.

Gooch is nearing seventy. He has lived in Virginia for almost two decades and is a staunch Anglican. At one time he was a member of the military and was shot in the ankle fighting pirates in Cartagena, New Granada, in today's Colombia. A haughty man, Gooch favors a white wig when presiding over the General Assembly.

Going unspoken is the financial aspect of religion in Virginia. The Anglican Church is a great source of revenue. Congregants are taxed, ordered by law to pay the church whether they attend services or not. This is called forced tithing. These moneys are used for traditional benevolence such as caring for the poor, but also for building roads and ferries, and even certifying that property boundaries are correct. As a member of Anglican vestry, men like Gooch can derive funds from the religious taxes. All ministers and church employees get a salary.

The governor's April 3 proclamation is posted throughout the state. All would-be ministers must now register with a county clerk, show their credentials, and pay for a license.

One of the governor's supporters is an Anglican rector named Patrick Henry, whose nephew will go on to become a hero of the Revolutionary War. Reverend Henry mocks the evangelical preachers and refuses to consider them spiritual equals. When the now notorious George Whitefield requests permission to speak at Henry's church in 1745, he is denied.

That does not deter Whitefield. He shows up anyway, attracting a large crowd. A furious Patrick Henry has no choice but to let Whitefield into his church. Thus, bad blood gets even worse. Predictably, Whitefield gives a stemwinder of a sermon. Sinners are "damned, double damned, whose souls are in hell, though they are alive on earth."

Reverend Henry is appalled, even conjuring up memories of the Salem witch trials, complaining that the evangelical preachers use their words to bring out the Devil in a congregation by leading listeners to contort in convulsions.

❖ ❖ ❖

What neither William Gooch nor Patrick Henry understands is that this religious controversy in Virginia is a pivotal moment in American history. There is rebellion against the British Crown through the opposition to the Anglican Church. That has happened before in New England, but not to this extent.

Reverend Patrick Henry's own sister-in-law leaves the Anglican Church to follow the ministry of a passionate new pastor in Hanover County. Sarah Henry brings her twelve-year-old son, Patrick, named after his uncle, to hear the oratory of Reverend Samuel Davies, an evangelical and dissenter from the Anglican Church. The young preacher has a powerful vocal style meant to captivate an audience, and the young boy will one day describe Davies as "the greatest orator I ever heard." The minister arrives in Virginia in February 1747 and will become one of the most influential figures in the life of the soon-to-be patriot Patrick Henry.

The boy is one of nine children born to thirty-nine-year-old Sarah and husband, John. Two of their daughters die young. The couple own the seven thousand acres of land that Sarah inherited. John acquires more each year through business deals.

With that kind of property, the Henry family is one of the elite, and own slaves.

So it is a powerful statement when Sarah stops attending the Anglican Church with her husband. Young Patrick Henry sees the discord in his family being caused by religion. And so do some other young people. More than one hundred miles to the west in Virginia, four-year-old Thomas Jefferson's family has chosen to remain with the Anglican Church. To the north, fifteen-year-old George Washington's family are also devout Anglicans.

But the redheaded Patrick Henry, a budding intellectual who will earn the nickname "Hot Head" for his hair color and volatile temper, is, along with his mother, a religious dissenter. To him, the Church of England and its offshoot in Virginia, the Anglicans, are obsolete.

✧ ✧ ✧

And so it is that religious power is breaking down in the prosperous colony of Virginia. The king's church is losing parishioners and authority to a new breed of preachers. It is the first major fissure between the Crown in London and the colonists three thousand miles away—and one that is metastasizing throughout the thirteen colonies. Families are splitting apart over worship—and freedom of choice is taking root.

In Virginia, young Henry, Jefferson, and Washington are witnessing the changing times in a very personal way.

In Pennsylvania, the older Ben Franklin is delighted by the religious sedition and senses more conflict to come.

He will be proved astoundingly correct.

Chapter Twenty

The town of Salem is still haunted.

The accusers and prosecutors in the witch trials are long dead. On present day Washington Street, the great courthouse where the trials were held on the second floor is showing its age and will soon be torn down. The Puritans no longer practice a dogmatic and cruel version of their faith, having been changed by the shocking brutality of the witch hangings. The city remains a backwater port compared with nearby Boston, but as the second half of the eighteenth century begins, Salem is finally beginning to prosper. The waterfront is home to nearly fifty wharves right now, capable of handling a large volume of shipping from all around the world. Young girls haunted by the Devil are a thing of the past.

Yet Salem has a new demon. A lawless terror can be found on the waterfront in the form of piracy. Thousands of pirates roam the Atlantic Ocean, killing with guns and swords as they attack and rob cargo vessels in the Caribbean and off the African coast. Their winters are spent in those warm equatorial waters, but summer brings a return to the busy New England shipping lanes. Famous pirates Blackbeard and William Kidd have made fortunes in the lucrative waters near Boston's North Shore. Salem's many wharves make it an illicit stopover for pirate ships in need of resupply and entertainment. The locals know their true identity but treat them like any other customers.

✦ ✦ ✦

With a pirate presence comes the "Witch of Wellfleet." Maria Hallett is a teenager when she takes up with the notorious Samuel "Black Sam" Bellamy. At age twenty-eight, Bellamy is thought to be the richest pirate of them all—plundering more than fifty ships.

Born in England, he joined the Royal Navy as a teenager but soon sailed for America to become a treasure hunter. But finding sunken gold was hard work and Bellamy had little success. He gravitated toward the world of piracy because that's where the money was. He signed on with the pirate ship *Marianne*—not as captain but as ordinary crew.

By all accounts, "Black Sam" was a charismatic man. Tall and powerfully built, he had a reputation for being tidy and articulate. He enjoyed the finest garments and gemstones and preferred to dress in black. "I am a free prince," Bellamy once stated. "I have as much authority to make war on the whole world as he who has a hundred sail of ships at sea and an army of 100,000 men."

The pirate uses that articulate charm to convince *Marianne*'s ninety-man crew to get rid of the captain—not by killing him but through a vote. The men do so, then place Bellamy in charge. The young pirate does not kill the deposed captain but allows him to go ashore in safety.

Bellamy then leads *Marianne* on a series of raids, capturing vessels laden with gold and ivory. The crew of each boarded ship are allowed the option of joining his pirate crew. He seeks men of action, not "sniveling puppies, who allow superiors to kick them about deck at pleasure."

The captain captures the eighteen-gun former slave ship *Whydah Gally* after a three-day chase. Black Sam fires a single shot across her bow, after which her captain lowers his flag in surrender. The 110-foot-long vessel with a speed of thirteen knots immediately becomes Bellamy's new flagship.

Most pirates are brutal, but Black Sam prides himself on treating his hostages kindly. However, in the world of piracy, even the most successful die young.

Enter seventeen-year-old Maria Hallett, who was born and raised in Wellfleet, Massachusetts, on Cape Cod. Bellamy and Hallett meet when the pirate comes ashore to do some business. She soon becomes his consort on land. But Maria's parents refuse to let the couple marry and Bellamy sails off, leaving behind a pregnant and lonely mistress. Because of her association with a pirate, Maria is shunned by many of the religious people in her community. She is suspect and widely talked about. "Goody," as Hallett is also known, secretly bears Black Sam's baby after he returns to sea. This is unacceptable in her community. So she hides the pregnancy and the infant after birth. Because she has no money, even feeding the infant becomes a challenge. One day, Maria leaves the child alone as she goes out to secure food. When she returns a short time later, the baby has choked to death while eating straw bedding.

Then another disaster strikes. It is April. Black Sam is sailing north to rekindle his romance with Maria Hallett and to begin a summer of plunder. Suddenly, a powerful Atlantic nor'easter appears off the coast of Wellfleet. A wave sixteen feet high descends on the *Whydah Gally*, drowning most of its crew, including Black Sam Bellamy—who never reaches his thirtieth birthday.

After word of the pirate's death travels the Massachusetts coast, a distraught Maria Hallett is accused of using "Devil powers" to conjure up the storm. Witnesses will claim to see her riding on the back of a whale. They will also state that she owns a black goat and a black cat, both signs of evil. Yet unlike the women of 1692, the "Witch of Wellfleet" is never prosecuted. There is no attempt to arrest her for being a witch. Goody Hallett lives a long life before dying unmarried. In her later years, she becomes a churchgoer and gives away all her worldly possessions.

Still, the tale of Maria bewitching the *Whydah Gally* continues to spread.

✤ ✤ ✤

In Boston, fifteen-year-old John Adams has no time for tall tales and witches. He is devout, describing himself as a "church going animal." Adams lives on a farm near Braintree and is the son of a Congregational minister. Yet the Harvard-educated Adams does not believe in the mysteries and superstitions of the Puritans, such as persecuting witches. His family is part of a congregation in Boston that believes in social justice and fellowship. But the young Adams is conflicted about religion in general: "This would be the best of all worlds if there was no religion in it," he will write, making a distinction between organized sects and simple faith in God.

But he then contradicts himself. "Without religion, this world would be something not fit to be mentioned in polite company—I mean hell."

Conflicted or not, John Adams is certainly aware of the battle between traditional Puritanism, with its witch history, and the much more liberal Unitarian movement. He is also under the influence of a twenty-nine-year-old Unitarian minister, one of his instructors at Harvard.

Jonathan Mayhew is the most prominent dissenter against the Church of England in Massachusetts. His powerful sermons put forth radical ideas against the Crown that might get him jailed in Virginia. Mayhew's words are not just spiritual wanderings but outright treason.*

---

* In particular, Mayhew is incensed that the Church of England has named King Charles I a martyr and saint. Mayhew believes that Charles's execution during the English Civil War was justified because he had infringed on the civil liberties of his subjects—and thus was neither a martyr nor a saint.

Preaching at the Old West Church on Cambridge Street in Boston on the anniversary of the beheading of King Charles I, Mayhew puts forth a radical new belief in personal freedom. He preaches that killing a king is *justified* if the monarch intrudes on individual liberty. "It is hoped that but few will think the subject of this sermon an improper one to be discoursed on in the pulpit," he begins, "under a notion that this is preaching politics, instead of Christ."

But Reverend Mayhew is clearly preaching politics—as John Adams well knows. The tradition of passive obedience to a flawed ruler has never before been challenged with such authority.

The minister's "Discourse Concerning Unlimited Submission," as the sermon is titled, is printed and circulated throughout Massachusetts. His words inspire Adams to believe Americans should be free from the tyranny of a king.

In time, Mayhew's speech will become known as "the morning gun of the Revolution," fueling rebellion against England. John Adams is so inspired by Mayhew's words that even in his old age he will give copies of the speech to friends as a gift.

✢ ✢ ✢

In Philadelphia, Benjamin Franklin still believes that all power comes from the king.

The avowed advocate of the British monarchy again sails to London in 1757 to present a local controversy to the Crown. Franklin's wife, Deborah, has chosen to remain behind in Pennsylvania, terrified of crossing the ocean by ship. She will run the family business in his absence. Neither she nor Ben could know this separation will last eighteen years!

Franklin takes up lodging at 36 Craven Street. The residence lies on a narrow lane just off the Thames River, a short walk from the royal palace and the heart of London. Franklin is now fifty-one and no longer the struggling printer who visited here three decades ago. He is portly and wears bifocals—a type of eyewear that Franklin invented, which corrects for both nearsighted and farsighted vision.

Because of his tremendous success in a variety of fields, Benjamin Franklin is now by far the world's most famous American, revered for his intellectual genius. England has named him a Fellow of the Royal Society for his advancements in science—in particular, his 1752 discovery that lightning contains electricity.

Franklin's friend Reverend George Whitefield is inspired by this scientific breakthrough to continue his attempts to coax his business partner toward a similar investigation of faith. Whitefield writes Franklin, admitting that since he "made a pretty considerable progress in the mysteries of electricity, I would now humbly recommend to your diligent unprejudiced pursuit and study the mystery of the new birth."

As he has for years, Ben Franklin ignores George Whitefield's advice.

✦ ✦ ✦

As Franklin makes himself at home in London, American independence is the last thing on his mind. He has come back to London to enjoy himself and to settle a dispute over who exactly owns Pennsylvania—a disagreement that can only be settled by King George II. If anything, Franklin wants the English king to have *more* say in American matters—not less.

Yet things will not go well for Benjamin Franklin in London. And that will change his perspective radically. After a few months, Franklin is distressed to find that America is looked upon as a backwater and that the English Crown has little interest in the welfare of the colonists. In fact, it is money derived from the colonies that is on the mind of King George. He needs to finance England's European conflicts and is not distressed about controversies three thousand miles away.

But he should be.

The seeds of American independence are being sown back in the colonies. What began with attacks on the Church of England by religious dissenters is spreading through philosophical young men like John Adams who believe it is time for a change.

In England, Ben Franklin wants nothing to do with radical change. He remains committed to the monarchy.

That, however, will soon change.

Chapter Twenty-One

Patrick Henry and his father have a problem.

The attorney Henry, now twenty-seven and married, stands on a speaking platform in the redbrick courthouse, arguing for religious freedom. He is six feet tall, a slender 160 pounds, and plays the violin in his spare time. He has been a small-town country lawyer for three years, without any major success. Dark suit and a white shirt, long red hair pulled back. He knows the words he will say this morning could send him to prison.

But Patrick Henry does not care.

It seems like the whole town is taking this Thursday off to see the spectacle. The courtroom is so full the doors have been left open for those outside to hear. Across the street is a tavern owned by Henry's father-in-law. The young lawyer and his wife, Sarah, live above the establishment.

Presiding over today's proceedings is Colonel John Henry, Patrick's father. He is a devout Anglican and leading member of Virginia's landed aristocracy. Fifty-nine years old, white hair, walks with a cane. His alignment with the British Crown is complete. Surprisingly, in the colony of Virginia there is no legal conflict in having a father make decisions in a case concerning his son. It is thought that a true gentleman will set aside any biases while presiding over a court of law.

Essentially, the issue at hand today is the salary of Anglican ministers, who are also known as parsons. Tobacco is currency in Virginia, no different from paper money. Whether they like it or not, every landowner throughout the state is considered to be a member of the Church of England and is taxed to pay the salary of their local parson. Tax collectors ensure payment. The penalty for refusal is confiscation of property, and even jail.

In 1696, the Virginia legislature, known as the House of Burgesses, passes a strong law stating that parsons could be paid in promissory notes for tobacco. The problem is the crop goes up and down in price. So when harvests are poor the clergy is happy. But when there is an abundance of tobacco the parsons get far less.*

Now, the House of Burgesses votes to place a cap on how much the ministers could be paid. This amount is two pennies per pound of tobacco. The parsons are enraged and send a delegation to England to have the law overturned. Enlisting the help of the archbishop of Canterbury and the bishop of London, they successfully persuade the aging King George II to rule in their favor.

These legal actions are known as the "Parson's Cause."

✤ ✤ ✤

Patrick Henry opposes the mandatory payments to clergy. He believes a religious tax of *any* kind is unjust. The Anglican Church,

---

* The House of Burgesses was part of the Virginia General Assembly, which was bicameral. It was the "popular" (elected) house of the bicameral assembly with the upper house appointed. The title for members of the House of Burgesses was formally Burgess (plural Burgesses). You can informally refer to the Burgesses as "members of the House of Burgesses" or, as you write, "legislators," more of a modern term. The House of Burgesses was the title used for the lower house of the Virginia General Assembly until 1776, when it became the House of Delegates. When the House of Delegates came into being, members were called Delegates.

acting on behalf of the British Crown, is depriving colonists of their rights.

Patrick Henry's father, the presiding judge, disagrees. After his son makes his case, John Henry rules in favor of the parsons—and the Crown.*

✢ ✢ ✢

But the case is not done. Now, a Virginia jury has to decide exactly how much money the parsons are owed.

"A king and those he rules share a solemn compact," Patrick Henry states in his closing arguments. "In exchange for their obedience, the King must rule in a way that brings happiness to his subjects.

"But gentlemen," Henry continues, turning to the jury. "I submit that for a sovereign to disallow such a wholesome law as the Two-Penny Act in such a manner is a misrepresentation of rule and breaks the compact between a king and his subjects. It may even be called tyranny."

Gasps fill the courtroom. Shocked cries of "treason."

But Patrick Henry is not done. The courtroom is filled with more than twenty members of Anglican clergy. Henry calls out several by name, noting their wealth, fondness for good wine, fox hunting, and, in the case of one minister, ample girth.

"Do not be deceived, gentlemen of the jury. This is not an issue from a few pence per pound of tobacco. This is a case concerned with freedom. Freedom for Virginia to govern itself. Freedom to choose who shall minister to our spiritual needs. Freedom from tyranny, in whatever form it may take. . . . Unless you wish to fasten the chains of bondage around your own neck,

---

* Colonel John Henry died in 1773, one decade after the Parson's Cause trial. As a boy, Patrick Henry was taught Greek, Latin, and mathematics by his father, as well as the virtues of self-reliance and speaking his mind. The two remained close, John Henry even giving his son a gift of 1,700 acres of land in 1765.

you must make an example . . . of the rights of free men to make their *own* law.

"Award damages as you must. But send a message to tyrants by awarding only one penny in damages."

The courtroom quiets as the jury retires to consider the arguments. They return just five minutes later.

"Have you reached a verdict?" Judge John Henry asks the foreman.

"Yes, we have," comes the reply. "We find in favor of the plaintiff . . . and award damages in the amount of one penny."

The parsons are furious. The jury decision nullifies the king's veto of the Two Penny Act. This is a major defeat for the Anglican clergy and a successful challenge to the king's authority. The packed courtroom cheers. Patrick Henry is lifted up and carried to the tavern on the shoulders of the jubilant crowd.

Rebellion is in the air.

✤ ✤ ✤

It will be thirteen years until a group of radical colonists gather in Philadelphia to argue for and against total independence from England. But a precedent has just been set by a ruling against the king's Anglican Church.

Word of the verdict quickly reaches London. Patrick Henry becomes a known subversive.

✤ ✤ ✤

On the day Henry gives his Parson's Cause speech, Thomas Jefferson is a college student in Williamsburg. He actually knows the lawyer: "My acquaintance with Mr. Henry commenced in the winter of 1759–60," Jefferson will write.

"On my way to the college, I passed the Christmas holidays at Colonel [John] Dandridge's in Hanover, to whom Mr. Henry was a near neighbor. During the festivity of the season, I met him in society every day, and we became well acquainted, although I was much his junior, being then in my seventeenth year, and he a married man."*

The six-foot-two Jefferson likes Henry, who shares his love for playing the violin. The two men consider themselves best friends, despite their age difference. But while Patrick Henry is openly questioning the role of the Anglican Church in Virginia, Thomas Jefferson is still publicly loyal to the Crown. The college student attends Anglican services, pays taxes to the parsonage, and maintains friendships with a number of clergy. He has an eye on a career in politics, and church attendance is mandatory for membership in the Virginia General Assembly.

However, in the process of getting his college degree, Jefferson has been introduced to the Deist movement to which Benjamin Franklin has long adhered. The teachings have not altered his church attendance, but he is fascinated by metaphysics and the connection between theology and morality.

Unlike Patrick Henry, Thomas Jefferson is not ready to make his views public.

But that day will come.

✦ ✦ ✦

All thirteen colonies now have religious controversies. Much of this is brought on by growing diversity. Massachusetts remains Puritan and Maryland is overwhelmingly Catholic, despite repression by the Anglican Church barring "Papists" from voting, holding public office, practicing law, worshipping in churches, or making converts.

---

* Colonel John Dandridge was the father of the woman who will become known as Martha Washington. Born in 1731 and widowed from her first husband at the age of twenty-six, she remarries two years later. Her second husband is a surveyor and soldier who fought in the French and Indian War. His name is George Washington, and he is a devout Anglican.

Rhode Island accepts all religions, as founder Roger Williams envisioned—though Williams is known to criticize Quakers. English philosopher John Locke wrote the constitutions of North and South Carolina, with a strong focus on religious tolerance as well.* And despite being a Quaker, William Penn founded Pennsylvania with an eye toward freedom for all faiths.

But there are continuing problems with religious differences.

✢ ✢ ✢

In New York City an alleged "Negro Plot" is uncovered. This is an attempt by Catholics to align with former slaves to burn down Manhattan. The growing city is more than 90 percent Protestant. To these people, the Catholic faith is deeply suspect after centuries of persecuting religious heretics—mostly Protestants. In a series of tribunals reminiscent of the witch trials, the suspected conspiracy in New York City leads to twice as many executions as in Salem. More than 150 Roman Catholics are arrested between March and August 1741. Under duress, most soon "confess" their guilt. Thirty-four Catholics and former slaves are hanged. Eighty more are banished from New York for life.

In Plymouth, anti-Catholic fervor is also a reality. Since 1623, on November 5, gangs of sailors and working-class men have celebrated "Pope Night." Hundreds turn out for a night of drinking and fighting as the pope is burned in effigy. In 1764, a carriage transporting the pope's effigy to the burning site runs over a young boy, crushing his skull.

Also in 1764, shortly after Patrick Henry's Parson's Cause victory, Presbyterians in the Pennsylvania town of Paxton rebel against Quaker authorities for not protecting them against Indian

---

* The full title was "Fundamental Constitutions of Carolina" written in 1669. There is some disagreement as to whether or not John Locke was the sole author—but he certainly was the primary writer associated with it. The "Constitutions" applied to land south of Virginia, which later became North and South Carolina.

attacks. In a massacre designed to taunt the nonviolent Quakers, Scotch-Irish settlers kill twenty Native Americans.

In Virginia, religious conflict grows worse. One sheriff ends a Sunday service by pulling the Baptist minister from his pulpit. The lawman then drags the pastor outside, where he pummels him and delivers twenty lashes with a horsewhip.

At the Mill Swamp Baptist Church in what is today the Portsmouth, Virginia, area, a gang of pro-Anglicans breaks into a service and drags two church leaders to the nearby Nansemond River. In a mockery of the Baptist practice of submersion in water, the ministers are dunked in the swampy muck almost to the point of drowning.

Strangely, the one religious group persecuted more than any other in Europe is left alone in America. By the 1770s, Jewish colonists will number between two thousand and three thousand out of a population of three million. First arriving in what will become known as New York City in 1654, when it was still known as New Amsterdam, Jews have quietly migrated throughout the colonies.

However, despite synagogues in Charlotte, Newport, Savannah, Philadelphia, and New York, Jews are not allowed the same rights as Christians to publicly observe their faith. In fact, in New England, those practicing the Hebrew faith are not welcome at all.

✢ ✢ ✢

In Salem, once home to all things Puritan, the city has undergone a remarkable change. There is a new god: prosperity. The city is now dependent on the sea, not farming, for its income. The thriving port has a population of just less than six thousand. Ships from around the world dock in Salem, unloading their cargo on long, busy wharves. Fishing boats bring back holds filled with cod caught off Newfoundland's Grand Banks. Seaside taverns fill daily with sailors speaking in their native Portuguese, various African dialects, Caribbean, and British accents. The Salem Marine Society, founded by sea captains, is a powerful group caring for aging sailors and their families. There's a new library. A newspaper. Homes of former "witch hunters" are being torn down. The Puritan faith no longer reigns supreme, the three Congregational churches now joined by Quakers and Anglicans. Salem is not looking backward at witches but onward to a wealthy future.

Yet the Devil has not forgotten about Salem.

✢ ✢ ✢

In England, the new king, George III, doesn't care very much about what's going on in the colonies. His concerns are more immediate: the Crown is going broke, and George needs money to fight a series of European conflicts.

The American colonies are the perfect place to get it.

The cost of maintaining ten thousand British troops to defend American soil is £225,000 per year.* George has no choice but to keep those soldiers on the payroll, even after the French and Indian War is over. Native American attacks on colonists are common, and pirates roam the East Coast.

The king has never been outside England. He was born in London and is preparing to move his family into new lodgings known as Buckingham House. George doesn't even know the names of the colonies. There are "Sugar Colonies," "Rice Colonies," and "Tobacco Ones." Massachusetts, to George, is a place "North of Tobacco."

In his ignorance, the king proposes a small tax for each colonist. This seems fair; he is protecting them.

However, many colonists don't see it that way. They have no love for or loyalty to George.

Which bothers him not at all.

He is coming hard for American money.

And that will change the world.

---

* More than $35 million in modern American currency.

Chapter Twenty-Two

Patrick Henry is now a Virginia legislator.

"Caesar had his Brutus; Charles the First his Cromwell; and George the Third," Henry thunders in the House of Burgesses. Thomas Jefferson, now twenty-two, sits in the spectator gallery here in the newly rebuilt Capitol Building, absorbing his friend's tirade.

But the orator's speech is cut short.

"Treason!" yells a fellow legislator. Then another.

But these men are shouted down. The majority of the thirty-nine lawmakers in attendance (out of 116 members) share Henry's outrage against the king. Especially the latest action.

England has imposed the new Stamp Act on the colonies. By order of the king, all papers in the New World, everything from newspapers to diplomas, will be taxed. A royal seal—"stamp"—must appear on every document. These cost a fee. All revenues revert to the Crown.

In the past year, King George III and Parliament have instituted the Sugar Act to increase duties on non-British goods entering the colonies. Also, the Currency Act prevents Americans from printing their own money. The colonies are also responsible for feeding and sheltering British soldiers through the king's Quartering Act.

But the Stamp Act is the worst. This is the first direct tax levied against the people. Citizens must pay out of their own pockets when they purchase a needed paper document.

Patrick Henry, elected to the House of Burgesses one year ago, fuels the anger. Boldly, he is introducing as many as seven new resolutions that declare Virginia free from British rule. This will become known as the Virginia Resolves.

Many in the crowded assembly, wealthy planters with strong alliances to England, oppose Henry. They want no part of rebellion. But Patrick Henry will not be dissuaded.

"If this be treason," he states, "make the most of it."

✦ ✦ ✦

Virginia is not alone.

In Maryland, the first public resistance to taxation begins in August. Businessman Zachariah Hood of Annapolis is returning from England, where he has been appointed the Maryland tax collector for the new Stamp Act. Jonas Green, publisher of the *Maryland Gazette*, prints news of Hood's new job and tells readers of his imminent return from London.

On August 26, with Hood still at sea, a lawyer named Samuel Chase creates an effigy of the new tax collector, which is hoisted up onto a gallows and burned.

One week later, as Hood's ship reaches Annapolis, an unruly mob waits on the docks, preventing him from disembarking. "He was insulted and spurned," one eyewitness will relate. "His effigy was placed upon a one-horse cart like a malefactor and was hauled through the streets of Annapolis while the bells tolled a knell."

Yet Zachariah Hood is determined to carry out his royal commission. The new stamps will be arriving soon from England aboard a British sloop of war. But before the ship can sail into the Chesapeake Bay, a furious gang of three hundred citizens surrounds

Hood's warehouse and burns it to the ground. They then walk to his home, breaking windows.

Finally, fearing for his life, Zachariah Hood flees Maryland for New York City.

When the *Hawke* arrives in port, there is no tax collector to receive the new stamps. Maryland governor Horatio Sharpe orders the ship to keep the documents on board.

"None of the stamps were ever used in Maryland," one Annapolis historian writes.

✤ ✤ ✤

Meanwhile in Boston, a group calling themselves the "Loyal Nine" secretly meets at the *Boston Gazette* newspaper. The goal is repealing the Stamp Act. But their ways are more militant. These middle-class businessmen plan on using violence to lure the masses to their cause. Though not a member of the Loyal Nine, a wealthy Bostonian named John Hancock has agreed to serve as one of its benefactors.

In August, a second group opposed to the Stamp Act is formed in Boston and then New York. The "Sons of Liberty," as these men call themselves, will one day use dire methods such as applying hot tar and feathers to their enemies. But in these early days, methods are less brutal. In Boston, the group meets at the Green Dragon tavern, once owned by Salem witch trial jurist William Stoughton.

"The Sons of Liberty on the 14th of August 1765, a day which ought to be forever remembered in America, animated with a zeal for their country then upon the brink of destruction, and resolved, at once to save her," Bostonian Samuel Adams will write in the *Gazette*. Adams, a local brewer and cousin of John Adams, also coins the group's motto: "No taxation without representation."*

---

* The phrase confronts London with the fact that Americans have no voice in the British Parliament.

The Sons of Liberty act quickly after their first meeting. An effigy of Andrew Oliver, the public administrator in charge of collecting the stamp tax, is hung from what is known as the "Liberty Tree" near Hanover Square. A sign is affixed to Oliver's likeness, warning everyone against removing it: "He that takes this down is an enemy to his country."

Thousands of citizens gather to parade through the streets of Boston to Andrew Oliver's home. As in Maryland, the mob soon assaults the house, tearing down fences, breaking windows, shredding furniture, and looting the large wine cellar. Fearing for his life, Oliver soon publicly vows to never serve as a stamp tax collector.

But the Sons of Liberty are not finished. Andrew Oliver's brother-in-law is Thomas Hutchinson, lieutenant governor and chief justice of the Superior Court of Judicature, the highest judicial position in colonial Massachusetts. The day after looting Oliver's home, the revolutionaries surround Hutchinson's residence and demand he denounce the stamp tax. The lieutenant governor is an opponent of the legislation, yet he refuses to give in to the mob because he is a staunch advocate for the king. Two weeks later, the Sons of Liberty return with axes and hammers. Hutchinson's front door is hacked into kindling and the mob pours in. Soon, forces loyal to the Crown come to Hutchinson's defense. What follows is a huge brawl, which ends only after the mansion is looted of all silver and hundreds of pounds of currency notes.

The attacks have the desired effect: thousands of common citizens rally to the anti–Stamp Act cause. Word spreads, and tax collectors throughout the colonies quit their jobs in fear. The town of Salem does not riot or burn effigies but chooses to send a sharply worded message to the Massachusetts colonial assembly that the act is "excessively grievous and burdensome."

In London, George remains defiant. He will not rescind the stamp tax. But he will punish the rebels.

✢ ✢ ✢

Also in London, three thousand miles away from the colonies, Benjamin Franklin approves of the Stamp Act.

At first.

But he is rethinking.

Franklin stands before the House of Commons. It is February 13, 1766. Word of mob violence in America is the talk of London. Alarmed members of Parliament are angry and want an explanation about this barbarous behavior. So they have called on Franklin to explain the ingratitude of his countrymen.

Benjamin Franklin is now sixty and reveling in his role as elder statesman. He surveys the room made of hand-carved oak. Members of Parliament sit on benches covered with soft green fabric. Franklin knows this is an important moment in his life.

As the American representative in England for the colonies of Pennsylvania, Massachusetts, New Jersey, and Georgia, Franklin at first believed the Stamp Act to be a fair method of funding the British military presence in America. He is also aware that the tax is very small compared to what British citizens pay the king.

Yet long before Parliament received the news of insurgency, word had reached Franklin that the colonists were rebelling against the tax.

He now stands before Parliament to explain why.

This is an inquisition. The House of Commons is upset that Americans are disregarding British law. The Speaker of the House leads the questioning. He sits in a high chair in the center aisle, feet balanced on a green step stool. Members step forward one by one to pose questions to Franklin.

Q. What is your name, and place of abode?
A. Franklin, of Philadelphia.
Q. Do the Americans pay any considerable taxes among themselves?

A. Certainly many, and very heavy taxes.

Q. What are the present taxes in Pennsylvania, laid by the laws of the colonies?

A. There are taxes on all estates, real and personal; a poll tax; a tax on all offices, professions, trades, and businesses, according to their profits; an excise on all wine, rum, and other spirit; and a duty of ten pounds per head on all Negroes imported, with some other duties.

The queries continue—lasting four hours.

Q. Did the Americans ever dispute the controlling power of Parliament to regulate the commerce?

A. No.

Q. Can anything less than a military force carry the Stamp Act into execution?

A. I do not see how a military force can be applied for that purpose.

Q. Why may it not?

A. Suppose a military force is sent into America; they will find nobody in arms; what are they then to do? They cannot force a man to take stamps who chooses to do without them. They will not find a rebellion; they may indeed make one.

Q. If the act is not repealed, what do you think will be the consequences?

A. A total loss of the respect and affection the people of America bear to this country, and of all the commerce that depends on that respect and affection.

✤ ✤ ✤

Benjamin Franklin is well known in London after almost a decade in the city. He socializes with many of the men in this room. Franklin also has a number of enemies, enough so that one eyewitness makes notations about which members of Parliament asking questions are friends and which are foes.

Franklin actually has a job in England. He is joint postmaster general to the Crown, responsible for the mail getting through in America. He is not the only person to testify; over the last three days, many British merchants have stepped forth to share their beliefs about the Stamp Act.

But it is Benjamin Franklin who changes minds.

Amazingly, the Stamp Act is repealed one month after his testimony.

To a pleased Ben Franklin, whose reputation in London soars even higher after his testimony, the situation has been satisfied "to what the profane would call luck, and the pious providence."

✤ ✤ ✤

Heading into the latter part of the eighteenth century, the pious still dominate the American colonies. But, once again, the specter of violence is most apparent in New England, which has discovered a new Satan.

King George III.

Chapter Twenty-Three

The king's men have their backs against the wall.

An angry mob confronts nine English soldiers on King Street, outside the Custom House. The veteran members of the 29th Regiment of Foot are unfazed. Each grenadier carries a musket, a bayonet, and ammunition—more than enough firepower to fight back if need be. They wear red uniforms, black-and-white leggings, black tricorn hats. These men now live in Boston with the mandate of controlling colonial dissent. Their leader is Captain Thomas Preston, a forty-eight-year-old Irish-born Protestant and career soldier. It is almost 5 p.m. The sun is about to set on this cold, snowy afternoon.

Yet even in the fading daylight, a growing throng of angry colonists show expert marksmanship, pelting the soldiers with snowballs, sticks, and trash. Citizens continue to arrive as word spreads throughout central Boston of a chance to humiliate the British. Many walk past the confrontation on their way home from work, then stop and join. The mob swells to two hundred, then three hundred.

The soldiers have no way to escape. They are quartered here to enforce the peace, but now there is no such thing in Boston. Colonists are outraged these troops live permanently in their city and homes. Bostonians consider the British force to be a foreign army and have been rebelling against the occupation since their arrival a year and a half ago.

The intensity of the dusk confrontation grows, and the soldiers are now surrounded and vastly outnumbered. They realize extreme action is their only escape.

✠ ✠ ✠

Standing at the very front of the mob is a forty-seven-year-old sailor named Crispus Attucks. He is not entirely a stranger. Born in nearby Framingham, he escaped from slavery in Massachusetts when he was twenty-seven—then went to sea. It is known that he works on whaling boats, one of the only trades open to black men. He makes rope for a living when ashore. Some say he is part Native American, while others claim he is a freed African slave.

Like many sailors, all of whom are considered the lowest rung of Boston society, Attucks is caught up in the rebellion captivating this waterfront city. He is angry that low-paid British solders often take second jobs, reducing his own chances of making money while ashore. Just last night, a soldier wandered into a pub where Crispus was drinking and demanded work. To the cheers of other sailors, the six-foot-two Attucks stood up and physically threatened the grenadier until the much smaller man slunk back out the door.

But lost wages are not the whaler's only complaint. Like any sailor, Attucks lives in fear that British press gangs roving the waterfront will club him over the head and drag him onto a Royal Navy ship, where he will be forced to work for the king. This is called "impressment," and there is little hope of escape from it.

Attucks knows he will soon leave Boston, shipping out in just a few days for the Carolinas. He just arrived from the Bahamas and is eager to set sail. But now, here in the heart of the city, he wields a club in anger, ready to use the weapon against the oppressive British presence.

Attucks does so without fear of reprisal, thinking himself just another anonymous member of the angry mob.

✤ ✤ ✤

Thirty feet away, Captain Thomas Preston unsheathes his curved saber. To frighten the Bostonians, he orders his men to make a show of loading their flintlock muskets. Ducking hurled debris and large sticks, the soldiers form a line abreast as they ram powder and ball into the long steel barrels. Two British grenadiers in particular, Hugh Montgomery and Matthew Kilroy, stare intently at Attucks. The sailor's considerable height terrifies them. At Captain Preston's command, each of the nine members of the 29th Foot raises his musket to shoulder, placing one finger on the trigger.

They await the order to kill.

✤ ✤ ✤

The Bostonians believe the British are bluffing. This is not a battlefield but a cobbled square in front of the colony's most esteemed building. Shooting a colonist could result in a charge of murder, even for a British soldier. Just eleven days ago, an eleven-year-old boy named Christopher Seider was killed while protesting in front of a loyalist's home.*

As darkness descends, the crowd now numbers four hundred

---

* Christopher was part of an anti-British protest in front of the home of customs officer Ebenezer Richardson. After the mob threw stones that broke Richardson's windows and struck his wife, he fired a gun into the crowd. Christopher was hit in the chest and arm. The boy died that evening. His family was too poor to afford proper burial, so patriot Samuel Adams covered the cost. It is estimated that two thousand people attended the funeral. Seider is considered the first person killed in the American Revolution. Richardson was not charged.

and begins taunting the British soldiers as they raise their weapons, daring them to shoot.

"Fire, damn you!" Bostonians yell.

"Ye dare not!" a protester screams, laughing in scorn.

Someone whose name is lost to history throws yet another large piece of wood at the British line, knocking one soldier to the ground.

As the grenadier rises quickly to his feet, an angry Captain Preston realizes he has run out of options.

✢ ✢ ✢

"Damn you, fire!" cries one of the soldiers. Captain Preston stands behind his line of soldiers, sword raised in exclamation. In the confusion, many will later claim he was the man giving the order. For the rest of his life, Preston will deny uttering those words, especially when he stands trial for murder.*

Crispus Attucks is killed first. Two rounds lodge in his chest. He drops to the snowy ground. The firing continues. Five more Bostonians are shot dead within seconds. The soldiers patiently reload and fire another volley, but now the crowd is fleeing—terrified they may be killed. In all, eleven colonists are shot dead or wounded.

The mob is gone. Days later, as the dead civilians are buried, hand-drawn images of their black coffins grace newspapers throughout the colonies. Large crowds attend the funerals.

One Bostonian, a local silversmith named Paul Revere, has had enough. He dubs the incident the Boston Massacre.

✢ ✢ ✢

Harvard-trained lawyer John Adams agrees to take the case after much thought.

---

* Years later, the diaries of Massachusetts governor Thomas Hutchinson will be made public. He wrote that soldier Hugh Montgomery admitted he had yelled the command to fire.

However, he is not going to prosecute—he will actually *defend* the king's men.

The "rabid churchgoer" is thirty-four years old. He stands just five-foot-seven with a smooth face, receding hairline, and a deep passion for books. Married to the former Abigail Smith, a third cousin who has borne him three children and is now pregnant with a fourth, Adams is certain that defending the British soldiers will be his professional demise. But he feels he has no choice. He writes to Abigail, "I have consented to my own ruin, to your ruin, and the ruin of our children, but the law will not bend to uncertain wishes, imaginations, and wanton tempers of men."

It is seven months after the massacre when the trial of the British soldiers begins. Massachusetts lieutenant governor Thomas Hutchinson, a staunch loyalist to King George III, has decreed that justice must be served. Most residents of Massachusetts still distrust Hutchinson for his support of taxation, many remembering the night they destroyed his mansion in a fit of rage.

John Adams is not a popular man as he chooses to defend the beleaguered British troops. Some soldiers are claiming the defense from prosecution as "benefit of clergy," a rare footnote to English law that holds religious leaders unaccountable for their actions. Some observers locally ask how an armed soldier could be a man of the cloth. But a new loophole in the law has also extended this defense to felons facing a first conviction. To prove they are God-fearing men, worthy of this plea, they must recite Psalm 51 before the court.*

The "benefit of clergy" defense is the brainchild of John Adams. Even if this does not result in acquittal, it will spare his clients the death penalty.

In the name of liberty, Adams believes it is vital that Massachusetts

---

* "Have mercy on me, O God, according to your unfailing love. According to your great compassion, blot out my transgressions."

deliver a fair trial. He will later write of the massacre, "On that night, the foundation of American independence was laid."

✢ ✢ ✢

Captain Thomas Preston is tried first.

The British officer doubts John Adams will remain impartial, so he is dumbfounded when the lawyer prefers truth to patriotism. Adams wears the black robe and powdered white wig required by all officers of His Majesty's court. Rather than show timidity about defending an enemy of Massachusetts colonists, Adams strides across the courtroom with authority. His carefully prepared defenses are based in fact and precedent. Wisely, the attorney has empaneled a jury from outside Boston proper, knowing locals will never listen to his arguments with a clear head.

Captain Preston loathes the colonists. In his own words, he says these "malcontents" are "using every method to fish out evidence to prove [the shooting] was a concerted scheme to murder the inhabitants."

John Adams does not believe that. He sees a spontaneous demonstration that got out of control.

Colonial America is not used to trials lasting more than one day. But the fate of Captain Preston is such a fiery topic that Adams layers a long defense. His arguments are direct. "Facts," Adams argues, "are stubborn things."

Preston is acquitted of murder, as are all eight British soldiers on trial. Soldiers Hugh Montgomery and Matthew Kilroy are found guilty of manslaughter, but the clergy defense Adams recommended prevents their execution. Instead, their thumbs are branded with *M* for murder.*

---

* That was their only punishment. The two soldiers found guilty of manslaughter did not spend time in prison. Both men remained in Boston to continue their army service. It is not known whether John Adams realized the "benefit of clergy" could have protected some of the witch hunters in Salem, as they were never prosecuted.

The victory brings disdain for John Adams throughout the colonies. He does not care. His firm belief in American independence is slowly starting to build. Adams's win in court sends a clear message to England that America is not a land of anarchy but a place where justice prevails.

Adams believes representing the British soldiers at their trial is "the greatest service I have ever rendered my country." He bases that opinion on what happened in Salem, writing, "Judgment of death against those soldiers would have been as foul a stain upon this country as the executions of the Quakers or witches."

✛ ✛ ✛

In London, it is Benjamin Franklin's turn to stand trial.

King George's Privy Council seeks to make an example of the prominent American. The date is January 29, 1774. Saturday. In an octagonal room within London's Whitehall Palace used for cockfighting during the reign of King Henry VIII, more than two hundred years ago, Franklin stands before these powerful men. He is almost seventy years old. Thickset—and set in his ways.*

The Pennsylvania printer has always been a logical man. He longs for reconciliation between the American colonies and the Crown. He considers himself not just a British subject but *British* by every definition of the word. Even as the Boston Sons of Liberty conducted a dumping of tea into Boston Harbor in a protest of yet another tax several months ago, Franklin has been able to defend the colonists' actions while also maintaining sympathy for the Crown.

Yet letters between the Massachusetts now-governor Thomas Hutchinson and his lieutenant Andrew Oliver have secretly found their way to Franklin. These private missives decry colonial

---

* The Privy Council is a group of senior advisers appointed by the king to assist the sovereign in legal matters. It also served as the High Court of Appeal for the British Empire.

protesters and discuss plans to end their rebellion. No one knows how or why the letters came into Franklin's possession.

But the Privy Council believes that Franklin, as joint postmaster general for the American colonies, is stealing the mail, then using it to advance America's political agenda.

Alexander Wedderburn, Britain's solicitor general, stands to begin the proceedings. In a series of carefully worded arguments, he mocks Franklin in front of the crowd. The forty-one-year-old Wedderburn makes puns about Franklin's job as postmaster general and his discovery of lightning as a source of electricity. "He will henceforth call it a libel to be called a man of letters." Wedderburn smirks and continues. "He stands in the light of the first mover and prime conductor of this whole contrivance against his Majesty's two Governors." The reference to "lightning" is one that few miss. Wedderburn, a Scottish member of Parliament, is known for his cold, haughty manner. Even good friends think him pompous.

The audience laughs at Wedderburn's denigration of Benjamin Franklin. The American is almost three decades older than the member of Parliament. Yet Wedderburn continues to speak down to Franklin, railing that he "has forfeited all the respect of societies and of men."

Benjamin Franklin does not let his embarrassment show. He stands upright for the entire hour of abuse and does not respond. His face remains impassive. Though Franklin has two prominent friends in the room, famous statesman Edmund Burke and theologian-chemist Joseph Priestley, he is very much alone.

After one very long hour, the humiliation finally ends.

Wedderburn asks if Franklin would like to respond.

The American says nothing.

Instead, head held high, Benjamin Franklin departs the room as quickly as possible. He walks back to his home flanked by the Strand, less than a mile away. The aging genius is shattered.

Franklin has never known such animosity. He is a learned man. In Europe and America, his name is synonymous with philosophy, science, and discourse. And yet he has just been publicly dismissed as a treacherous fool.

The news gets worse in the morning. Franklin is informed by messenger that he is out of a job. He has been fired as His Majesty's postmaster general for the colonies.

Despite seventeen years in London and a misguided belief that he could keep the bond between England and the colonies intact, Franklin knows he is defeated.

Henceforth, from this cold January day in London, he will do everything in his power to make King George III pay for this public humiliation.

A furious Franklin boards a ship for America.

Time to go home.

The Pennsylvanian is known for many traits.

Vengefulness is not among them.

Until now.

Chapter Twenty-Four

King George is getting tough.

The HMS *Lively* sails into Boston Harbor carrying the new military governor of Massachusetts. Three thousand British soldiers in bright red uniforms line the docks to greet Lieutenant General Thomas Gage. As *Lively* ties off at the wharf and Gage steps ashore, the soldiers fire their muskets in thunderous salute and chant a single loud "huzzah!" Longtime governor Thomas Hutchinson has been recalled to London for good, his authority compromised after the letters that caused Benjamin Franklin's public humiliation in London were published in Boston by patriot Samuel Adams for all citizens to read one year earlier—enraging the colonists even further.

The date Gage lands in Boston is also the date of a letter from Samuel Adams to the Boston Committee of Correspondence protesting the Boston Port Act—yet another act of colonial defiance.

General Gage is not just the thirteenth governor of the province of Massachusetts Bay; he is a *military* man. The wealthy, middle-aged career officer is arriving in Massachusetts to crush the growing colonial rebellion. No longer will a civilian tepidly administer King George's taxes and edicts. From this day forward, armed soldiers will enforce the law. Gage will see to it.

Unlike the citizens of Boston, the people of Salem could not be happier.

The port city is dependent on British commerce. Therefore, authorities in Salem defer to the Royal Navy. In an effort to distinguish their loyalty to the Crown from the revolution brewing fifteen miles south in Boston, Salem's leaders send a message of welcome to General Gage.

"We, merchants and other, inhabitants of the ancient town of Salem, beg leave to approach your Excellency with our most respectful congratulations on your arrival in this place. We are deeply sensible of His Majesty's personal care and affection for this province."

General Gage is so impressed by the greeting that he pays a visit to Salem just three weeks after his arrival. Deciding to keep his distance from Boston, Gage temporarily locates his headquarters near the site of the witch trials. He places two regiments of infantry within the city limits and declares Salem to be the provincial "capital" of Massachusetts.

In a spirit of mockery, leading rebel leaders from Boston travel to Salem. Among them are Samuel Adams and John Hancock. Audaciously, they hold their "government" meetings in a Salem courthouse. Among their duties is selecting delegates to attend what is being called the first Continental Congress, soon to take place in Philadelphia. When Governor Gage learns of these gatherings, he sends his assistant to put an end to them. The rebels respond by ignoring secretary Thomas Flucker—then lock the door.

Yet for all his might, Governor Gage is slow to take further action against the rebels. He is known for being a quiet man. So, due to his silence, rebellion continues throughout the summer. There are no laws being broken in the colonial gatherings, just peaceful assembly. Short of using military force, which Gage is reluctant to do, there is little the governor can do to stop the sedition.

Yet as the summer passes, there is growing tension between the British and Americans—a sense of menace. Gage and his men no longer feel the warm welcome previously extended by Salem's leaders. Instead, many citizens glare and yell insults, taunting the British with cries of "lobster back" for their red uniforms. By the time Gage and his troops march back to Boston on August 27, handbills decrying British rule are posted everywhere in previously loyal Salem. The taxes that citizens must pay has turned the tide against the Crown.

Thomas Gage knows trouble is coming. He quickly puts his men to work, treating Boston as enemy territory. "The unusual warlike preparations throughout the country make it an act of duty in me to pursue the measures I have taken in constructing what you call a 'fortress' in Boston," he will tell a gathering of loyalists. Indeed, the entire city is now on a wartime footing, cannon and soldiers everywhere to be seen.

Within six months of his celebratory arrival, Governor Thomas Gage knows he is being outwitted by the colonists and their infuriating ability to pursue their radical agenda without violating the law. Officials in London are growing increasingly concerned, even demanding that Gage "arrest and imprison the principal actors." However, the governor is reluctant to do so, fearing this will only lead to mob violence that could soon spiral out of control.

Yet Thomas Gage is not without wiles. He has a spy within the rebel movement. Benjamin Church is thought by all to be a patriot. The physician is a member of the Sons of Liberty and treated victims of the Boston Massacre. He is also deeply in debt, married to an Englishwoman, and keeps a mistress. In exchange for money, Dr. Church betrays his colonial friends by providing Gage with names of key individuals and locations where rebel weapons are stored.*

It is Church who tells the general that colonists are now arming themselves with muskets, gunpowder, and cannon. It is known that stores of ammunition and cartridges are being secretly cached by the rebels. Calling themselves Minute Men, they are secretly training to quickly deploy against the British. Unless these resistance groups are immediately disarmed, the results could be catastrophic. Gage's four thousand soldiers would be sorely overmatched if thousands of armed colonists rise up in revolt.

The governor has no other choice: he must find those hidden guns. Military force will be required. Church has reported that these weapons can be found in the cities of Lexington, Concord—and the port city of Salem.

General Thomas Gage knows precisely where he will look first.

✢ ✢ ✢

Sunday, February 26, 1775, is a cold, gray Sabbath. In the Salem blacksmith shop of Robert Foster, seventeen cannon barrels are in the process of being affixed to caissons and limbers for battlefield mobility. Some are new, commissioned by a wealthy local benefactor. Others are ship's guns, captured from French privateers, now being converted to land warfare. All are "twelve-pounders," so called for the weight of their cannonball.

Yet the forge is not lit this afternoon. Foster is in church, like most Salemites. The British know this. They heard the bells toll for the afternoon service. In fact, they are depending on the regular

---

* Church's deception will be discovered when one of his coded letters is intercepted several months later. He is jailed, then later released due to poor health and exiled to the Caribbean. The ship on which he sailed is lost in a storm, and Church's body is never found.

attendance habits of the faithful. Little do the soldiers know, but many Salem men now bring muskets to church.

Five miles down the road in Marblehead, 240 British soldiers under the command of Lieutenant Colonel Alexander Leslie arrive by ship from Boston. The vessel is HMS *Lively*. Leslie is forty-four, still in America twelve years after fighting the French and Indian War. He is known for his lack of patience and fits of rage. Governor Thomas Gage, a longtime friend, personally gave him the verbal order to execute the raid on Salem.

Disembarking, the British assemble in columns and begin the march north. In addition to their muskets, the soldiers carry shovels and picks to "spike" the cannon. A fife and drum band plays "Yankee Doodle." Leslie and the men of the 64th Foot move quickly, hoping to raid Robert Foster's blacksmith shop before church services end. Hopefully, this will prevent any mob from getting between them and the seventeen cannon.

But news travels faster than a marching soldier.

By the time Leslie and his men reach the North River on the outskirts of Salem, the city has been alerted. Church bells peal, warning of the British approach. The services have been cut short and waterfront taverns are empty because it's Sunday. Mothers and young children have been told to stay indoors. Now, the pious and profane alike stand ready to block British troops from entering Salem. Their jeers and taunts are furious, daring the soldiers to shoot. Many locals are also armed. These are militia—the Minute Men—about whom spies have warned the British.

Making matters more difficult for Lieutenant Colonel Leslie is that the drawbridge over the river is now raised. Young boys and sailors worked together to pull the chains lifting the span, and now heckle Leslie from atop the structure. There is no other way across. The river is more than three hundred yards wide.

Leslie demands the bridge be lowered by order of the king. "Down with that draw!" he yells.

Believing Leslie intends to open fire, a man named John Felt warns the British officer.

"Fire and be damned! You've no right to fire without further orders. If you fire you'll all be dead men," Felt yells at Leslie. The large man with the booming voice has lived in Salem for much of his life, and now prevents death and destruction.

A standoff ensues. Lieutenant Colonel Leslie sees a solution on the banks of the river in the form of small dories, but the locals quickly realize his plan and hack the bottoms of the boats with axes. One Salem man is busy chopping a hole to destroy his own boat even as twenty soldiers try to jump on board.

The British are exhausted. Their day began long before sunrise. During the long journey by ship from Boston to Marblehead, none were allowed on deck for fear colonial spies might see them. Huddled together in the hold, some grew seasick. Upon disembarking, the soldiers are thirsty, hungry, and tired. The raw winter wind cuts through their wool uniforms.

Yet as miserable as the soldiers might be, there seems no end to the colonists' energy. Cries of "cowards" and "lobster coats" echo across the North River. In the blacksmith shop of Robert Foster, just one hundred yards away but unseen by Leslie and his men, the heavy cannon are being placed on carts for the journey to a new hiding spot. This is a long process and requires a great deal of manpower—each barrel weighing more than a thousand pounds.

Hours pass.

Lieutenant Colonel Leslie grows more furious. He has lost the confrontation, and there is no easy way to depart without losing face. To Leslie's horror, a new wave of colonial militia is approaching, traveling from Marblehead. The British are now surrounded.

Reverend Thomas Barnard of Salem steps forward with a plan. He states that the drawbridge will be lowered so the British can inspect the blacksmith shop for cannon. But Leslie must give his word that he will leave if he does not find anything.

Both men know this is a ruse. Clearly, the cannon have been moved. But the good reverend's plan offers the British a chance to march away without humiliation.

Leslie agrees to the compromise. He strides across the lowered bridge with his men and inspects Foster's shop. Finding nothing, the British turn around for the long march back to Marblehead.

To their shock, the road is lined with armed colonists, who taunt the soldiers every step of the way. The British shoulder their weapons throughout the long retreat. They wisely choose not to open fire.

But next time—things will be different.

Chapter Twenty-Five

I t's war.

Formal fighting between the Americans and the Crown is now more than two years old. Philadelphia is so far untouched by the conflict, but word has reached the city that George Washington, commander of the Continental Army, has been defeated by British general William Howe in the Battle of Brandywine Creek, thirty miles away from Philadelphia, which is now defenseless. It is only a matter of time before enemy troops occupy America's first capital city.

The nation is no longer a collection of colonies. The people have renamed it the United States of America. They have also declared their freedom from England, issuing a document of liberty, crafted on Chestnut Street at the Pennsylvania State House. Fifty-six patriots affix their signatures to this Declaration of Independence and will henceforth be known as America's Founding Fathers.*

A two-thousand-pound copper and tin bell tolled to summon Philadelphia residents for the first public reading of the declaration. The State House Bell, as it is known, has a large crack and is used sparingly. Loyalists rejoiced when George III ascended to the

---

* Among the patriots who did not sign the Declaration of Independence are George Washington, James Madison, Patrick Henry, and Alexander Hamilton.

throne in 1760, with the bell pealing in his honor. But, four years later, the king was reviled as the bell rang to publicly protest the Stamp Act.

In 1775, the bell once again alerted Philadelphians that British troops had fired on Americans at Lexington and Concord. That confrontation began the war of revolution.

The "Liberty Bell" will not be so named until 1835, but its significance is already apparent to Philadelphians. They also understand that the bell will be melted down to make British cannon after the city is occupied. So it is placed on a horse-drawn cart and escorted out of town, destined for a secret location.*

It is that way for the Founding Fathers, as well. Signing the Declaration of Independence is an act of treason. Their lives are in jeopardy if they are captured by the British.

On the run, the rebellious Founders must avoid capture while at the same time forging a new country. That will become an exceedingly difficult task, as Americans are divided on many issues.†

✦ ✦ ✦

Thomas Jefferson is safe, at least for the moment.

Now thirty-four and the author of the Declaration of Independence, Jefferson returns to his western Virginia plantation after signing the document. He spends hours each day reading the words of philosophers and other great thinkers throughout history. Jefferson has recently focused on the ideas of a man close to him in Virginia—a lawyer named James Madison. The twenty-six-year-old attorney argues that religious liberty is an inalienable right: "All men are equally entitled to the free exercise of religion, according to the dictates of conscience," Madison writes.

---

* The Liberty Bell was hidden beneath the floorboards of the Zion Reformed Church in what is now Allentown, Pennsylvania.

† The population of the new United States in 1777 was approximately 2.5 million. It is estimated that half supported the Crown, not wanting to be independent.

James Madison stands just five-foot-four and weighs one hundred pounds. His writing is ponderous. The lawyer's views on freedom of religion are clear but controversial. The Virginia General Assembly—no longer known as the House of Burgesses—is struggling with the issue. Some of Madison's ideals are written into the state's new Declaration of Rights. Yet, amazingly, the state of Virginia still recognizes the Anglican Church as the official religion. Therefore, all Virginians are forced to pay taxes to its clergy, most of whom support King George.

Thomas Jefferson wants that to change.

Writing with quill and ink, he pens the new legislature's Bill Number 82, which calls for establishing religious freedom.

"The opinions and belief of men depend not on their own will but follow involuntarily the evidence proposed in their minds; that Almighty God hath created the mind free," Jefferson writes. He is fierce in his belief that there should be no "official" religion in America.

"No man shall be compelled to frequent or support any religious worship, place, or ministry whatsoever, nor shall be enforced, restrained, molested, or burthened in his body or goods, nor shall otherwise suffer, on account of his religious opinions or belief."

But Jefferson's bill fails. The Virginia General Assembly takes no action. On June 18, 1779, with Thomas Jefferson now serving as the state's governor, the bill is once again introduced. It fails again.

There is one large problem standing in its way.

His name is Patrick Henry.

✢ ✢ ✢

Thomas Jefferson and Patrick Henry now despise one another.

This did not occur due to a single incident. It happened over time. James Madison is the current object of Jefferson's intellectual admiration, even as Henry has fallen far in the governor's estimation. Jefferson is in attendance at Saint John's Church in Richmond on that night in 1775 when Henry gives a rousing speech demanding "liberty or death." Yet Thomas Jefferson is not impressed. Having observed his former friend in the legislature, and then again as his predecessor in the governor's seat, Jefferson believes Henry revels in theatrics instead of deep commitment.

"His imagination was copious, poetical, sublime," Jefferson will write of Patrick Henry. "But vague also. He said the strongest things in the finest language, but without logic, without arrangement, desultorily."

Jefferson will also write a shocking private note to James Madison. The topic is Patrick Henry: "What we have to do, I think, is devoutly to pray for his death."*

The greatest divide between Jefferson and Henry is religion. In a contradiction of his "Parson's Cause" speech, Henry still *favors* taxation to fund state-sponsored churches. Anglicans and Presbyterians take his side in this debate. Among them is George Washington, who continues to participate in the Anglican Church.†

Thomas Jefferson and James Madison believe churches should be funded like businesses. Citizens should pick the church of their choice—or attend no church at all. Baptists, Methodists, Quakers, and Lutherans rally to that cause. Catholics in Maryland, persecuted since 1704 and double taxed for their faith, are also keen to support this freedom.

It was religious persecution that originally brought the pious

---

* The anti-Henry note was written on December 8, 1784, and can be found in Madison's papers in the Library of Congress.

† During the Revolutionary War, the term *Anglican* caused a division between loyalist and patriot practitioners of the faith, many of whom began calling themselves "Episcopalian."

to America. Now, more than 150 years later, beliefs in the proper method of worshipping God remain divisive. Despite the Declaration of Independence's statement that mankind is entitled to "life, liberty, and the pursuit of happiness," a debate continues about whether this applies to matters of religion.

In New England, the Puritan grip on the population is slipping. Prosperity has made the fire-and-brimstone clergy almost obsolete. Also, the legacy of the witch executions remains a stigma on the Puritans, whose extreme views have moderated but only a bit.

In fact, all throughout the new nation, religious controversies continue to brew.

Finally, on January 16, 1786, James Madison pushes Thomas Jefferson's bill through the Virginia General Assembly. It will become known as the Virginia Statute of Religious Freedom. Patrick Henry is once again serving as governor but has no vote. Henceforth, the Anglican Church is "disestablished" in Virginia. It is no longer the official state religion.

Jefferson, now the American minister to France, is relieved— calling his state's debate over religious freedom "the severest contest in which I have ever been engaged."

✤ ✤ ✤

Despite Jefferson and Madison's victory in Virginia, not every state enjoys religious freedom. On May 25, 1787, the Founding Fathers meet at the Philadelphia State House to begin the Constitutional Convention. American independence is now assured, so delegates gather to vote on the structure of a new nation. George Washington is the convention's president. The first priority is finding common ground on the subject of religious freedom.

Rhode Island protests, choosing not to attend the convention because its delegates fear a federal government that would control the new states.

And so it is that the Founding Fathers are far apart on many issues. But one subject is particularly intense: the future of religion in America.*

---

* The British surrender to George Washington at Yorktown in Virginia on October 19, 1781. The Treaty of Paris was signed on September 3, 1783—in it, Britain formally recognized American independence.

Chapter Twenty-Six

The most famous American in the world is hot.

Philadelphia is a muggy mess. Warm rain pelts the city on this first day of the Constitutional Convention. Eighty-one-year-old Benjamin Franklin, inventor and scientist, is home after nine years as American minister in civilized Paris, only to find his adopted hometown smelling like a sewer. The population of what is now America's largest city stands at forty thousand. Leafy tree-lined boulevards bustle with commerce. But the city lacks proper sewage facilities, causing outbreaks of illness and filling the air with a sickening odor—a stench made far worse in the humid heat.

Fifty-five delegates have traveled here, taking lodging where they can. Days will be spent in the Pennsylvania State House arguing about America's future while evenings will be occupied close by at the City Tavern, continuing those debates. Some will skip the pub, preferring to walk to Ben Franklin's home just two blocks from the State House, where a free-flowing keg of beer waits in the garden.

Many, in fact, will skip the convention altogether, leaving the hard work of crafting a constitution to others—enjoying a holiday in Philadelphia until the time comes to vote.

Ben Franklin long ago lost his skills as a politician—indeed, Georgia delegate William Pierce observes that "he does not shine much in public council. He is no speaker, nor does he seem to let politics engage his attention. He is, however, a most extraordinary man, and tells a story in a style more engaging than anything I ever heard."

Franklin is held in such high esteem that his participation in the convention adds authority to the proceedings. The bald and portly widower is no longer just "Benjamin Franklin" but "Dr. Franklin," the honorary title added a quarter century ago to celebrate his lifetime of accomplishments. A majority of delegates wish for him to serve as convention president, watching over the proceedings. Whoever assumes this prominent role will have a significant influence on America's future, shaping the constitution by determining the flow of daily debate. The president will set the tone, managing conflicts and seeking compromise on pressing matters. Given the respect accorded the calm and thoughtful Franklin, his weighty intellect, and his utter lack of political aspiration, he seems perfect for the task.*

The structure of the American government will be at the forefront, with "federalists" arguing for a powerful national presence while "anti-federalists" favor more power vested in the individual states rather than centralized, national power. Representation is also an issue, with small states not wanting larger states to have numerical superiority in making legislation. Slavery is another key matter, dividing northern and southern states. The new nation is trying to decide how slavery might be treated under the constitution—fugitive slaves and the slave trade most notably. (The words "slavery" and "slave" are never mentioned in the US Constitution.) And the

---

* Franklin was awarded honorary doctorates from Scotland's University of Saint Andrews in 1759 and England's Oxford University in 1762.

key issue that emerges is how slaves are going to be counted for congressional representation.

There is also the troubling issue of religious freedom, a matter over which Franklin would be perfect to preside, for he has contemplated and written about faith often during his long life. He still occasionally attends services at nearby Christ Church.

Finally, there is a movement to add a "bill of rights" to the constitution to ensure individuals are not denied liberties by powerful politicians in individual states. The Salem witch trials are used as an example of local governments out of control. Ben Franklin's personal memories of Cotton Mather and his connection to the witch hunt add perspective no delegate can match.

✤ ✤ ✤

Upon their arrival in Philadelphia, almost all the delegates have come to Franklin's house to pay respects. He offers them brown beer or hot tea, depending on their preference. George Washington, representing Virginia, made Franklin's elaborate home his first stop upon reaching the city.

The two men know each other well from the Continental Congress in 1776—when American independence from Britain was declared. "We are either a united people, or we are not," Washington argued about the goals of writing a constitution. "If we are not, let us no longer act a farce by pretending to it."*

Benjamin Franklin is a realistic man. He knows his life is almost over and his abilities declining. Despite pressure from Washington and the other delegates, Franklin declines the presidency. He will attend but not preside over the convention.

✤ ✤ ✤

---

* George Washington did not sign the Declaration of Independence because he had left Philadelphia to be with his army in New York. In a letter signed July 6, John Hancock notified the general of the declaration's passage by the Continental Congress.

As the proceedings are about to start, rain pours down. Dr. Franklin decides against making the short journey to the State House. His health is failing. Walking, particularly in bad weather, is too difficult. So on the days he chooses to be in attendance, he will be carried through the streets of Philadelphia in a sedan chair by servants, looking very much like America's lone royal figure.

So it is that the Constitutional Convention will start without Ben Franklin. But he sends a message to the delegates, nominating George Washington as convention president.

"The nomination came with particular grace from Pennsylvania," writes James Madison, "as Doctor Franklin alone could have been thought of as a competitor. The Doctor was himself to have made the nomination of General Washington, but the state of the weather and his health confined him to his house."

George Washington's presidency of the convention is approved by a unanimous vote.

It is the only matter on which all the delegates will agree.

✢ ✢ ✢

James Madison knows government can be oppressive.

A learned man, he understands the witch accusations and executions that took place in theocratic New England during the first century of its settlement by the English. He also knows about the continuing battles with Native Americans and the massacres that have occurred on both sides. Finally, he believes that religious zealots remain a dire threat to the new country. Therefore, Madison, one of the leading architects of the constitution, devises a compromise to limit the power of both federal and state governments. His good friend Thomas Jefferson, now the American minister to France, agrees. But both men understand there will be fierce opposition as states all too often violate the rights of individuals in the name of God. Madison has a plan to end that oppression.

The Virginian is an intense man. He has no hobbies, preferring to spend leisure time reading Latin and Greek. In his youth, Madison graduated from the College of New Jersey, later to be known as Princeton, where he knew a future American vice president named Aaron Burr. Still single, the thirty-six-year-old Madison has devoted his adult life to creating the new American nation. On matters of faith, he considers himself an Episcopalian. In fact, a cousin sharing the same first and last name is the first Episcopal bishop ordained in Virginia and oversees the Diocese of Virginia.*

James Madison is so excited to attend the Constitutional Convention that he arrives in Philadelphia eleven days early. As the convention gets underway, the Virginian takes careful notes cataloging all aspects of the debate. George Washington, meticulously dressed, sits at the front of the room in a wooden chair. An image of the rising sun is painted on the back of the top rail. He has decreed that the delegates deliberate in complete secrecy and keep their comments private throughout their entire lifetimes.

There are ten newspapers in Philadelphia, but none of them are allowed to cover the proceedings. Thus, Madison's detailed minutes will become the primary record of the discussions. In order for the constitution to be ratified, two delegates from each of the thirteen states must agree. If that happens, the constitution would then be voted on by the states themselves in order for it to become law.

But there is chaos. Many delegates simply don't show up for the debates. Some days fewer than forty choose to attend. Only thirty delegates will remain in Philadelphia all four months. New York's Alexander Hamilton, George Washington's military aide during the Revolutionary War and another prodigious note taker, will

---

* James Madison will marry a widow seventeen years younger than him in 1794. The former Dolley Payne has two sons from her first marriage and was born a Quaker. Their marriage would produce no children, but the couple will be well known for their affection for one another.

leave Philadelphia for six weeks without explanation but return in mid-August. The rest of the New York contingent, angered by James Madison's proposed governmental structure, will leave Philadelphia on July 10 and never return.

✛ ✛ ✛

Meanwhile, back in Virginia, James Madison's war with Patrick Henry continues. The Anglican Church had been the "established church" (or official state religion) of Virginia since Jamestown. Jefferson's Statute of Religious Freedom ended that. Henry now proposes to make Christianity the official religion of Virginia. He is calling for a state tax to fund teachers who would be teaching about Christianity. Madison and Jefferson object so strongly because they oppose government-sanctioned—or -supported— religion. Henry has refused to attend the Constitutional Convention because he fears it is a plot by the wealthy to devise a strong central government of which *they* would be the rulers. Many other famous Americans are also not in Philadelphia, among them John Hancock, Thomas Jefferson, John Adams, and Samuel Adams.*

But Patrick Henry's absence feels personal. His feud with Madison has only grown more bitter. Henry becomes one of the leading anti-federalists, opposing ratification of the Constitution. In an affront to Madison's fight for religious freedom, Henry has continued his efforts to seek a method of taxing Americans to fund churches. Two years ago, he introduced a bill that would make Christianity the official state religion of Virginia.

James Madison immediately called Henry's proposal "a dangerous

---

* Samuel Adams boycotted the convention, believing that creating a strong central government would infringe on personal liberty. John Hancock did not attend due to poor health. Thomas Jefferson was in Paris. John Adams was in London, America's first ambassador to Great Britain. In a letter to the Massachusetts militia, written on October 11, 1798, Adams would praise people of faith, stating, "Our constitution was made only for a moral and religious people. It is wholly inadequate to the government of any other."

abuse of power." The bill was eventually voted down, though it was close.

Madison now takes the same approach to the constitution. He believes "injustice" could very well emerge if the delegates do not accept complete freedom of religion and speech.

✛ ✛ ✛

Although he is not saying much, Benjamin Franklin is siding with James Madison. In Paris, it was Dr. Franklin's habit to wear a hat made of raccoon fur to cover his bald head. Now, in the searing Philadelphia heat, such vanity is ridiculous. Franklin would normally spend a withering day like this walking around his home naked, believing it good for the body to let air circulate over the skin. But here he sits in the Pennsylvania State House, fully dressed and perspiring, and what little breeze comes through the window is foul from the stench of raw sewage.

Now, Franklin has something to say. George Washington, six-foot-two and formidable, watches as Franklin rises to his feet. Three dozen delegates, most of whom remain completely silent during the contentious debates, are stirred by the wizened figure.

"The diversity of opinions turns on two points," Franklin begins, then makes a grand detour. "When a broad table is to be made, and the edges of the planks do not fit, the artist takes a little from both and makes a good joint. In like manner, here both sides must part with some of their demands in order that they may join in some accommodating proposition."

Franklin is talking about representation in the Congress—and, from Franklin's perspective, the need to compromise.

That proposition, under fierce debate, is how the new Congress would be populated.

The matter becomes bitter. The smaller states will not submit to less representation than the larger states.

Soon, the small meeting room at the State House becomes the

scene of yelling and threats as the matter ends some friendships. Delaware even threatens to leave the union to align with another country. Says delegate Gunning Bedford Jr., "The small ones would find some foreign ally of more honor and good faith, who will take them by the hand and do them justice."*

Into the fray steps the second-oldest man at the convention, sixty-six-year-old Roger Sherman of Connecticut. Sherman, like Patrick Henry, believes the new America should be a Christian nation. Sherman is a Congregationalist holding firm Calvinistic beliefs. The nation is only 16 percent Anglican, but more than 50 percent of the American population practices the same faith as Sherman. In Connecticut, where eleven alleged witches were murdered, that number is far higher. The Puritans hold on despite their violent legacy.

However, like Roger Sherman, James Madison is an ardent defender of personal liberty. He does not want the federal government to dictate how Americans should live but believes the local government should have a strong say in matters of faith and personal conduct. Sherman argues that church and state should be "mutually beneficial" and that taxes should be collected to support local ministers. He says there is no room in this world for any faith other than Christianity. This alarms Madison, Jefferson, and Franklin—all of whom do not want any government mandate on religion. The three men fear that if the individual states are not somewhat controlled by a strong federal government, the abuse of mandatory religion could very well happen.

Madison, the absent Jefferson, and Franklin win. Each state would have two senators and a number of representatives based

---

* Gunning Bedford Jr. of Delaware was one of the leading advocates at the convention for the small states. As for leaving the Union, as such, the Union was a very loose association of the individual states under the Articles of Confederation. Whatever national government existed was very weak by design. Most power was left to the states. Ultimately, though, all five Delaware delegates signed the US Constitution, and Delaware was the "First State" to ratify it.

on population. As any new law would have to have the approval of *both* houses of Congress, the smaller states are protected.

On July 16, 1787, the basic structure of the new federal government is agreed on. However, the "individual rights" of Americans are not yet defined. Said Thomas Jefferson, "A bill of rights is what the people are entitled to against every government on earth, general or particular, and what no just government should refuse."

Two years later, James Madison will craft a set of seventeen new amendments to the US Constitution known as the Bill of Rights. The House of Representatives and Senate will agree on twelve. Ten of these amendments will be passed after two more years of debate.*

✣ ✣ ✣

Throughout August and September 1787, every word of the new constitution is debated. But the essential points of the document have been agreed on. On September 15, the delegates finish their work.

Let the party begin.†

✣ ✣ ✣

It is Saturday night. The City Tavern is jammed with the delegates and other interested parties, including some members of George Washington's army unit that crossed the Delaware with him, defeating the Hessians in Trenton. It is a grand occasion, beer and

---

* Madison proposed the original seventeen Bill of Rights amendments in the House, where he was a member. The House and Senate ultimately agreed on twelve, which were sent to the states for ratification. Ten of those twelve were ratified—hence, the ten amendments comprising the Bill of Rights.

† Thirty-nine of the fifty-five delegates signed the new US Constitution. Those choosing not to sign stated disagreement with governmental structure, lack of a bill of rights, and the ongoing practice of slavery as reasons. The document needed the approval of nine states for ratification. Eventually, all thirteen original states voted in favor, with Rhode Island the last to agree.

wine flowing nonstop. Indeed, the bar tab will run to more than £89 and four shillings.*

Washington is hailed by the group. There is widespread public belief that he should be named America's first president, should the ratified constitution make that position a reality.

The evening is long. A sit-down dinner is served. Glasses are broken in celebration—which the bartenders quickly add to the tab.

Yet amid the celebration, a melancholy lingers over General Washington. He misses his wife, Martha. And he has no intention of running for president. He is vainglorious but just as often modest and believes himself too old at age fifty-five to run the country. More than anything, Washington looks forward to "living and dying a private citizen on my own farm."

Through the past decade of constant travel, George Washington has made church attendance a weekly priority. Though raised Anglican, services for that faith have not always been available. So he has made do, worshipping in churches dedicated to Presbyterians, Quakers, Roman Catholics, Congregationalists, Baptists, and Dutch Reformed worshippers. Here in Philadelphia, he prefers to worship at Christ Church, the nation's first Episcopal congregation. Benjamin Franklin sometimes attends, as does John Adams when visiting the city.

The party rages on long after Washington steps out into the night. The convention is not over, and he still has work to do. "I returned to my lodging, did some business," he will write, "and retired to meditate on the momentous work which had been executed."

---

* That is $18,000 in modern American currency. The bar tab paid for seven large bowls of spiked punch, eight bottles of hard cider, eight bottles of Old Stock whiskey, twelve bottles of beer, twenty-two bottles of porter, fifty-four bottles of Bordeaux, and sixty bottles of claret. The tab was paid for by the First Troop Philadelphia City Cavalry, a military unit that served under Washington and is still in existence today. It is worth noting that this group is one of the oldest military units in America.

The date is September 15, 1787. Signing of the constitution will take place Monday. Washington knows that at least one-third of the delegates will refuse to sign because they don't agree with something in the document.

But whether the final vote passes or fails is out of George Washington's hands. He has done his job. Tomorrow is Sunday. Despite tonight's raucous festivities, the general will rise early and attend church. He may or may not see Benjamin Franklin sitting close by on the hard wooden pews.

But Washington suspects, come Monday, the octogenarian will have the final word about religion and the United States.

✦ ✦ ✦

Indeed, Dr. Franklin does get the last word.

September 17, 1787. Time to sign. The convention has reached its final day. Forty-four delegates are in attendance. Franklin is not much of a speaker, so he gives the task of reading his speech to James Wilson, his fellow delegate from Pennsylvania.

"I cannot help expressing a wish that every member of the convention . . . put his name to this instrument," Franklin says, knowing some in this room will prefer not to sign the constitution. His words tell of "heat and opposition" to the topics discussed over the past four months. But he saves his final and most direct observations to address religious freedom.

"Most sects in religion, think themselves in possession of all truth, and that wherever others differ from them it is an error. [Sir Richard] Steele, a Protestant, in a dedication tells the Pope, that the only difference between our two churches in their opinions of the certainty of their doctrine, is, the Romish Church is infallible, and the Church of England is never in the wrong."

Wilson reads Franklin's final sentence, directed at George Washington: "On the whole, sir, I cannot help expressing a wish, that every member of the convention, who may still have objections to it, would with me on this occasion doubt a little of his own infallibility, and to make manifest our unanimity, put his name to this instrument."

✢ ✢ ✢

Madison, the absent Jefferson, Franklin, as well as George Washington again emerge victorious. The new constitution, although flawed in some areas, is the most liberating government document in the world. For the first time, citizens of a country are not controlled by kings, tyrants, or profiteers. The American Experiment is just beginning, and it will lead to the most powerful nation the world has ever seen.*

But in the background, deep problems remain. Nearly a million slaves will be imported into the original colonies and the United States. Some religious philosophers believe slavery is prompted by the Devil. Some religious philosophers, writers, and politicians of the day still describe slavery as a "positive good."

Religion, particularly Christianity, will continue to dominate the United States. But from this point forward, no specific faith will be imposed.

✢ ✢ ✢

America moves forward. There is prosperity and strife. Violence and peace. The United States expands westward, carrying traditions from the first settlers.

One of those traditions is the struggle between evil and good. America, basically, remains a devout Christian country. God and the Devil are debated every Sunday.

In fact, Satan becomes a commercial force in stories such as "The Devil and Daniel Webster."

---

* Jacob Shallus, assistant clerk of the Pennsylvania State Assembly, was paid $30 to write the US Constitution's 4,543 words on four sheets of vellum parchment.

With the many different religions now being practiced through-out the country, the intensity of the interest in the occult, witches, and belief in demonic possession varies from place to place.

✤ ✤ ✤

As many historical occurrences fade into obscurity, one does not: the witch executions at Salem. That horror becomes even more vivid in literature and theological lessons. The Devil and demonic pos-session are known throughout the new nation—as hell becomes a frightening scenario.

And here on earth, Satan's disciples are not limited by any gov-ernment.

They roam at will.

Chapter Twenty-Seven

Modern times.

It is approaching the witching hour as thirteen-year-old Ronald Hunkeler is getting ready for bed on this Saturday night. Ronald is thin, small, weighing ninety-five pounds. He is blond-haired and an only child. The boy attends Bladensburg Junior High School, where he is in the eighth grade.

The house at 3807 Fortieth Avenue is six miles from Washington, DC. Nondescript. Two stories. Ronald's parents are out for the evening. He remains at home with his grandmother. A third influential family member is not here tonight: Ronald's eccentric aunt Tillie. She lives in St. Louis but visits often. Tillie, who believes in an active afterlife, often uses a Ouija board to commune with the dead. Other times, she listens closely for the sound of rapping on walls, known to be a sign that the spirit world is trying to be heard.*

This practice of communicating with the departed goes back to the Old Testament. There is a warning in the Book of Deuteronomy,

---

* A Ouija board is a flat piece of wood with letters of the Latin alphabet. Individuals place their hands on a heart-shaped piece of wood known as a planchette and ask questions to the spirit world. The planchette is thought to move to each letter in response, spelling out the answers.

written centuries before the birth of Christ, calling an attempt to speak with the dead "an abomination unto the Lord."

The Book of Leviticus, written by Moses about the same time, is even more explicit. It is from the words of Moses that the Salem witch trials derived authority: "A man or a woman that has a familiar spirit, or is a wizard, will surely be put to death."*

None of that means anything to Aunt Tillie and young Ronald, who is certainly not a biblical scholar.

But Tillie and Ronald do have a secret. She is instructing the boy on the art of channeling the dead.

And he is an eager student.

✢ ✢ ✢

The first sign of trouble is dripping water.

Source unknown, the sound is so powerful that Ronald and his grandmother stop listening to the radio and walk through the house looking for the leak. The water appears to be coming from the roof over an upstairs bedroom. The two enter and are overwhelmed by the dripping noise. But as they search the floors and ceiling for moisture, none is found.

Yet the sound of dripping grows louder.

A picture of Jesus hangs on the bedroom wall. Suddenly, it begins to shake, the frame banging against the plaster.

Then comes the scratching noise.

It originates from beneath the bed. Ronald gets down on his hands and knees to look. As he peers into the dark space, the sound gets louder. Standing up, he tells his grandmother it's probably a rat or raccoon that found a way into the gap between floors. This being the middle of winter, it makes sense that an animal

---

*The Bible contains sixteen references to demons and sixteen more about Jesus combating demonic possession. When the Old Testament Israelite king Saul asks a "witch" to channel the ghost of the prophet Samuel, the irritated "ghost" predicts the ruler will soon die in battle—which he does.

would seek warmth. A short time later, the scratching, dripping, and shaking of Jesus's picture end.

Absolutely nothing to worry about.

❖ ❖ ❖

One night later, the scratching sound resumes.

Ronald's father, Ed Hunkeler, calls an exterminator. Floorboards are pulled up to check for signs of rodents, but nothing is found. Just in case, rat poison is placed under the floor.

The poison has no effect. Every night from 7 p.m. to midnight for the next week, the scratching sound resumes. The Hunkelers ignore it, believing the trouble will soon end.

And it does.

Then Aunt Tillie drops dead.

❖ ❖ ❖

A lonely, intellectual boy, Ronald Hunkeler has few friends other than family members. He mourns Aunt Tillie, whose mysterious death took place after a recent return to St. Louis. She is quickly buried in a Missouri cemetery. Ronald never has a chance to say goodbye.

He channels his grief in a way that Tillie would have approved: conjuring up her spirit on the Ouija board. Every day after school, Ronald fills hours holding séances, attempting to contact the beyond. His father and mother do not pay attention, thinking it is a harmless diversion. Everyone has forgotten about the scratching under the floors, as if it had never happened.

But there is trouble at school. Ronald's desk is moving on its own, suddenly gliding away and crashing into other students. Teachers think Ronald is propelling the desk with his feet, not believing his insistence that he has no power over what is happening. This becomes a major problem.

Back home, as Ronald lies in the darkness of his bedroom, new sounds emerge.

And they are terrifying.

At first, it's the squeak of shoes, as if someone is walking around the room. The noises return the next night. And the night after that. After almost a week, Ronald finally admits to his mother and grandmother that he is hearing strange new sounds. Yet no one else in the house has heard anything. So both women come into Ronald's bedroom that night and lie down with him in the dark. Soon, the noises begin—not squeaking shoes but actual footsteps marching up and down the side of the bed, growing louder as the minutes pass.

"Is that you, Tillie?" cries Ronald's mother, Odell. "If it is, knock four times."

All three lying on the bed hear the unmistakable sound of four slow raps on the wooden floor.

Then each feels a weight pushing down on them, making it difficult to breathe. They are pressed down into the bed, unable to sit up.

The scratching sound starts again—this time coming from inside the mattress.

The bed begins to shake, slowly at first, then violently.

The quilt atop the mattress is yanked out from under them and hangs suspended in the air. In a few moments, it falls to the floor.*

✣ ✣ ✣

The marching footsteps continue every night for three weeks.

But, now, the terror is not just confined to bedtime. The Hunkeler family begins to see unusual occurrences throughout the day. Books and clothes suddenly fly across the room. A heavy chair in

---

* The account of what happened to the Hunkeler family became public in the August 10, 1949, edition of the *Washington Post*.

which Ronald is sitting begins to levitate. A vase hurls itself into a wall and shatters. If this is the ghost of Aunt Tillie, she is far more angry than she ever appeared in her lifetime.

Ronald can no longer attend school. His desperate parents take him to seek psychiatric help at the County Mental Hygiene Clinic. There, the doctor sees nothing unusual—only stating in his report that the teenager is "high strung."

The Hunkelers leave the clinic distraught.

Things get worse. The family is awakened to the sound of Ronald screaming and using angry words he has never used before. Rushing to his bedside, they witness a large set of drawers slide across the room, blocking the door and preventing them from leaving.

The boy is now screaming on a nightly basis. Ronald can barely sleep, and when he does he appears to be having mumbled conversations with someone else. His appearance suffers; dark circles now ring his eyes, and his days are spent in anxious worry.

✛ ✛ ✛

Ed and Odell Hunkeler are Protestant and believe in heaven and hell. Exasperated, they reach out to their minister, Luther Miles Schulze, the forty-three-year-old pastor at Saint Stephen's Lutheran Evangelical Church.

The reverend visits the Hunkeler home. He witnesses the shaking bed, the flying books and clothes, furniture moving around the room. He notes that the floors are "scarred from the sliding of heavy furniture" and that a picture of Jesus shakes whenever Ronald walks past it.

Schulze is appropriately sympathetic. Yet unlike Catholics, the Lutheran faith has no belief in demonic possession. So he offers to pray for the boy. Nothing more.

The reverend thinks the events are elaborate pranks, parlor tricks contrived by the thirteen-year-old. To prove these cannot be duplicated elsewhere, he asks if the family will let Ronald spend the night at his home.

They agree.

✢ ✢ ✢

Bedtime.

The minister's wife says good night and retires to their bedroom. Schulze and Ronald lie down on matching twin beds in the guest room. The lights are turned off. At first, silence. Just a normal night. But shortly after midnight, Schulze awakens to the sound of Ronald's bed vibrating loudly. "It was like one of those motel vibrator beds," the pastor will later state. "But much faster."*

Schulze suggests Ronald sit in a large chair in the corner of the room. The minister keeps the lights on. Within moments, the chair slowly begins to tilt. Ronald pulls his knees to his chest as he falls to the floor.

Schulze can only watch in confusion as Ronald starts sliding all around the floor, then shifts under the bed. Schulze yells at the teenager to stop.

"I can't!" Ronald yells back.

Soon, the boy is being lifted off the ground and pressed hard against the bottom of the bed. Mattress springs cut into his face, leaving him bleeding. Reverend Schulze finally pulls the teenager from the room.

"You have to see a Catholic priest," he tells Ronald. "The Catholics know about things like this."

---

* Reverend Schulze first detailed his involvement in the Ronald Hunkeler case in March 1949, writing to Duke University's Parapsychology Lab, telling of the unexplainable things he had witnessed. Schulze then went public, speaking to the Society of Parapsychology at the Mount Pleasant Library in Washington, DC, during the summer of 1949.

Chapter Twenty-Eight

Not every Catholic believes in demonic possession.

Father Edward Albert Hughes knows nothing about exorcism. The priest is thirty on the morning the Hunkeler family visits his rectory at Saint James Catholic Church. The handsome, square-shouldered Hughes looks more like a movie star than a parish priest. He has a fondness for making jokes and putting his parishioners at ease. If he thinks it is unusual that Lutherans would come to him for help, he does not say so. But as everyone sits down to discuss Ronald's affliction, the priest notices the room growing colder. Ronald, himself, is in a trance-like state. All at once, he begins swearing at the priest. Also, a telephone on the table begins to rattle.

Father Hughes is terrified. He wants the Hunkelers out of his office immediately. He stands up and gives them a bottle of holy water and a blessed candle to provide protection. He says that's all he can do other than to pray for them.

One day later, Odell Hunkeler places an urgent call to the rectory at Saint James. She has followed the priest's instructions and sprinkled holy water in every room in their home. She lit the special candle normally used during Holy Mass. But something hurled the glass bottle of water to the floor, shattering it. The candle became a torch, shooting flames so enormous she feared the house would burn down.

Reluctantly, a frightened Father Hughes drives to the Hunkeler residence. He confronts Ronald, who stares at him with impassive eyes and says, "*Oh, sacerdos Christi, tu scis me esse diabolum. Cur me diogas?*"

Like all Catholic priests, Hughes has trained in Latin. He still speaks the language every day while saying Mass. So he understands every word that Ronald Hunkeler is speaking to him.

"O priest of Christ," the words translate. "You know that I am the devil. Why do you keep bothering me?"*

✥ ✥ ✥

As the situation escalates, Ronald Hunkeler is admitted to Georgetown University Hospital, a Catholic institution. He is evaluated by psychiatrists. His parents use a false name to keep the situation secret. Word is starting to get out about crazy things taking place in the Hunkeler home. Rumors are going around that their house is haunted. The police have made visits.

Ronald now rests in a hospital bed, his torso, arms, and legs secured to the frame with restraints. Nuns in white habits are his nurses, and a crucifix hangs on the wall. The staff is already reporting unusual occurrences in the private room, with a tray flying from one nun's hands and smashing against a wall. Ronald's bed is often seen shaking visibly and moving itself around the room. Bloody scratch marks appear on the boy's chest during routine examinations. He also speaks in foreign languages, including Aramaic, which has not been spoken since the time of Jesus.

---

* Father Hughes followed proper channels and sought the permission of the archbishop of Washington, Patrick A. Doyle, before attempting to help Ronald. Multiple eyewitnesses testified to the severe changes in Hughes's physical and mental state after the Hunkeler case. Those testimonies are in newspapers like England's *The Guardian* and *The Washington Post* and *New York Post* in the United States.

All of this confuses and frightens the nuns attending to Ronald. They summon Father Hughes to the hospital. He arrives and kneels before the teenager's bed.

Father Hughes then says in Latin, "*Exorcizo, te, immundissime spiritus, omnis incursio adversarii, omne phantasma, omnis legio*"—"I cast thee out, thou unclean spirit, along with the least encroachment of the wicked enemy, and every phantom and diabolical legion."

Immediately after the Latin prayer, Ronald breaks his restraints, wrenches a bedspring free, then violently slashes the priest. The deep cut opens a wound down the length of Hughes's left arm.

Father Hughes cries out, terrified, and flees the room. He is so shaken that Catholic officials place him on an indefinite leave of absence from Saint James Church. His wound requires one hundred stitches to close. Soon, Father Hughes suffers a nervous breakdown. His hair turns white. "He was strikingly changed after that," said one former parishioner who witnessed the difference in the priest. "A very dark, very thin, very attractive man, he was considerably aged afterwards."*

✢ ✢ ✢

Odell and Ed Hunkeler are in despair. They cannot stay in their home. They have relatives in St. Louis and wonder if they should go there. A scream interrupts their conversation. Odell runs to Ronald's bathroom, where he is preparing for bed. He lifts his pajama top to reveal the word *Louis* scratched into his ribs in bloodred letters. On his hip, another set of scratches, this time showing *Saturday*.

Apparently, whatever is attacking young Ronald knows that St. Louis is home to some experts on "demonic possession."

They are called Jesuits.

---

* The *Washington Post* followed up with a story on August 20 chronicling the bizarre situation at Georgetown University Hospital.

Chapter Twenty-Nine

MARCH 16, 1949
ST. LOUIS, MISSOURI
10:45 P.M.

I t has been nine weeks of hell for the Hunkeler family.

And now, Father William S. Bowdern, Society of Jesus, reads the prayers of exorcism. Bowdern is fifty-two, a stocky chain smoker with dark hair. He is a World War II veteran known for his keen intellect. The priest kneels by Ronald's bed at the home of the boy's St. Louis relatives. Bowdern is dressed in a black cassock and white surplice. A purple stole drapes around his neck. On his head, the priest wears a four-peak black hat known as a biretta. He recites the Litany of Saints, then says a quiet "Our Father." This is the prelude to the official "rite of exorcism." At his side is Father Raymond Bishop, a fellow Jesuit, keeping a written record of all that will occur.

✣ ✣ ✣

Ronald and his parents have been in St. Louis for nine days. They are staying in a two-story brick home with a white front door and colonial-style windows. The boy's battle with "demons" grows more intense. Traveling west has done nothing to suppress what is attacking him. If anything, things are even more frightening. When Ronald's mother suggests the boy enroll in a local school, the word *NO* appears scrawled on his wrists. Two aunts, four uncles, and four cousins bear witness to the scratches, as well as to flying furniture and shaking mattresses. In desperation, a female cousin attending Saint Louis University, a Catholic Jesuit institution, asks a priest for assistance. Father Raymond Bishop consents and goes to see Ronald with a container of holy water.

"The boy was dozing when the bottle of St. Ignatius holy water was thrown from a table two feet from R's room," Father Bishop's official report will read. "A bookcase was moved from alongside the bed and turned completely around facing the entrance to the room. The stool from the table moved from the table to the bed, about two feet. The stool was moved back to the position in a few minutes, and in a few moments it was turned over."

Catholic priests are cautioned against confusing strange behavior with demonic possession. So on March 10, Father Bishop requests that another priest join him in visiting Ronald. For the next five nights, Father Bishop and Father Bowdern sit with the boy at bedtime. Bowdern is a top Jesuit scholar, a man immersed in the ways of the order since he joined it at age seventeen.

By Wednesday, March 16, Bowdern has made his decision about Ronald Hunkeler: the time has come for an exorcism. He asks for, and receives, permission from the local archdiocese "to read the prayers of exorcism according to the Roman Ritual."*

That rite begins tonight.

✚ ✚ ✚

In the Book of Mark, Jesus has a conversation with a "demon" inhabiting the body of a Gentile man. The evil spirit gives his name as "Legion"—implying that the possession involves hundreds

---

* Roman Catholicism is not the only religion that believes in demonic possession. In Islam, evil spiritual bodies known as *shayatin* and *jinn* are believed to inhabit humans. Regional faiths throughout Africa show a profound belief in demons taking on human form. In the Caribbean, the Haitian practice of voodoo actually *invites* the *Loa* spirit into their bodies in order to see the future. Even the peaceful Buddhist faith believes in a *mara* (an evil spirit) that afflicts humans.

of evil spirits. Jesus then orders the demons to leave the afflicted individual—which they do, according to Scripture.

This act, taking place on the shores of the Sea of Galilee, is history's first exorcism. The developing Catholic faith accepts an active evil in the world. In the prayer of Saint Michael, it is said that demons "prowl about the earth seeking the ruin of souls."

Over the centuries, the Catholic Church will codify the casting out of evil spirits, adding ritual and prayer. The Catholic Catechism reads, "When the Church asks publicly and authoritatively in the name of Jesus Christ that a person or object be protected against the power of the Evil One and withdrawn from his dominion, it is called exorcism."

Shakespeare will write about possession in *King Lear* and *Twelfth Night*. When Martin Luther's 1517 schism separates Catholics from Protestants, the practice of exorcism becomes limited to the former. Thus, when the Puritans of Massachusetts Bay Colony are confronted by witches in Salem, the death penalty is invoked instead of an exorcism ritual.*

The Vatican has never wavered in its support for demon expulsion, though it is not a common practice. First, a doctor must be consulted to rule out mental or physical illness. Signs such as supernatural strength, scratches on the body, speaking in foreign tongues, and rooms that suddenly turn cold must be observed. Exorcism is rare and kept quiet to avoid inciting public scrutiny. A special Vatican course trains priests in the rite, which can involve multiple daily attempts to cast out a "demon." Yet this training is not *required* to perform an exorcism.

So it is that an untrained Father William S. Bowdern begins trying to heal Ronald.

---

* The Pentecostal movement of the twentieth century saw a return to the casting out of demons by some Protestant sects. In 2019, the Vatican allowed individuals from other Christian denominations to take part in its official exorcist training course. In 2017, Pope Francis encouraged priests to pursue the use of exorcism in rare cases.

✛ ✛ ✛

The first round is brutal.

"R was awake and the overhead light in the bedroom was kept burning," Father Bishop writes in his notes. "R kept his hands outside the bed covers."

As Father Bowdern begins the lengthy exorcism prayers, Ronald cries out. The priests immediately witness scratches emerging over the length of the boy's torso and legs.

"The most distinct markings on the body were the picture of the Devil on R's right leg and the word *HELL* imprinted on R's chest in such a way that R could look down upon his chest and read the letters plainly. The image of the Devil and *HELL* appeared at the repetition of the [Latin prayer] *Praecipio* demanding the evil spirit to identify himself," Bishop writes.

The night becomes an odyssey. As the priests look on, Ronald appears to be fighting someone. He must be physically restrained, the clerics throwing their bodies on the boy to stop the thrashing. At other times, he sings in his sleep, songs like "Swanee" and "Old Man River" in a high falsetto.

Father Bowdern asks how many demons are inside Ronald. A single line suddenly scratches the boy's right leg. A mysterious "X" also appears. The priests are unsure whether this means one evil spirit or ten. Through the course of the evening, twenty-five different scratches appear on Ronald's body, each causing him to double up and cry in pain. They all disappear within hours.*

When Ronald finally speaks, he begins flailing his arms violently, as if in a fistfight. A third priest enters the room—a physically powerful twenty-seven-year-old seminarian named Walter Halloran. He is here to help restrain Ronald.

---

* The archbishop of St. Louis, Joseph Ritter, requested that the exorcism be chronicled as it happened—thus, Father Bishop's extensive notes.

The boy finally falls asleep. Father Bowdern sprinkles holy water to wake him up. Halloran pins Ronald's arms until the boy opens his eyes.

"R was asked what he was doing and what he saw. He said he was fighting a huge red devil who felt slimy and was very powerful. The Devil was trying to get him through the iron gates at the top of a pit that was about two hundred feet deep and very hot. R wanted to fight that devil and felt that he was strong enough to overpower his enemy. R mentioned that there were other smaller devils," Father Bishop records.

The ordeal continues. Ronald spits at the priests with great accuracy, even with his eyes closed.

At 7:30 a.m., the boy finally begins "a natural sleep." The exhausted teenager rests well past noon. "Then he ate an ordinary meal and participated in a game of Monopoly."

✣ ✣ ✣

The nights become predictable: priests arriving at bedtime, then sitting with Ronald until he falls asleep. Sometimes there are hours of violent episodes. To steel himself for the spiritual battle, Father Bowdern eats and drinks only bread and water—a "Black Fast," as it is known—a habit he will continue for the entire ordeal.

✣ ✣ ✣

Saturday, March 19, marks the third night of the exorcism.

The priests arrive at 7 p.m. The exhausted Hunkeler family, who have all been losing sleep throughout the ordeal, retire at eight. Father Bowdern begins the nightly recitation of the exorcism rite, beginning with the Litany of Saints. Ronald begins barking like a dog and bares his teeth.

Bowdern asks for a sign that the demon is present, whereupon Ronald doubles over with stomach pain and begins spraying a long stream of urine. The boy then begins singing "in a clear voice and with real finesse," in the words of Father Bishop. The song is "Blue Danube." When Ronald awakens, the priest hums the tune and asks where the boy learned to sing it so well.

Ronald Hunkeler claims to have never heard the song before.

Then the boy begins taunting the priests: "Get away from me, you assholes. Go to hell you dirty sons of bitches. God damn you, sons of bitches. God damn you, you dirty assholes."

✛ ✛ ✛

Father Bowdern is growing thin from fasting and the nightly exertions. His skin is reddened and swollen with styes and boils.

Ronald's mother, Odell Hunkeler, is also unwell. In an attempt to help her rest, the exorcists decide to admit her son to Saint Alexian Brothers Hospital. The beds there have restraints and a ward where the teenager can scream without being heard. "But he feared the surroundings of the hospital: the barred window, the bare room, the straps on the bed, and the knobless door," Father Bishop records.

"His whole reaction was one of intense fear."

Yet tonight is a breakthrough.

Ed Hunkeler has joined the exorcism team for the evening. Ronald's father is forty-nine and works in the Washington Navy Yard back home in Maryland. Uprooting his family for the treatment of Ronald's bizarre condition places considerable strain on their finances, but he will do anything to see his only son healed. Ed was born Catholic and has not forgotten the rituals of the faith. As Father Bowdern completes the prayers of exorcism for the fifth time, everyone in the room kneels to say the Rosary. Ronald stays in bed but does not fall asleep. After completion of the religious procedure, the clergy leave—but Ed stays behind. He is the more lenient of Ronald's parents, far less strict than his wife and fond of pampering the boy. Ed reads aloud to his son from a book of prayers, then rests on a divan next to Ronald's bed.

For the first time in months, Ronald Hunkeler sleeps through the night.

He is discharged from the hospital the next morning.

✥ ✥ ✥

Two nights later, Ronald shatters Father Halloran's nose.

"R went into a tantrum. He fought and kicked and spit so that three men could barely hold him," Father Bishop writes. "The first blows were accurate, quick, and deadly, although R's eyes were shut. R urinated rather copiously and on coming to himself complained of the burning sensation. There were four or five such urinations during the evening. Several times there was passing of wind through the rectum."

The hope felt at the hospital is now replaced by a new level of degradation. Ronald talks of life in hell, stating that he has already glimpsed into the future. In eight years, he declares, the priests will be joining him. He stipulates the year 1957. The boy then brags about his penis and takes off his pajama bottoms, gyrating his nude loins at the exorcists.

This is the worst of it, the priests tell one another in the morning.

It is not.

Ronald spends the next night "screaming, barking, singing, urinating, and passing foul air." He brags about his penis and taunts Father Bowdern about his failing attempts to exorcise the demons. "Cut out the damned Latin," the teenager barks. "Get away from me, you goddamned bastards."

But unlike other nights, Ronald does not fall into an exhausted sleep.

"You like to stay with me," the demon says flirtatiously to the priests, letting them know he isn't going anywhere.

"Well, I like it, too."

One night later, Ronald adds a new threat: "Father Bishop, all people that mangle with me will die a terrible death."*

✠ ✠ ✠

The decision is made to baptize Ronald into the Catholic faith.

The ceremony will take place first thing in the morning on Friday, April 1. Father Bowdern is exhausted, his physical appearance declining as the exorcism takes its toll. He and the other priests have wrestled with Ronald time after time. The boy has urinated and spit on them. Baptism is an attempt to confirm the presence of God in Ronald's life, performed with the hope of creating a spiritual opposition to the evil within the boy.

Ronald's parents and other family members begin the drive to Saint Francis Xavier College Church, where Father Bowdern is the pastor. During the journey, the boy begins having hot and cold flashes. Suddenly, in a strange new voice, he yells, "So you are going to baptize me? Ha, ha!"

Ronald then grabs the steering wheel and attempts to crash the car. "His uncle was forced to pull up to the curb in an effort to subdue the violence," Father Bishop will record. "R stiffened and fought. It was a major task to remove him from the front seat and force him into the back of the car. Even with careful supervision, R leaped up to seize the wheel from the aunt as she drove."

Everyone in the vehicle notices that the radio stops working whenever Ronald has a spell. As soon as the teenager returns to normal, the music resumes.

✠ ✠ ✠

Monday, April 11. Ronald is returned to Saint Alexian Brothers Hospital. The daily routine of exorcism prayers has continued un-

---

* That prediction did not come true. No one associated with this case died in 1957. In the 1960s, Father Halloran joined the army as a chaplain and served in Vietnam with honor.

abated. Yet it is not working. The priests, by now, are used to the "filthy talk and damning threats," which seem to grow more vulgar each night.

For the first time, Father Bishop mentions the Devil by name in his report. "At midnight, the Fathers planned to give R Holy Communion, but Satan would have no part of it. Even while the institution of the Holy Sacrament was explained to R, his body was badly scratched and branded. The word 'HELL' was printed on his chest and thigh."

Father Bishop continues: "One new phase was the display of the Devil's power over the senses and external personality of R. In one instance, he said he would have R awaken and the boy would be pleasant and attractive. The promise was true. A few minutes later, the Devil said he (through Ronald) would have R awaken, but this time he would be offensive. True to the promise, R came out of the spell very irritable, and he complained very bitterly to those who held him."

Another attempt is made to give Ronald the Holy Eucharist.

"I will *not* let R receive Holy Communion," a voice tells the priests.

✣ ✣ ✣

Easter morning passes. It is day thirty-one of the exorcism.

A new statue of Michael the Archangel, a Catholic saint known to be effective in battling demons, has been placed in Ronald's room. Once again, the evening prayers of exorcism are offered in Latin, with several priests in attendance. Since the exorcism began five weeks ago, a number of Jesuits have been present as eyewitnesses.

"At 10:45 p.m., the most striking of events occurred. R was in a seizure but afterward lay calm. In clear, commanding tones, and with dignity, a voice broke into the prayers. The following is an accurate quotation: 'Satan! Satan! I am Saint Michael and I command you, Satan, and the other evil spirits to leave the body in the name of Dominus, immediately: NOW! NOW! NOW!'"

As Ronald begins thrashing on the bed in "the most violent contortions of the entire period of exorcism," the Jesuits once again grow exhausted trying to restrain the boy.

Then Ronald becomes calm. He tells of a bright white light. A man with wavy hair wearing a white robe that fits closely to his body. The man is holding a fiery sword and pointing it down into a pit, where he can see the Devil and his minions.

"As the devils disappeared into the pit, R felt a pulling or tugging in the region of his stomach. He said it was the most relaxed feeling he has had since the whole experience began in January."

✛ ✛ ✛

It is over.

"Since Monday at 11:00 p.m., there have been no indications of the presence of the Devil," Father Bishop writes.

✛ ✛ ✛

April 29, 1949. Father Bishop files his confidential report. It is more than three months since Ronald first heard the sounds of running water and scratching in his bedroom. The exorcism has been witnessed by multiple people, all of whom are cited in the report.*

Father Bishop sums up the situation this way:

> Dear Brother Cornelius:
> The enclosed report is a summary of the case which you have known for the past several weeks. The Brothers' part in this case has been so very important that I thought you should have the case history for your permanent file.

---

* The names of the following priests from the Society of Jesus are listed on the official report: George Bischofberger, Raymond Bishop, Joseph Boland, William S. Bowdern, Edmund Burke, John O'Flaherty, William Van Roo, Walter Halloran, and Albert Schell.

We have been informed by the Chancery Office on two different occasions, March 16 and April 27 that the case is not to be publicized. I fear that the news has already broken in various parts of the city through individuals asking for prayers and perhaps through some who took part in the case. The difficulty of keeping some of the facts secret is practically beyond our control right now, but insofar as we are able, we should not make this case public.

❖ ❖ ❖

The Hunkeler family returns to Maryland, where Ronald enters Gonzaga High School in the fall. His story is kept relatively quiet, although word does get out and people occasionally come by to pray with Ronald's parents. In August, when the *Washington Post* reports on the exorcism, the teenager escapes scrutiny because the Catholic Church has ensured that he remains anonymous.

Soon, the sensational story about demonic possession in the Washington suburbs is mostly forgotten.

But not by everyone.

Chapter Thirty

AUTUMN 1949

WASHINGTON, DC

DAY

Ronald Hunkeler resumes being a normal teenager.

At the same time, a twenty-one-year-old Georgetown University student is fascinated when he reads and rereads the *Washington Post*'s exposé on the terrifying events involving a boy in Maryland. "In what is perhaps one of the most remarkable experiences of its kind in recent religious history, a fourteen-year-old Mount Rainier boy has been freed by a Catholic priest of possession by the devil, Catholic sources reported yesterday," begins the story written by Bill Brinkley.

The student, William Peter Blatty, wants to know more. But details are scant. Ronald Hunkeler is not mentioned by name—future accounts will call him "Roland Doe" or "Robbie Mannheim." Indeed, the boy's identity will not be revealed publicly until after his death almost seventy years from now. Every effort is being taken to scrub any trace of the Hunkeler family and location of their home from the record.*

But Blatty has an inside source: he attends classes taught by Father Eugene B. Gallagher, who recently lectured on the topic of

---

* Several investigators seeking to know more about the 1949 exorcism will discover Ronald's true identity. However, they will refrain from making that public until his death out of respect for his privacy.

exorcism. During one seminar, it comes to light that the diary of events written by Father Raymond Bishop during Ronald's ordeal has been transformed into a training manual. Titled "Case Study for Jesuit Priests," the day-to-day accounting of the possession ritual is kept secure by the Jesuits.

Blatty knows that Father Gallagher has a copy. The aspiring writer badgers his instructor, asking to read the sixteen-page document. The priest refuses.

✢ ✢ ✢

William Peter Blatty graduates from Georgetown in 1950. The years pass. He works as a beer truck driver and a door-to-door vacuum salesman, and he serves for a time in the air force. But he never forgets the existence of that journal nor the amazing story of an exorcism taking place so close to his home in Washington, DC. Eventually, the aspiring writer digs deeper, learning that at least two copies of the journal are in the hands of priests, and two more are held by the local archdiocese. Blatty manages to read the diary and attempts to speak with Father Bowdern about the Hunkeler exorcism. The priest refuses.*

✢ ✢ ✢

Twenty-two years later, William Peter Blatty is a successful Hollywood comedy writer. His mother's death in 1967 has sparked Blatty's return to the Catholic faith of his childhood. In an effort to show "that God exists and that the universe will have a happy ending," he decides to write a "supernatural detective story that was filled with suspense with theological overtones." Blatty bases the book on the 1949 exorcism. He changes the main character from a boy to a girl. Halfway through the novel, the writer is excited, sure

---

* It is unknown exactly how William Peter Blatty got hold of the diary. The best evidence is that someone at Georgetown let him see it.

in his belief that the book will become a bestseller. He will later insist that it was never his intent to scare anyone.

But sales are dismal when *The Exorcist* is published in June 1971. Blatty's publisher pays for a twenty-six-city book tour, with an average of twelve to fifteen radio and newspaper interviews a day. "I got very nice reviews," Blatty will remember. "But no one was buying the book."

One prominent department store, the May Department Stores Company, returns every single copy.

And though the author has previously written more than a dozen scripts made into films, attempts to sell his screenplay version of *The Exorcist* are rejected by every studio in Hollywood.

Then comes New York. Blatty's publicist arranges a preinterview for a potential appearance on *The Dick Cavett Show*. That broadcast is second only to Johnny Carson's *Tonight Show* in late-night popularity. But despite the author's high hopes of promoting his book on national television, the *Cavett* producer tells him it is unlikely he will be selected.

But a short time later, while he is eating lunch with his editor, she is called to the phone. A few moments later, the woman asks a stunned Blatty, "Can you get over to the *Dick Cavett Show* right now?"

A guest has canceled and Blatty will now be on the program. And more luck awaits. Dick Cavett is not pleased with the first segment of the program and, after a commercial, is expecting the second guest, actor Robert Shaw, to appear. However, Shaw is deemed too inebriated to go on. So Cavett still has almost an entire show to tape with only William Peter Blatty left as a guest.

"Well, Mr. Blatty, I haven't read your book," Cavett apologizes.

"That's OK. I'll tell you about it," the author replies, then spends the next forty-one minutes promoting his book on national television in front of millions.

A short time later, *The Exorcist* reaches number one on the *New*

York Times bestseller list, where it remains for seventeen straight weeks. It goes on to sell thirteen million copies worldwide. Warner Brothers Studios pays $641,000 for the movie rights.

Blatty's book will enthrall readers all over the world.

But it is the motion picture that will terrify them.

✤ ✤ ✤

Filming begins on August 14, 1972. Director William Friedkin has had no trouble assembling a cast. Big names like Marlon Brando, Jack Nicholson, and Paul Newman are considered for roles as the priests based on Father Bowdern and Father Bishop. Those parts, instead, go to Swedish actor Max von Sydow and a playwright named Jason Miller. Thirteen-year-old Linda Blair plays Regan, the possessed teenager based on Ronald Hunkeler, beating out five hundred other children for the role. The shoot will be demanding for the young girl, filled with long days on a refrigerated set wearing just a nightgown. In one scene in which she is fastened to a rig to help her "levitate" above a bed, she will cry out in pain when her lower spine is accidently strained—yet Friedkin keeps the cameras rolling, despite her tears. He believes this realism makes the movie more intense and will leave that scene in the completed film. By the time filming ends, Blair will be so traumatized she will claim she never wants to act again.*

Much of the shoot takes place in and around Georgetown University, where Father Edward Albert Hughes first attempted to heal Ronald. The 105-day filming schedule stretches to 200 as the production falls behind. The eccentric Friedkin likes to keep the actors on edge, so he randomly fires blasts from a real shotgun before a take. But he soon finds that tactic unnecessary because unexplained occurrences are providing all the stimulation he

---

* Linda Blair did go on to have a successful acting career, even doing a sequel to *The Exorcist* that starred Richard Burton.

needs. "We were plagued by strange and sinister things from the beginning," the director will remember. He is six feet tall, thin, and wears wire-framed glasses. "It is simply the hardest thing I've ever done in my life."

A series of bizarre events occur, giving rise to an alleged "Curse of *The Exorcist*." For example, nine members of the production die *during* filming, including actors Jack MacGowran and Vasiliki Maliaros. Ironically, their characters also die in the script. In addition, actor Jason Miller's five-year-old son is hit by a motorcycle. The boy's life hangs in the balance for weeks.

On top of all that, a pigeon flies into a circuit box during filming. As Friedkin looks on, both bird and the electrical outlet catch fire, setting the set ablaze. All is lost, with the exception of the bedroom where the movie exorcism takes place. Friedkin then brings in a Catholic priest to bless the set. Reverend Thomas Bermingham refuses at first but accedes when several members of the cast implore him to do it.*

Like Linda Blair, actress Ellen Burstyn, who plays the possessed girl's mother, suffers spinal trauma when a harness that is supposed to fly her across the room crashes. Max von Sydow's brother dies the first day of filming. Blair's grandfather dies during the production. One set carpenter accidently cuts off his thumb. A gaffer slices his big toe. A broken sprinkler system floods the set, causing a two-week delay. And a ten-foot-tall statue of the Archangel Michael, which was packed into a fifteen-foot-long box for shipping to a location shoot in Iraq, somehow ends up in Hong Kong—causing another two-week delay.

"There were strange images and visions that showed up on film that were never planned," Friedkin will say. "There are double exposures at the end of one reel that are unbelievable. I had to do a tremendous amount of re-shooting."

---

* Father Bermingham was an adviser on the film and had a small role in it.

✢ ✢ ✢

Then there is a report concerning actor Jason Miller and a real-life priest. As the story goes, the cleric approaches Miller at random, a total stranger who knows nothing about the filming of *The Exorcist*. He looks at the actor and quietly says, "Reveal the devil for the trickster that he is. He will seek retribution against you or he will even try to stop what you are trying to do to unmask him."

The priest then hands Jason Miller a religious medallion.[*]

As production winds down, William Friedkin meets with journalists to begin promoting the movie. One year ago, he won the Best Director Academy Award for *The French Connection*, so his skills are well known to the press. He spent a year researching the occult, filling his New York City apartment with books on witchcraft, hypnosis, and psychiatric disorders. He can speak knowledgeably about the Salem witch trials. So it is surprising when Friedkin admits that the pressure affecting him most during the making of *The Exorcist* is not being millions of dollars over budget—it is the strange occurrences he has witnessed.

"I'm not a convert to the occult," the thirty-eight-year-old director tells the media. "But after all I've seen on this film I definitely believe in demonic possession. There are things that cannot be treated by medical or psychiatric means. It seems strange, foreign, and impossible but it exists. The film has no message. It's an actual case history."

Unfortunately, history will soon repeat itself in a haunting way. The Devil is not yet finished with Ronald Hunkeler.

---

[*] This report appeared in two British newspapers. The authors of this book cannot verify that this took place. Jason Miller died in 2001, at age sixty-two, of a heart attack.

Chapter Thirty-One

DECEMBER 26, 1973

SILVER SPRINGS, MARYLAND

DAY

A secret life is about to be unmasked.

The now thirty-eight-year-old NASA engineer works at the Goddard Space Flight Center in nearby Greenbelt, Maryland. Ronald Hunkeler holds college degrees in chemical engineering and psychology. Since beginning his employment with the space agency, he has worked to put men on the moon as part of the Apollo project. He is the married father of three children, of whom the oldest is named Michael, for the archangel.

The Exorcist arrives in theaters today. In the twenty-four years since his possession, Ronald Hunkeler has largely been able to shut the trauma out of his mind when he is in public. However, in private, he is prone to unexpected rages that are affecting his marriage and child-rearing.

Ronald's wife and a few close colleagues do know the exorcism occurred, but it is not something he speaks about. However, the success of William Peter Blatty's book has resurrected demon possession as a topic of worldwide conversation. And now the movie can only add to that awareness.

It is known that the film was produced in nearby Washington. Newspapers are reporting that the movie and book are based on a 1949 exorcism that occurred in this area. Ronald Hunkeler's name is still not public, but he lives in dread that it soon will be. This anxiety is affecting him deeply. It is almost as if the Devil is back.

✣ ✣ ✣

Everyone is talking about *The Exorcist*.

"In a quiet Beverly Hills, California, neighborhood, residents have been awakened at dawn as thousands of people gather for an 8 a.m. showing at a theater seating 1,450. Every day 5,000 moviegoers stand in the long queue wrapped around the Sack 57 Cinema in Boston. Four Manhattan theaters have lines extending for blocks from noon to midnight," reports *Time* magazine.*

"I want to see it before it's banned," one Bostonian tells *Time*.

The real exorcists, Father William Bowdern and Father Raymond Bishop, live long enough to see their exploits on film. They will attend the premier, quietly admitting that the terrors on the screen are far *less* scary than what actually happened.†

All over the world, the film is scaring the hell out of those who see it. Some audience members faint or become hysterical. "I think it's part of the religious trend that's going on, the craving for the supernatural, the interest in the nonmaterial," states the Most Reverend Arthur Michael Ramsey, archbishop of Canterbury.

After each screening of *The Exorcist* ends, fear continues. Televangelist Billy Graham states, "There is a power of evil in the film, in the fabric of the film itself."

Graham believes that watching *The Exorcist* is an open invitation to demonic possession.

William Peter Blatty disagrees. "There has been a devil theory

---

* Bill O'Reilly saw *The Exorcist* shortly after it opened in 1973 at the Sack 57 Theater. He was a student at Boston University.

† Father William Bowdern will die in 1993 at age eighty-five. Father Raymond Bishop will pass in 1978 at age seventy-two. Father Walter Halloran, who had his nose broken by Ronald Hunkeler, will pass away in 2005, the last Jesuit involved in the rite to die. The cause of death for each priest will be natural causes brought on by age.

that sinister forces were annoyed by the film. I don't attach any significance to it. Still, I would like to think that somebody down there doesn't like me."

✤ ✤ ✤

Much to Ronald Hunkeler's chagrin, the exorcism phenomenon grows. High school teenagers in the town of Mount Rainier come out at night, flocking to a vacant lot at the corner of Bunker Hill Road and Thirty-Third Street. The house that once stood here was burned down after a firefighting exercise in 1962. However, the kids think this is the site where Hunkeler's exorcism took place.

In fact, this is not the true location. But the revelers do not care. They drink beer and build wooden crosses, apparently celebrating the exorcism. Even though police shoo them away, the teenaged crowds keep returning, sure in their belief that the Devil once dwelled where they are standing.

✤ ✤ ✤

The actual Hunkeler homestead in nearby Cottage City, Maryland, is the scene of many violent disturbances. Father Frank Bober, a former pastor of Saint James Catholic Church in Mount Rainier, is approached by reporters from the *Washington Post* in 1985. They have questions about unexplained phenomena near the home. "Not far from where the boy and his parents lived, police found a woman in a plastic bag, her body decomposing," the priest remembers. "A couple doors away from that house, a guy went crazy and decapitated his mother. A few doors down, children were arrested for hacking off appendages of their parents. So that entire area there seemed to be plagued by very bizarre criminal elements."

Father Bober, who was a good friend of Father Albert Hughes, the priest attacked by Ronald Hunkeler at Georgetown University Hospital, then tells about a letter he received from a convicted felon after the *Washington Post*'s 1985 story. The man is serving a life sentence for murdering his mother. "I did this and I loved my mom," the killer admits, adding that there is "something extraordinarily uncomfortable" about the area around the Hunkeler home.

"Some power just took over me and I hacked her to pieces."

✢ ✢ ✢

Ronald Hunkeler's life unfolds but his personal demons become too much for his wife, who divorces him in 1986. Also, two of his children will not speak to him. It is a tragic situation.

In 2001, after forty years with NASA, Ronald retires. He now has a female partner, who worked with him at the space agency. The two buy a house, approximately forty miles from his boyhood home. But Hunkeler cannot escape his legacy.

In fact, on occasion, strangers still approach Ronald Hunkeler asking if he was the exorcism boy. Flustered, he denies being involved with anything like that.

But his youthful trauma continues to haunt the grown man.

There is no escape.

Chapter Thirty-Two

MAY 10, 2020

MARRIOTTSVILLE, MARYLAND

DAY

Ronald Hunkeler is dying.

The now eighty-four-year-old retired engineer has experienced a stroke and soon it will kill him.

His partner is doing the best she can to keep Ronald comfortable, but it is clear the end is near. She is a short, slender, attractive woman who knows what the thirteen-year-old Ronald endured seventy-one years ago. She has kept his secrets for decades. But many questions remain unanswered.*

✣ ✣ ✣

As Ronald lies in his bed, the doorbell rings. His partner answers. A Catholic priest stands on the porch. She is stunned. Although Ronald converted to Catholicism during his exorcism, he did not practice the faith throughout his adult life. There are no plans for a religious funeral. The engineer will instead be cremated.

In addition, no one called a priest.

What is said between the woman and the priest remains un-

---

* Ronald Hunkeler grew so paranoid about people recognizing him as the subject of the exorcism that he made a point to spend Halloween night at a location other than his home, fearful that trick-or-treaters would make a point to visit the "*Exorcist* house."

known. She never divulges that. But she admits the cleric into the house.

The home is spacious, with a brick facade, large airy rooms, hardwood floors, and tall windows to let in the light.

The priest goes to Ronald's bedside. The blinds are open and sun streams into the room. The unnamed cleric performs the Sacrament of the Sick, as the "last rites" are also known. He asks for Ronald's confession and anoints his head with oil. "Through this holy anointing may the Lord in his love and mercy help you with the grace of the Holy Spirit," prays the father.

"May the Lord who frees you from sin save you and raise you up."

Then, as Father Bowdern did in 1949, the priest attempts to give Ronald the sacrament of Holy Communion. This time, there is no interference.

Ronald Hunkeler dies shortly after the priest's visit—three weeks shy of turning eighty-five.

✠ ✠ ✠

One year later, a *New York Post* reporter tracks down Hunkeler's companion. She has never publicly spoken about the exorcism situation and what happened to Ronald. The journalist asks her to describe his final moments.

She is terse, saying that she will talk only if her identity is kept secret. The reporter agrees. The woman sighs and ends the conversation this way: "I have no idea how the Father knew to come but he got Ron to heaven.

"Ron's in heaven and he's with God."

Author's Note

Demonic possession.

The concept has been around since the time of Moses: an active evil in the world that can directly alter human lives. In Scripture, the evil one actually confronts Jesus with temptation.

Some believe; many others do not. But as we chronicled, demonic "situations" have led to executions and tortured lives throughout history and extending into the modern age.

Today, there is a new kind of witch hunt. Accusations mean guilt. The press drives that every day. No one is executed, but lives are ruined in terrible ways.

And there is no forgiveness for actual transgressions. The cancel culture makes sure of that. Demonization has cast a terrible fear across the land.

Roseanne Barr recently lamented that "witch-hunters" destroyed her career by intense canceling after some terrible comments she made about former Barack Obama adviser Valerie Jarrett. Barr apologized for her invective and stated she was loaded on Ambien when she attacked Jarrett on social media.

It didn't matter. Roseanne was banished by the entertainment industry. She said this to the *Los Angeles Times*: "It was a witch-burning and it was terrifying. I felt the devil himself was coming against me to tear me apart."

Harry Potter author J. K. Rowling was demonized for promoting traditional gender. The trans fanatics immediately called for a symbolic lynching—so much so that there is a podcast entitled *The Witch Trials of J. K. Rowling*.

Although very different from the Salem hysteria in form, the spirit of no forgiveness and celebrating unproven allegations binds the modern cancel culture and Salem together. Instead of insane clerics and corrupt officials, our current witch hunt is led by dishonest media, both traditional and social, and a legion of despicable attorneys who seek to extort money by peddling unexamined accusations, often with full knowledge that careers will be destroyed and families torn apart.

We see examples almost every day.

Unlike seventeenth-century Salem, there are guilty people today who should be held to account for their misdeeds. But the demonstrable fact in the United States is that due process is often ignored in the court of public opinion. Denials never deter the destroyers.

Like the powerful Mather preachers, corporations are taking the lead in the mass denial of due process. Let me give you a vivid example.

New York Post columnist Phil Mushnick has chronicled the case of tennis analyst Doug Adler. While working for ESPN, which is owned by the the Walt Disney Company, Adler described player Venus Williams as using "guerrilla tactics" while rushing the net.

Adler was clearly referring to guerrilla warfare, where hit-and-run attacks are used. This was at the Australian Open in 2017.

But smear merchants on Twitter, including a tennis stringer for the *New York Times*, accused Doug Adler of using the word *gorilla*. Because Williams is black, racism was charged. Adler was almost immediately fired by ESPN. Few outside of Mushnick dared to defend him. Adler's career was shattered.

Shortly after his dismissal, Adler suffered a heart attack. He survived, but you get the picture. Cancel culture hysteria and a cowardly corporation ruined an innocent man's life. But Adler is not alone.

Literally no one is safe from the new witch hunt.

✦ ✦ ✦

November 2018. Heavily armed police burst into Kimberly Winters's home and arrest her. She is a teacher at Park View High School in Loudoun County, Virginia. Winters proclaims her innocence but is strip-searched and booked, charged with sexually abusing a male student. Her mug shot is released to the press. She is fired from her job.

She is not guilty.

Prosecutors quickly drop the case; there is no evidence other than an accusation. Kimberly Winters sues the county. It takes a jury less than two hours to award her $5 million.

Here's what Kimberly told the *Washington Post*: "It became so humiliating I literally couldn't go out of my house. This has been going on for four years. The repeated trauma of having to relive this created this tremor. My entire body shakes."

Why is this happening?

You would think the legacy of Salem and the intense struggle to eliminate fanatical religious mandates from our Constitution would have fostered an indelible cautionary outlook on American society. But that is not the case.

Fear has returned. It is a mirror of Salem. Many good people turn away from the cancel culture corruption rather than criticize it.

There is an active evil in our country. It is present for all to witness. There are now thousands of cases of shattered lives with more emerging every day.

Something is generating all this.

Something.

BILL O'REILLY
LONG ISLAND
MARCH 2023

Afterword

Witch City is thriving.

More than three hundred years after the witch trials, here is the city motto: Salem—Still Making History.

Located a forty-minute drive from Boston, Salem is now a city of forty-five thousand people. Yet a million tourists from around the world show up each year. In fact, it is estimated that more than $100 million is spent annually in Witch City by people enthralled with its past.

Halloween and the "Haunted Happenings" is the busiest and most profitable holiday. This is the largest celebration of Halloween on the planet, with parades and shows and exhibitions to scare the children. In fact, some believe that Salem's history has become a cult situation. The city fathers aggressively protect the image of Salem, so as to not disturb the money flow.*

Tourist revenue centers on the 1692 executions. Some experiences are historic, like the Salem Heritage Trail, taking visitors past the Witch Trials Memorial and the Witch House on Essex Street, once home to "hanging judge" Jonathan Corwin. Disney is also involved. The movie *Hocus Pocus* was filmed on location in Salem and is marketed to children. In addition, a statue of *Bewitched* star Elizabeth Montgomery stands in the center of town, in honor

---

* No one from the Salem mayor's office would speak on the record to the authors of this book.

of the television show that filmed several episodes of one season in Salem. This was a gift to the city of Salem by the TV Land network as a way to promote its new program lineup, including *Bewitched*. At the time, the nine-foot-tall, three-thousand-pound bronze statue was a controversial gift because people felt it made light of the tragedy of the witch trials.

That sentiment has changed.

"This bronze beauty has quickly become a staple in our magical city," reads Salem tourism board literature.

✛ ✛ ✛

Predictably, Salem is now saturated with modern witches and warlocks. The city is a haven for men and women who practice the black arts or at least pretend to. The Witch City Mall sells séances, psychic readings, and future predictions with tarot cards. Other business owners throughout Salem promote themselves as psychics, vampires, and proponents of "witchcraft and magic." The pentagram, the mark of the Devil, is featured prominently on signs. Obviously, all this present commerce trades on the gruesome deaths of twenty innocent individuals.

But that is in the past.

Salem's true legacy is kept well hidden. "By European standards this was a very small witch hunt," notes Professor Emerson W. Baker, a historian from Salem State University and one of the leading proponents of remembering those executed in the witch trials. "There were outbreaks in Germany where more than three thousand people died. Yet no one calls Cologne the Witch City.

"We think of Salem this way because the trials were a fall from grace. Before then, Salem was literally the city upon a hill, a model of Christian charity. To see its daughters accusing mothers and grandmothers of witchcraft was a real blow to the reputation of the town," Baker told us.

Even now, the witch trials divide Salem due to efforts to promote the city as a scary but benign tourist destination. The locals are split between those who enjoy the crowds—particularly the profit center of Halloween—and citizens upset about the city making a fortune on the back of murder.

Adds Professor Baker, "The town is not reconciled to that."

✢ ✢ ✢

In 1711, Massachusetts began awarding money for restitution to the families that were harmed during the witch hunts. That continued until the 1740s. The process was known as restoration of "innocency." In every case, those requesting compensation received it.

Then there's the matter of religion. There were no real witches in Salem in 1692, but a large godless community has descended on the town. Salem is still home to a strong Congregationalist Church population, yet an estimated 10 percent of the residents call themselves Wiccans—followers of modern neo-pagan rites. Many of these worshippers were not born in Salem but have traveled here to make a home.

"Some say it is because of the witch trials and the symbolism of living in a town known for witchcraft," says Baker. Noting that Salem calls itself a "No Place to Hate" community. welcoming all people, all races, all backgrounds, and all lifestyles, he adds, "Others come to Salem because it is now a place of religious freedom and toleration. A town that rushed to judgment in 1692 has learned to be more tolerant. Most of these Wicca[ns] come seeking a place where people aren't judged. It has become the Wicca[n], neo-pagan, haunted happenings destination."

Professor Baker adds that until the influx of tourism, the postindustrial city where the board game Monopoly originated was in decline. Salem had begun using the label "Witch City" in 1892, before the two hundredth anniversary of the trials. Arthur Miller's play *The Crucible*, first performed in 1953, used the witch trials as an allegory for the McCarthy era. But extensive marketing of that name didn't begin until 1970, the year *Bewitched* was filmed in Salem.

Yet as the popularity of promoting witches proved a financial boon to the city, more questions were raised about honoring those executed in the trials. In addition to kitsch and crystals, those visiting Salem can also find prominent memorials. In 1992, Holocaust survivor and Nobel laureate Elie Wiesel dedicated the Salem Witch Trials Memorial, a three-sided granite wall with stone benches displaying the names and execution dates of the victims.

Twenty-five years later, on July 25, 2017, a new memorial was dedicated at Proctor's Ledge, site of the hangings at the bottom of Gallows Hill. This is the place where the victims took their last breaths. But the monument is often overlooked because there are few parking spaces. The city asks visitors to avoid Gallows Hill, reminding them they will be towed if they park at the nearby Walgreen's drugstore.

Which is a lot better than being hanged.

Yet people come anyway. Some leave offerings. New Age folks prefer crystals. Other visitors leave notes, many written with great emotion to honor the fallen. A very active community of victims' descendants is still emotional about the witch hunt.

"Descendants are effusive in their thanks for the memorial at Gallows Hill," says Professor Baker. "Many descendants say their visit was the conclusion of unfinished business."

Baker himself was shocked to discover, while doing research on the topic, that he is related to a witch hunt victim.

And he does not think that is unusual.

"The witch trial is all-encompassing," he says. "The people of Salem had children, then their children had children, and through the centuries those generations married and moved away, their families spreading across the nation.

"If you dig deep enough into your family tree, you will most likely find that you are related to someone who took part in the Salem witch trials. Even if your descendants were not born in the United States, they might have married someone with a connection. Three hundred and thirty years after the trials, that's a lot of generations.

"It's our American story."

+ + +

The professor's words are true. The Salem witch trials are a unique part of US history. There is no question the Puritans lost their way and committed atrocities, but justice did ultimately prevail and a terrible situation was used for good as the Constitution prohibits an established or official church. The First Amendment guarantees religious freedom. There is no prohibition of fanaticism. In modern times, Salem has turned what was a dark experience into a prosperous one. Yes, citizens are divided over that prosperity, but it is relatively harmless at this point. There is no question that Salem would not be an affluent suburb if not for the witch legacy.

History, as they say, is complicated. For every horror, a benefit emerges. In totality, the province of Massachusetts Bay paved the way for the abolitionist movement that sought to free slaves. The lessons learned at Salem were part of that—demonstrating man's inhumanity to man.

Also, the city acknowledges that the definition of a "witch hunt" has expanded to include the "social targeting" that is now a part of modern society. In fact, the Salem Witch Museum exhibits actually tell visitors about the role of social and political witch hunts throughout history and in contemporary life.

The Salem Award for Human Rights and Social Justice was established in 1992 to recognize individuals or groups who are confronting fear and fighting injustice.

So the witches did not die completely in vain. The course of the most powerful nation on earth was changed by the murders at Salem. Americans today can worship as they please, with no government intrusion.

We the people can also make up our own minds about good, evil, God, and the Devil. Americans possess the absolute right to believe or not believe.

Something witch hunters and demons of all types cannot be happy about.

Postscript

We dispatched the villains of Salem in earlier pages, but it is worth noting the fates of some patriots who forged this nation.

Benjamin Franklin's health issues deepened after the Constitutional Convention. The gout that made walking so painful was compounded by a worsening case of the pleurisy he had battled for fifty years. While lying in bed with a high fever, an abscess in his lungs burst. Franklin began violently vomiting large amounts of blood. This was followed by an inability to breathe, whereupon a calm settled over him as he lapsed into a coma. At 11 p.m., on April 17, 1790, Benjamin Franklin died. He was eighty-four.

The famous man's funeral was the largest ever held in America at the time, attended by twenty thousand mourners. In the Philadelphia harbor, ships lowered their flags to half-mast. Franklin's coffin was borne from the Pennsylvania State House to Christ Church, where it was laid to rest in the cemetery as church bells tolled. Franklin's wife, Deborah Read, is buried at his side, along with his son Francis Folger, who died at the age of four.

The members of the US House of Representatives wore black crepe as a sign of mourning after Franklin's death. In Paris, where he had long served as US minister, the National Assembly also declared a period of mourning, stating that Franklin was a "mighty genius, who, to the advantage of mankind, compassing in his mind the heavens and the earth, was able to restrain alike thunderbolts and tyrants."

✢ ✢ ✢

George Washington fulfilled his goal of returning to his home at Mount Vernon after the Constitutional Convention. But the general could not remain inactive long. In 1788, he accepted the position of chancellor at the College of William and Mary in Williamsburg. The following year, Washington was unanimously elected America's first president by the Electoral College, which casts votes based on each state's representation in Congress. The popular vote in America was not formally counted until 1824.

During his presidency, Washington established traditions that continue to this day. He chose to be known as "Mr. President" rather than "His Excellency" or "His Highness." In addition, he established a "cabinet" of advisers on a number of topics. The first cabinet was comprised of only four members—secretaries of state, treasury, and war, and the attorney general. There is a constitutional reference to the president being able to seek written advice from heads of the executive departments—but Washington initiated a more formal, regular structure. He also instituted an inauguration speech. And he delivered the Annual Message to a joint session of Congress—this annual message became known as the State of the Union in the twentieth century. In addition, Washington chose the site of the White House in what would become the District of Columbia and laid the cornerstone in 1792.

Washington was reelected to a second term in 1792 but chose not to run for a third. He was sixty-five when he retired to Mount Vernon, planning to spend the rest of his life managing the plantation. However, on December 12, 1799, after a long day on horseback, the general fell ill with a sore throat. His condition worsened and he died on December 14, shortly after 10 p.m., from quinsy, an abscess of pus on the back of his throat caused by infection. Fearful of being buried alive, one of Washington's final wishes was that his burial be delayed three days after his last breath to ensure he was dead.

George Washington is interred in a vault at Mount Vernon, Virginia. Martha Washington, who survived him by three years, lies by his side.

✢ ✢ ✢

Thomas Jefferson was elected America's third president in 1800, at the age of fifty-seven. After serving two terms, following the precedent set by George Washington, Jefferson returned to his plantation at Monticello. He sold his vast collection of books to restore the new Library of Congress after the British burned down the Capitol in 1815. He also founded the University of Virginia. Jefferson's days were spent managing the estate and responding to the large number of letters he received from well-wishers. His wife, Martha, had died in 1782, so a solitary Jefferson took to sleeping with a slave named Sally Hemings, thirty years his junior. She was fourteen at the time this first occurred. Hemings would give birth to six children, all of them fathered by Thomas Jefferson.

Later in life, Jefferson ended a long-running feud with John Adams. The two men corresponded, exchanging 380 letters on matters of liberty and freedom.

Jefferson and Adams shared a mutual acquaintance in United States District Court judge John Davis. On January 10, 1824, Thomas Jefferson put his definitive thoughts on Christianity into an extraordinary letter he sent to Davis. Said Jefferson, "In efforts to restore us to primitive Christianity, in all the simplicity in which it came from the lips of Jesus. Had it never been sophisticated by the subtleties of commentators, nor paraphrased into meanings totally foreign to its character, it would at this day have been the religion of the whole civilized world. But . . . the maniac ravings of Calvin, tinctured plentifully with the foggy dreams of Plato, have so loaded it with absurdities and incomprehensibilities, as to drive into infidelity men who had not time, patience, or opportunity to strip it of its meretricious trappings, and to see it in all its native simplicity and purity. I trust however that the same free exercise of private judgment which gave us our political reformation will extend its effects to that of religion."*

In his early eighties, Jefferson developed health problems, which included arthritis and intestinal and urinary issues that made him unable to get out of bed. The former president passed away on July 4, 1826, the fiftieth anniversary of the signing of the Declaration of Independence.

He was eighty-three years old. He is buried at Monticello.

✛ ✛ ✛

James Madison served as Jefferson's secretary of state before being elected to the presidency in 1808. His time in office was marked by a second major conflict with Great Britain. The War of 1812 saw British troops invade the new American capital in Washington, DC, and set the White House and Capitol ablaze. Madison and his wife, Dolley, fled before the British arrived, returning to find the presidential residence in ruins. The couple moved into temporary housing. The outgoing Dolley and the subdued Madison oversaw the reconstruction of the city of Washington before leaving office in 1817.

Following his presidency, James Madison retired to his plantation home at Montpelier, twenty miles away from Monticello in Virginia. He died in 1836 at the age of eighty-five from congestive heart failure. Dolley Madison passed in 1849. Both are buried in the family cemetery on the Montpelier grounds.

✛ ✛ ✛

---

* That letter is now in private hands.

Patrick Henry was offered a seat on the Supreme Court by President George Washington in 1794. Henry turned him down. Washington then offered to make Henry his secretary of state or minister to Spain. Henry refused. Finally, when President Washington chose not to seek a third term in office, a movement to draft Henry as a candidate began. Once again, he declined the opportunity.

By March 1799, Henry had been out of politics for almost a decade, but at George Washington's urging he successfully ran once again for the Virginia General Assembly. Three months later, at the age of sixty-three, Henry died of an acute intestinal disorder. His plantation, Red Hill, housed sixty-seven slaves. Despite being publicly opposed to slavery, Henry's will did not free any of the slaves upon his death. Instead, the slaves and the remainder of his estate were divided between his second wife and six children.

Patrick Henry is buried at Red Hill, just outside Brookneal, Virginia.

✣ ✣ ✣

John Adams received the second-most electoral votes in the 1792 presidential election, earning him the position of George Washington's vice president. He later went on to serve as second president of the United States. During this time, Adams and his wife, Abigail, were the first presidential couple to live in the White House. However, he was defeated by Thomas Jefferson in 1800. A furious Adams returned home to Massachusetts, where he owned a farm outside Quincy known as Peacefield. During this time, Adams worked on his memoirs and devoted himself to daily farm chores. Meanwhile, his son John Quincy Adams was elected to the Senate in 1802, then went on to serve as minister to Russia under James Madison, as well as secretary of state in the James Monroe administration. John Quincy was elected to the presidency in 1824. Like his father, he served just one term in office.

In 1818, after fifty-four years of marriage, Abigail Adams died of typhoid.

Her husband lived eight more years, passing just hours after Thomas Jefferson on July 4, 1826. President John Quincy Adams, noting the coincidence of two Founding Fathers dying on such an auspicious day, called the moment "visible and palpable remarks of divine favor."*

John and Abigail Adams are interred in the crypt at United First Parish Church in Quincy, Massachusetts. John Quincy Adams and his wife, Louisa Catherine, are also buried in that church.

---

* James Monroe, considered the last of the Founding Father presidents, also died on the Fourth of July. Monroe passed from tuberculosis in 1831.

Acknowledgments

Bill O'Reilly: As always, my assistant, Makeda Wubneh, was invaluable in this project. She has allegedly ignored demonic possession by working with me for thirty-three years. Jonathan Leibner and Martin Dugard also made this book come alive.

Martin Dugard would like to thank Bill O'Reilly, Eric Simonoff, Jon Leibner, and Calene Dugard.

Index

Cushman, Robert, 10
Custom House, Boston, 197

Dafoe, Daniel, 146–47
Dandridge, John, 185, 186n
Danforth, Thomas, 116–17
Davies, Samuel, 172–73
Davis, John, 277–78
Declaration of Independence, 213–14, 213n, 217, 278
Deism, 149, 149n, 158, 186
Delaware, 226, 226n
Delaware River, 227
democracy, 38
demonic possession, 231, 232–37, 238–40, 241–51, 242n, 265
Denham, Thomas, 158
Deuteronomy, 233–34
Device, Jennet, 123n
The Devil and Daniel Webster, 230
The Dick Cavett Show, 254
disease, 38
Disney, 269–70
dissenters, 10, 13, 170, 171–72, 178, 178n, 181
dogs, accused of witchcraft, 137
Dorchester, Massachusetts, 48
Doyle, Patrick A., 239n
Drake, Francis, 114
due process, 266
Duncan, Geillis, 4–5
Dutch Reformed worshippers, 228
Duxbury, Massachusetts, 112–13

Eastey, Mary, 117
Edinburgh, Scotland, 1–7
Electoral College, 276
Elizabeth I, 1n
Endicott, John, 33
English, Mary, 138
English, Philip, 138
English Civil War, 171, 178n
English law, 75n, 76, 102n, 105, 194
Episcopalians, 216n, 223
exorcism, 240, 241, 243n, 244n, 258–61, 262n, 263
The Exorcist, 255–57, 258–61, 259n

Falmouth, Massachusetts, 128
Farrar, Isaac, 136
federalists, 220–21, 226
Felt, John, 211
First Encounter, 22

Fisk, Thomas, 77
Fletcher, Benjamin, 116
Flucker, Thomas, 207
forgiveness, 105
Fort Hill, 22
Fortune, 27
Foster, Robert, 209–10, 211–12
Founding Fathers, 143–44, 213–14, 217–18, 280, 280n. *See also specific individuals*
Francis, Pope, 243n
Franklin, Abiah, 148
Franklin, Benjamin, 98, 142–45, 147–51, 151n, 179–81, 226, 228, 275
British monarchy and, 179–80, 181, 203–4
Constitutional Convention and, 217–22, 224–27, 229–30
Deism movement and, 186
discovery of lightning as source of electricity, 204
"A Dissertation upon Liberty and Necessity, Pleasure and Pain," 158
as grand master of Freemason lodge, 162
honorary awards to, 220n
as joint Postmaster General, 196, 204–5
in London, 157–58, 179–80, 195–96
opens his own print shop, 157
before Parliament, 194–95
in Philadelphia, 152–58, 159–67, 174, 219–24
Stamp Act and, 194
takes over *Pennsylvania Gazette*, 160–61
trial of, 203–5
in Virginia, 170
walk across New Jersey, 152–54, *153*
Whitefield and, 164–66
Franklin, Francis Folger, 163–64, 164n, 275
Franklin, James, 145–47, 148, 149–51, 151n, 161, 163–64
Franklin, James, Jr., 151n
Franklin, Josiah, 147, 148, 148n
Franklin, Sarah, 164
Franklin, William, 163
Freemasonry, 162
French, 12, 46, 111, 112, 126, 129, 209
French and Indian War, 186n, 189, 210
Friedkin, William, 255–57
Fuller, Samuel, 14

Gage, Thomas, 206–7, 207–9
Gallagher, Eugene B., 252–53
Gallows Hill, 70, 86, 272
Gardner, Nathaniel, 148

About the Authors

Bill O'Reilly is a trailblazing TV journalist who has experienced unprecedented success on cable news and in writing eighteen national number-one bestselling nonfiction books. There are more than nineteen million books in the *Killing* series in print. He lives on Long Island.

Martin Dugard is the *New York Times* bestselling author of several books of history, among them the *Killing* series, *Into Africa*, *Taking Paris*, *Taking Berlin*, and the upcoming *Taking London*. He and his wife live in Southern California.